THE TRANSFER MARKET
THE INSIDE STORIES

THE TRANSFER MARKET
THE INSIDE STORIES

ALAN GERNON
FOREWORD BY JIM WHITE

First published by Pitch Publishing, 2018

Pitch Publishing
A2 Yeoman Gate
Yeoman Way
Worthing
Sussex
BN13 3QZ
www.pitchpublishing.co.uk
info@pitchpublishing.co.uk

ISBN 978-1-78531-452-0

Typesetting and origination by Pitch Publishing

Printed and bound in Great Britain by TJ International Ltd.

Contents

Foreword

'WHERE'S the yellow tie?' Seriously, there's not a day that goes by here in London and elsewhere when I'm not asked that question randomly by a dozen people or more!

It's clear that most football fans love transfer deadline day and I've been privileged to take the watching millions through all the drama and excitement it generates on Sky Sports News for over a decade now.

Great moments. Like Berbatov to United at the same time as Robinho to City. Fernando Torres joining Chelsea from Liverpool for £50m – was that REALLY him arriving at Stamford Bridge in that blacked-out people carrier?

Who can forget those pictures of Peter Odemwingie turning up at Loftus Road in west London, hoping to sign for QPR from West Brom only for him to turn around after no deal was ever on the table!

Great deadline day moments and there will be many more like them.

Some players excel following a big money move, none more so than Gareth Bale when he moved from Tottenham Hotspur to Real Madrid in 2013 for a then world record £85.3m. Bale got the move of his dreams. I'll never forget the look on his face as my cameraman and I met him at Luton Airport en route by private jet to Madrid, a mixture of shock and bottled-up elation. He has gone on to be magnificent in the colours of arguably the world's top club.

But not all players hit the heights Bale has achieved. How could they?

For many others, what unfolds is far from the move they'd been hoping for.

In Alan Gernon's new book *The Transfer Market*, he meticulously examines every aspect of the transfer, the move itself and the implications involved for the player.

How does the player cope with the move? Did he even want that move in the first place?

Following on from the success of his previous book, *Retired*, which explores what can happen to a typical footballer when he calls time on his career, Alan's *The Transfer Market* delves into areas most fans may not hear or even think about.

On this fascinating subject, Alan Gernon digs a lot deeper than anyone else has attempted to.

The man with the yellow tie on Sky just tells you about it first.

Jim White, Sky Sports & talkSPORT broadcaster

Introduction

THE young African man stood trembling in the parked plane's toilet at Birmingham Airport. He knew there was someone waiting for him, someone he'd never met before, but he couldn't move. The noise, the lights, the people – it all added up to potential sensory overload for someone who had only previously visited Europe for a few days.

Meanwhile, in the arrivals hall, Lorna McClelland was getting anxious. All the other passengers had disembarked and she had been waiting for over an hour. As she was about to give up, her new colleague arrived. They walked slowly to her car, where inside he sat hunched over with his hands over his ears in an unsuccessful attempt to block out the airport din. Concerned, she pulled over a few minutes into their journey and he revealed that he'd never been to such a large airport and was terrified. Aston Villa's player welfare officer quickly realised that the club's new signing was going to take some time to adjust to life in England.

His was just one of over 10,000 transfers across the football world that year. What I saw was quite different to what Lorna had seen. I'd read a headline a couple of days earlier linking Villa with a highly rated African prospect. That's all I observed until his first few lacklustre performances at the club. I didn't see the personal consequences of this life-changing move on this overwhelmed young man. I didn't see his struggle to adapt to a foreign country and an alien culture. I didn't see the tears, the self-doubt and the homesickness. I saw the headline, the money and the glamour. I never contemplated what it might be like for a man in his early twenties to chase his dream on a new continent and how difficult it might be for him to settle in, despite the fee agreed between his new and previous employers. Or whether he'd even had any say in the matter.

'Every transfer is a story. You always want the truth to come out.'

Arsène Wenger was bullish in his comments when questioned about *The Telegraph's* undercover sting of Sam Allardyce in September 2016.

He was, however, correct. Every transfer is a story, although we may only get to read or hear about the big-money moves. Not all transfers are Pogba-esque. Despite the vast sums of cash swirling around the English game, the majority of moves involve little or no money. But behind each move isn't just one story but many.

The story of a journeyman making a final move before his inevitable retirement. The story of a former hot prospect realising a move down the leagues is about all he can hope for. The story of a player, who has been loyal to his club, suddenly told that he is surplus to requirements. The story of a young man unexpectedly traded at the drop of a hat by his employer to another, often with the prospect of a move to a strange town, city or country. The story of a footballer with the pressure of a large transfer fee hanging over him. The story of the agents behind the deals. The story of a player's family and a move's effects on their lives. The story of how the media feed on all of the above. The story of the clubs. The story of countless others who live off this market in human personnel.

It's often easy to glance at the latest transfer gossip and fail to acknowledge that it's human beings we're reading about.

When new signings are unveiled they usually mouth the same sort of platitudes. 'I've dreamed of playing for this club since I was a boy,' or 'They're a massive club and I'm delighted to be here,' for example. But you never really hear what they actually think. What the move means to a player on a personal level. Having to move away from his young family. The wrench of leaving a club you've been at since you were six years old. The sudden realisation that you're on your way down the football ladder.

In what was an unlikely setting to all but confirm the world's record transfer, three Mancunian laundry ladies posed in front of industrial washing machines, with a grinning Paul Pogba sporting a Manchester United training top. A few days earlier a Miami barber had hinted at the conclusion of the deal, posting a picture on Instagram of him cutting the French midfielder's hair accompanied by the caption, 'Had to change up Pogba's hair colour for his new team #ManchesterUnited.'

The drawn-out transfer was officially announced a few hours after the laundry ladies' encounter with the star came out in the wash. This time, it was by more contemporary means – an Adidas-sponsored video featuring Pogba with UK grime artist Stormzy. While Pogba's protracted transfer stole the headlines in 2016, his £89m move wasn't typical in the world of football. How many other deals can you remember from that year? N'Golo Kanté leaving champions Leicester City for champions-elect Chelsea? John Stones's £50m switch from Everton to Pep Guardiola's Manchester City? Sadio Mané becoming the latest player on the Southampton to Liverpool conveyor belt? That's four deals, including Pogba's, and you'll probably recall a few new arrivals and outgoings at your own club.

The big names dominate the headlines but there were 14,591 international transfers in 2016 involving 178 associations and 4,379 clubs. While a record US$4.79bn was spent, this translates to just over US$325,000 per transfer. Most players are moving for a relative pittance. That's if any money is involved at all. The same year, only 14 per cent of worldwide transfers involved the payment of a fee.

While Pogba broke the world transfer record in 2016, it only took a year for it to be blown out of the water. Neymar's move from Barcelona to Paris Saint-Germain more than doubled the record, with the Ligue 1 giants meeting his seemingly prohibitive buyout clause.

Things were a lot more prosaic in the lower leagues of English football. Transfermarkt.com estimates that the average League Two signing in the 2016/17 season cost their club £627 – or roughly what Paris Saint-Germain reportedly pay Neymar every 12 minutes. This is based on disclosed transfer fees for the division. Indeed, in theory, you could buy 315,789 League Two players for the price of the Brazilian. Or, closer to home, the starting XIs in all of the 24 clubs in the fourth tier would cost about the same price as Leeds United paid Leicester City for Allan Clarke. In 1969.

This is the level the majority of professional footballers are at. And the level that the majority of football transfers are at. A 2016 report by FIFPro, the worldwide representative organisation for professional footballers, suggests that 45 per cent of footballers worldwide earn less than US$1,000 net per month, with a further 21 per cent earning between US$1,000 and US$4,000 after tax on a monthly basis. And it's not just in footballing outposts – 32 per cent of European respondents reported these earnings. In the country that gave us Pelé, Socrates, Romario, Ronaldo Luís Nazário de Lima, Ronaldinho and the aforementioned Neymar, almost 85 per cent of Brazil-based footballers earn under US$1,000 every month. It may come as no surprise then that, according to 2018 research by the CIES Football Observatory, part of the Switzerland-based International Center for Sports Studies, Brazil boasts the most expatriate players worldwide with 1,236 professional footballers playing in the 78 associations represented in the study.

The FIFPro report defines these third-tier footballers as 'representing the majority of players, who are under constant pressure to extend their careers in professional football and face precarious employment conditions, including a large degree of personal and contractual abuse.' One of those interviewed put things starkly, 'There is no stability. You have one-, two-, three-year contracts your whole career so you're always looking over your shoulder, thinking"where am I going next?"'

FIFPro represents 60,000 footballers across all continents and their report is the largest data collection about footballers' working conditions ever produced. This third tier of footballers equates to around 45,000 players, more than the average attendance at Chelsea's Stamford Bridge or Juventus's Allianz Stadium during the 2017/18 season.

An elite two per cent – the individuals we read or hear transfer stories about – earned above US$720,000 net annually. This top tier is 'formed by the global elite of players with superior talent and skill. They enjoy very good working conditions at the highest level and a very strong market position,' the report said. This elite equates to approximately 1,200 players, slightly less than Morecambe FC's average home crowd at the Globe Arena during the 2017/18 campaign or Finn Harps's average home attendance in the League of Ireland the previous season.

The transfer market for those at the bottom is a world away from the razzmatazz of Sky Sports's deadline-day coverage. Almost 30 per cent of those who were transferred for a fee were pressured into joining a club against their wishes or a club not of their choice.

When some footballers sign for a new club and hold aloft a scarf it might as well read, 'I didn't want to leave my last club', 'The best my agent could get,' or 'My twelfth club already!' rather than the name of their new employer. Uncertainty is rife. One player I spoke to admitted that his main thought every day is about the instability of his job and that it sometimes gets him down. He often wonders why he can't have, 'A normal job where I know what I'm going to be doing next year, where I'm going to be living.'

Even the elite players are affected. In 2017, Tottenham Hotspur and France captain Hugo Lloris said, 'We know the transfer market is not an easy period for players, for their minds, for their preparations, too, for their bodies.'

I've been a sucker for transfer gossip since I was a kid. Ceefax, ClubCall, the tabloid back pages, Sky Sports News, the internet. But it was probably a camping trip as a teenager that ensured I never missed my daily fix of transfer tittle-tattle again. It was the days before the internet and social media, and some friends and I had just finished school and headed off with a tent, some supplies and little access to the outside world – and more importantly page 312 of Ceefax – for a few days. Upon my return, I was flabbergasted to learn that then Tottenham chairman Alan Sugar (no knighthood those days) had been successfully courting Jürgen Klinsman on board his Monte Carlo yacht. Not only had Spurs lured the German striker in my absence, but they'd also landed Ilie Dumitrescu – a star for Romania at that summer's World Cup in the United States (US). These were exotic signings at the time and prompted Gordon Taylor, the chief executive of the Professional Footballers' Association (PFA), to claim that with the likes of Klinsmann and Dumitrescu in the English top flight there would be, 'Less emphasis on crash, bang, wallop and more on the passing style.'

My interest in the whole transfer business was probably sparked on Christmas Day 1987. At 3am I raced into our front sitting room, where we always decamped solely for the festive period, to survey my bounty. I was not disappointed. The perennial favourite Subbuteo, with Watford's Luther Blissett on the front, took centre stage but my eyes were drawn to another, lesser-known board game, Team Tactix, endorsed by the late Liverpool and England midfielder Emlyn Hughes. The box promised over £100m worth of top soccer players, featuring the 25 best-supported teams in British football. If it were nowadays, the £100m would only get you Kyle Walker and Raheem Sterling.

The 275 player cards all included a value for each and what was called a Factix. Nottingham Forest's Gary (sic) Birtles (£350,000) had 'a way out dress sense' and was spotted by Brian Clough when 'the half time Bovril was better than he was.'

Manchester City's Mick McCarthy (£350,000) was apparently known as the 'quiet man' who 'couldn't stand people with bad manners.' Which might explain that whole business with Roy Keane. Watford's David Bardsley had earned a reputation as a compulsive changer of cars, which may have come in handy for his Hornets team-mate John McClelland who 'refused to learn to drive and walks everywhere.'

The Factix for Queens Park Rangers's £250,000-rated Wayne Feredey (sic) rather dubiously stated 'his time over 100m would have won him a medal at the 1980 Olympic Games'. Nicknames were a common filler, with 'snappy dresser' Jerry Murphy also known as Smurph to his Chelsea team-mates, while they dubbed Colin Lee (£200,000) Quincy after the TV doctor as 'he has a detailed knowledge of injuries'. Watford's Tony Coton (£300,000) earned the sobriquet Droopy as 'he resembles a shaggy dog', while fellow keeper John Lukic (£300,000) was apparently known as Bogdan at Arsenal due to his Yugoslav heritage.

But I had no interest in these Factix, just the values. The game was basically Monopoly with footballers, a precursor to Fantasy Football. You had 90 minutes to 'compile the best team in British soccer'. A bit like that transfer deadline day when the Abu Dhabi United Group bought Manchester City.

For months, possibly years, this was all I played, as the Subbuteo Club Edition gathered dust in my bedroom. It was analogous to my later fascination with the buying and selling of footballers – scanning the transfer gossip rather than match reports in the papers and online.

What struck me looking through these player cards over 30 years later is the abundance of footballers who'd made the jump from non-league or lower-league football to the top tiers in England and Scotland and the dearth of overseas players. I can only find eight from outside the United Kingdom and the Republic of Ireland, or less than three per cent, including Danes Jan Mølby, John Sivebæk and Jesper Olsen, Australian Craig Johnston, the Argentinian Ossie Ardiles, South African-born Mich D'Avray, Dutch international Johnny Metgod and Surinamborn Romeo Zondervan.

In contrast, the same 25 teams' starting line-ups last weekend, at the time of writing, included 122 overseas players – or just under 45 per cent. And that doesn't include eight current Premier League clubs, who mustn't have been among the 25 best-supported teams in Britain back in 1987.

To put that into perspective, a 2018 report by the CIES Football Observatory found that expatriates represent just over 21 per cent of footballers globally. Every one of these 122 players had left their home country for a new club, a new land, a new beginning. A total of 107 different foreign FIFA-affiliated nations had been represented in the Premier League between 1992 and the summer of 2018, while footballers from 111 nations outside of the UK and the Republic of Ireland have played at least one Championship game since its inception in 2004.

To me, though, transfer gossip had always been just names, clubs and figures. Until recently. As the clock struck midnight, I made my nightly visit to the BBC website's transfer gossip page to get my fix. I usually spend about ten minutes reading the latest rumours and clicking through on links for some of the more attention-grabbing stories. I often wake up the following morning with a dozen tabs open on my phone's web browser, having fallen asleep halfway through a story about Papy Djilobodji, or Steve Bruce re-signing someone. I've done this nightly since the page's introduction in 2002, meaning I've wasted over a month of my life, at least, reading chitchat about the transfer market. A lot more, I'd estimate, considering how slowly the pages of its predecessor, Ceefax, took to rotate. Having satisfied myself that I was now up to date with the potential suitors for the latest Portuguese wonderkid I had never even seen play, I continued browsing the web. My Facebook timeline displayed a series of words from *The Dictionary of Obscure Sorrows*, a website that 'defines neologisms for emotions that do not have a descriptive term'.

One of these newly coined words caught my eye. Sonder, it explained, 'is the realisation that each random passerby is living a life as vivid and complex as your own – populated with their own ambitions, friends, routines, worries and inherited craziness – an epic story that continues invisibly around you like an anthill sprawling deep underground, with elaborate passageways to thousands of other lives that you never knew existed, in which you might appear only once, as an extra sipping coffee in the background, as a blur of traffic passing on the highway, as a lighted window at dusk.'

Essentially, everybody has a story. Arsène Wenger was correct. Every transfer is a story. But every transfer is about the human stories. I scrolled back to the BBC's transfer gossip page and experienced a moment of sonder, I guess is the right word for it, thinking about that Portuguese wonderkid's life. Did he really want to join Swansea City? Had he even heard of them? How would his parents feel about their 19-year-old son leaving for a new country, a new language, a new challenge? How did the story originate?

Like a lot of football fans and media, I had been guilty of forgetting the human aspect of a footballer's life regarding transfers. I got the sudden realisation that these players I'd been reading about for years are each living a life as vivid and complex as my own – populated with their own ambitions, friends, routines, worries and inherited craziness. Rather than appear only once, as an extra reading the back pages of a tabloid or as a supporter in Row Z, I wanted to discover what the transfer market actually means to the life of a typical footballer.

The Players and Their Families

RICHIE Ryan put down his phone and surveyed the boxes littered throughout the kitchen of his Jacksonville home. Inside, was his life. His family's lives. The life of a footballer. Four months after moving, they'd still remained unopened. There was no point opening them now, either. He was on the move again. They were on the move again. This time to Miami FC. The life of a footballer.

'When you think about it, it is a bit mad,' he reflects.

Richie's career began at Sunderland, where he made his debut in the Tyne-Wear derby, and has taken him to 11 clubs across five countries. Now 33, he'd just joined United Soccer League (USL) club FC Cincinnati when we spoke.

'That's the first time anyone's ever asked me that,' he laughs, when I question him about the instability of a footballer's life.

'In the Premier League and the Championship, a lot of players sign three-, four- or five-year contracts so they have that stability. But I think in the lower leagues in England, Scotland, Ireland and over here in America, players generally just sign one-, maximum two-year contracts,' he says. 'So, it is hard to have that stability, especially for players with families, wives and kids. Do you up and move the family for the sake of a year or two or do you keep them where they are and go on your own? That can then bring other difficulties, being away from the family. There's definitely a lot to take into consideration.'

He admits that it is difficult to put down roots when your immediate future is at the whim of your current employer. 'I can speak from experience. The longest I spent at any one club was Sligo Rovers and that was three and a half years,' says the Irishman. 'You can't really build any foundations if you're going to be moving around that much. Even since I've got to North America I'm at my fourth club since February 2014. It's for different circumstances, and not through choice, that I've moved around so much, but it's just the joys of the transfer market – anything is possible.'

When Belgian winger Adnan Januzaj reportedly spent almost £3m on a Cheshire mansion in 2017, he didn't expect Manchester United to sell him to Real Sociedad just days later. His costly investment highlights the precarious nature of life as a footballer, yet I was still surprised to speak to many players who rented rather than bought property for this very reason.

'Sometimes you're better off buying a house but there's no point in me and the family buying a house somewhere where we might be for a year and a half or two years,' says Richie. 'I could have gone to Jacksonville and bought a house and been there for four months, been left with a house there and not knowing what to do with it and the hassle of looking after it. When you think about it, it is difficult to set up home because you can't really afford the possibility of being on the move again when the next transfer window comes.'

Mark Roberts has had a much-travelled career since starting out at Crewe Alexandra. Taking in 12 clubs, the short-term contracts and uncertainty in the lower leagues in England led him to rent for much of it.

'When I left Fleetwood Town, my wife and I were getting married that summer in France, and then went for our honeymoon to Vietnam and Cambodia,' says the defender and non-executive director at the PFA. 'So, we were away for three weeks but I'd already signed for Cambridge United. As I didn't know anyone at the football club you realise you're putting a needle in a map and hoping that you find a place that you'd choose to live had you explored the area properly. I had been to Cambridge to visit but I didn't really know the area. So I was in my hotel room on honeymoon Googling places, thinking, "God, I need to get this sorted as I'll be back to pre-season soon." You're hoping that the place that you choose is going to be right for you, and when you have a family, for them too. From my experience, there are people at clubs who'll suggest areas but it's left to you to go and find that place to live.'

He regrets not investing in property earlier in his career but believes the insecurity of the profession makes it a risky proposition. 'Hindsight's a wonderful thing,' he reflects. 'I rented at Stevenage for the whole of the time I was there but ended up sharing the flat I lived in with a friend who was also from the north-west. When you see how property prices escalated I wish I'd bought. If I'd bought then it would have been something that would have been very profitable for me on a personal level. But you never know your future in football and I didn't expect to stay there for the length of the time I did when I signed there on that first day.

'It's a decision you've got to make based on the facts at that time. When I moved down to Cambridge with my wife we were renting again. I'd signed a two-year contract with an option of a third year so we were both throwing ourselves into it as a couple. We then found out, on the plane home from our honeymoon, that my wife was pregnant. And quite quickly when we moved down we found out we were having twins so that changes the whole family dynamics completely. We decided to rent down in Cambridge as we had bought a property together back in the north-west, while I played for Fleetwood Town. Obviously, that meant renting out our home and sorting that all out too while you're living and playing at the other end of the country.'

Moving house often tops the list of the most stressful life events a person can endure. It might seem absurd that it trumps the likes of divorce and the loss of a loved one but there's no doubt it can be distressing. However, it's usually a personal decision to up sticks with the majority of people moving for lifestyle reasons, access to shops and amenities, to be closer to friends and families, to reduce running costs or simply for the need of a bigger home.

Footballers often don't have this luxury. Their lives are nomadic, with a move to another city or country just a poor performance, a managerial decision, a phone call away. Sure, the riches on offer would help limit the downsides – but not every professional footballer is earning a Premier League salary.

It's not just the footballer and his spouse who will be affected. Players will typically have young families, with constant moves having an effect later in life. A 2010 study in the *Journal of Personality and Social Psychology* revealed that those who moved repeatedly in childhood were likely to perform poorly in school and were more likely to report lower life satisfaction and psychological well-being as adults. They also had fewer quality social relationships in adulthood.

When Leroy Rosenior joined Bristol City in 1992, it was his first move away from London after spending the first ten years of his career with clubs in the capital. His son, Liam, was a ten-year-old at the time and admits the move had a big impact on family life. Now a professional himself, Rosenior junior acknowledges that the life of a footballer means that, sometimes, family matters have to take a back seat.

'I've had it both ways. My dad was a footballer and I was lucky enough to be a footballer myself. Family life, when you're a footballer, almost has to come second,' says Liam. 'That's a really hard thing to say. The fact that it can change at any moment is difficult as well. Obviously, in the olden days you'd have the transfer window, but before that, it was pretty open. Literally, in one day you could find yourself at a different club and in a different city when your kids are happy at school and your wife has got friends and family around. And then you go to a completely different environment and change schools again. And the kids find it really tough, as any family would.

'It happened once when I was a kid. My dad played most of his career in London. Even when he moved clubs in London he made sure that we would stay in the same school, up until the age of ten. That was his desire to stay in the same area. When he got towards the end of his career, when he couldn't be as choosy, we moved to Bristol. My mum had made a lot of friends in London. My family are from London and all our close family were there. And then you find yourself in a new school, a new environment, having to make new friends. And, obviously, my dad had to get used to playing in a new team. It's a massive change. I think when we speak about transfers we speak about the glamorous side of things. At the same time, it's less glamorous when you're living out of a hotel with your parents for a while.'

He agrees that settling down is next to impossible for footballers, who can move unexpectedly to a new club, a new city, a new country, overnight.

'It is difficult because it is a short career so you have to maximise it. You have to think of footballing reasons and financial reasons,' Liam explains. 'And it also depends if you have children of school age or family around that need your help. I know players that have had to look after their parents and then have had to move away from them. It's a big decision for the whole family, including the extended family. At the same time, you have to make a decision for footballing reasons and you have to maximise a short career.'

Just days after Brighton & Hove Albion secured their Premier League status in May 2018, Liam was called into manager Chris Hughton's office. He got the talk that every player fears

– his contract was not being renewed. Even at the age of 33, with seven clubs on his CV, it was an emotional moment and his immediate thoughts surrounded breaking the news to his wife and family who were happy and settled in the area and the children in school.

'It's an uncertain time, for sure. Again, the first thing that I'm thinking of is my family,' he says. 'I've got an 11-year-old, a nine-year-old and a seven-year-old who I love spending my time with. I'm now in a position where I don't know where I'm going to be next year. I could be in England. I could be in another country. They are so settled at school and my daughter is starting secondary school, so I may have to consider commuting or even moving away from my family just to make my career work. This comes to all players. Especially at my age now, when you're coming towards the latter stages of your career, you want to settle down and make sure your family has a base, but if you're in football as a senior player, a coach or a manager, you know that things could change very quickly. From my point of view, it's a very uncertain time.'

In the summer of 2017 alone, Premier League clubs released over 120 players – more than enough to fill ten teams – to uncertain futures.

Former Scotland international Steven Caldwell echoes Richie's and Liam's sentiments. The defender played for nine clubs, including loans, during his 18-year career and also admits that football often comes first, before family.

'Transfers affect your family life a great deal. When I left Sunderland, my wife was five or six months pregnant. That was huge,' recalls Steven. 'We get to Burnley and we're in a hotel and were frantically looking for a house as we wanted to be in a home before our little boy was born. It was not just about focusing on football straight away. We didn't know Manchester, where we were looking to move to. We were speaking to people to see what was best, where we should go and to get all this done before he was born in June. We'd four or five months to get it done. That was stressful as well.'

Steven was released in 2011 by Wigan Athletic and, unsure of his next destination, set up a base in the north-east as his eldest child was starting school. 'I knew I was leaving, but I didn't know where I'd end up,' he says. 'Then I signed for Birmingham City, which was rather far away. So, the kids were at school in Newcastle and I was jumping back and forward and staying in an apartment in Birmingham, which was tough on the family life as well.

'You can't really set down roots as a footballer. You always have to remain impartial about where you live. If you're serious about your career, and I'd say 99 per cent of footballers are, then it's always about what's best for you and your career. You have to be very selfish and make sure you're in a place that suits you. Obviously, that has an effect on your life and your kids. Once you start making decisions thinking about your kids, you start to lose that edge. At Toronto FC, I probably should have left and played for another Major League Soccer (MLS) team but I didn't as I love the city and I wanted my kids to stay and grow up here. I made a choice to hang in but maybe it would have been better to move on at a point. I'm pretty settled here still.'

These days, most top clubs have a player welfare or liaison officer on hand to assist a player and his family to settle in their new surroundings. Steven believes this is one of the most pivotal roles in any football club and is crucially important – for both the footballer and his new employer.

'As soon as you get that player in, if you settle them quickly, a happy player will probably play better quicker. I was always lucky. At Birmingham City we'd a great player liaison officer,' he says.

'At Toronto, it's unbelievable. We have a handbook that we hand out to new players that tells you everything about the city – restaurants, hotels, places to go. We also have an incredible network of support, with someone who'll help you with house-hunting, based on schools and things like that. They're absolutely brilliant at that. It's really important that you have that as it settles the player quickly and allows them to concentrate on football. Your wife may be anxious and it affects you, as she just wants the best for the family. When you've got someone to raise these concerns with, you can just focus on training and playing games.'

When one former Premier League star I spoke to moved between top-flight clubs, his son was just six months old. The player admits that a move up north caused a bit of a strain on family life.

'You're in a hotel room with a little six-month-old and you've got a game the next day, it's not ideal,' he laughs. 'You don't have home comforts. I'm not knocking it as it is part and parcel of the game, but it does put pressure on your marriage and relationships. Even though you are together, you're living quite separate lives. Marriage-wise, if you keep moving around it does put a strain on the relationship. You have to put football first because that is your livelihood. Your partner doesn't always understand the pressure and assumes that everything is alright. I remember coming through at my first club and looking at the older players and wondering why they didn't want to go home. They'd be the last ones out of the shower, the last ones getting dressed and the last ones leaving to go home. As the years go by, and you go to different clubs, you see the same thing. It got to the stage where I was that player that didn't want to go home. It is a vicious circle that needs to be addressed. I'm going through a divorce right now.

'A lot of the time, it depends on whether you can fit in straight away. I was quite fortunate that I knew people at clubs I joined beforehand, but I did know players who moved to clubs who found it very difficult to settle down. If you're a foreign player, you've got to learn the language quickly. Even if you're an English player, you might sign for a manager who then leaves. And then you're in the loop again and you don't know what is going on. Despite the money, a lot of the time it can be lonely.'

It was a Saturday evening in January 2013 and Ángel Di María was having dinner with his family inside his Cheshire home when burglars attempted to smash their patio doors with scaffolding poles. Traumatised by the incident, he and his family moved to a hotel not long afterwards and, within months, he'd also left Manchester United. With footballers' lives and moves in the public eye, such incidents are never far from the back of some players' minds.

'You're always paranoid as to whether someone's following you,' continues the former Premier League player, who wishes to remain anonymous. 'Our lives, in general, are quite publicly out there, so people know where we are, more often than not. You're a living target really. There is a paranoia that comes with it. There may not be anyone really targeting you, but you're paranoid. When workers come to our house, you get paranoid about who they're talking to and who you can trust.'

That six-month-old son is now 13 years old and the player, now retired, remains settled in the north, where he admits he would never have ventured if it weren't for football.

'It's been good for us,' he says. 'The other side of it is, you come out of football and, apart from my kids, I've got no one really up here. I'm in Manchester and all my family are in London. You've got to find other work and, if you're going through a divorce, you've got to find another house. Do you find somewhere that's close to your kids or do you just uproot and go back down south? It is quite difficult.'

Over 16 years on, Roy Keane's departure from the Republic of Ireland's World Cup squad in Saipan still looms large in Irish culture. It was such a national, divisive issue in Ireland that then Taoiseach Bertie Ahern offered to step in as a mediator and a long-running comedy musical based on the events, *I, Keano*, sold over half a million tickets in its first two years. Even as I write this, in June 2018, Roy Keane has revisited the saga stating that he 'let people off lightly. There could have been a lot more trouble.'

Such was the animosity between Keane and the then national team manager Mick McCarthy that it seemed unlikely they'd ever speak to each other again. It took four years and a deal for a Scottish centre-back for them to make peace.

McCarthy had worked with Neill Collins at Sunderland and was eager to bring him on loan to Wolves. The only sticking point was that Keane was now The Black Cats's manager. The call was made, the hatchet was buried and the defender was on his way to Wolves, who he subsequently joined on a permanent basis.

It was the sixth of 11 clubs for Neill, who was delighted with the chance to play again under Big Mick.

'I was a huge Roy Keane fan growing up,' says Neill. 'Signing for Sunderland under Mick was quite strange but I realised quite quickly what a stand-up person he was.'

He believes that the unstable nature of a footballer's career can lend itself to marriage difficulties. With one in three players divorcing within a year of retirement, the constant moving around can have a huge impact.

'At the end of the day, you're talking about human beings,' stresses Neill. 'Your life involves upping sticks and moving constantly, you make friends and forge relationships and before you know it you're away again. These are all things to take into account, particularly when you have children to consider. It's definitely a recipe for success when you can settle down somewhere you're comfortable and enjoying it. I can understand why it's part of the reason for the divorce rate being so high.'

Many players now set up a base away from their families, who may be settled in a particular area. Research has shown that the risk of divorce increases when spouses live apart. A 2013 study funded by the US Department of Defense found that the divorce rates among service members were directly related to the length of time they spent away from their spouses.

Leroy Lita has played for 14 clubs during his career and believes family matters are of greater concern further down the football pyramid. 'If you're moving to a Manchester United, your family are coming with you no matter what,' laughs the former Reading striker. 'If you're talking about a lower level, you have to think about stuff as kids are at school and wives are happy where they are. But if you're moving to a big club it's not even a question. You don't go home and ask, "Babe, can I move to Manchester United?" Obviously family is very important but if it's a big club, you're going. If it's a smaller club at a lower level, players really think about their families a lot more.'

Northern Ireland goalkeeper Michael McGovern admits he's been quite lucky with moves so far in his career. He has spent the majority of it in Scotland, before his heroics at Euro 2016 – most notably against Germany – earned him a move to Norwich City.

'My career has been quite different to the boys at Norwich. I played in Scotland for most of my career and in Scotland, with most of the teams, you can get away with not moving house too much as the country's not the biggest of places,' explains Michael. 'Ross County, Inverness and Aberdeen would probably be the three which are central belt. I played for Ross County when I was starting out. I was at Celtic for seven years and I couldn't get a game there because I was the third-choice goalkeeper. It was very difficult. So I had to go to Ross County to get some games, really. I was actually 25 by the time I got to play first-team football, it came to me quite late. I had to travel as my wife was a teacher at the time and couldn't leave her job. So I travelled three and a half hours up and down to Dingwall. I was going up on Monday morning, leaving at 5am and then coming home on a Tuesday after training. We were off on a Wednesday so I'd go back up on a Thursday and then maybe back down on Friday if the away game was in the central belt. There was a lot of travelling involved in that one.

'That was when I was younger, but now I've got kids. If I'd have moved in January – and you never know what could have happened – I would have just commuted, no matter where it was. My wee boy has started school now and, if it was a loan, for example for six months, I wouldn't have been able to justify making a move and I wouldn't have wanted to take him out of school. I'd have just gone home as much as I could, really,' he concludes.

To a man, the players I spoke to acknowledged the privileged position they're in – paid to play the world's most popular sport. However, the human effects of the transfer market paint a far from glamorous picture. During the 2018 World Cup, Tottenham and England full-back Danny Rose admitted that he wouldn't be, 'Shouting from the rooftops to recommend to people's children to be a footballer. There's so much more to football than what people see.'

Italian midfielder Raffaele De Vita, currently in his second spell at Scottish Premiership club Livingston, admits that life as a footballer sometimes gets him down, when even planning to start a family can be difficult.

'I'm fortunate because there are people stuck in jobs that they don't like and who wake up in the morning and can't wait for the day to be over. But my main thought every single day is about the instability of the job,' says the 30-year-old. 'Sometimes I even think why can I not have a normal job, where I know what I'm going to be doing next year, where my house is going to be. I've been in the UK for 15 years and every year I think, "Can I maybe settle and try and buy a house here?" Then, next minute, you're not in the manager's plans any more and you have to move. Basically, you just can't plan anything. Everything is season after season. Never mind in five years, I don't know what's going to happen next year.'

Bournemouth goalkeeper Asmir Begović has played in England for 13 years and says that when you've been around the game for a while, you know that one phone call can change a lot of things.

'You just know it's a reality and you're always a little bit on edge,' says the 31-year-old. 'As you get older you try your best to put down roots and create a base. And then what happens is that a lot of players end up moving by themselves if their family is settled. Once you have kids settled in school who have their friends and comfort levels then it becomes very difficult to keep moving your whole family to different places. It can be tricky and affect the player's performances. Of course, you try and be as professional as possible, to try and make a living and give your best for your team, for your club, and do the best job you can. I've seen many players living outside their continent while their family is at home and, depending on finances, you can't just keep dragging your family with you everywhere.

'The more traumatic and difficult moves came a little bit earlier in my career. As I got older, they got a little bit more straightforward. There are definitely issues that go around the game, though, and there are definitely some elements that people don't see all the time, which makes it such a tricky thing to do – to keep moving.'

Martin Roderick was a self-proclaimed 'young, failed footballer' at Portsmouth, where he served a two-year apprenticeship before being awarded two one-year professional contracts. His manager at the time, the late 1966 World Cup winner Alan Ball, would tell him, 'Son, I can't play you as I don't know how you're going to play from one week to the next.' He admits this was down to a lack of maturity on his part, at a time when he was already realising that he didn't enjoy the lifestyle of a footballer very much at all.

'I wasn't as good as some of the people I was with,' acknowledges Martin. 'Some of the lads would probably say I was very talented but incredibly inconsistent.'

Following his release from Pompey, he played a season for Wycombe Wanderers, who at the time were in the Conference – 'It was a team full of people like me who had experience in the

Football League but had dropped out relatively early' – before following in his two sisters' footsteps to university.

Martin continued playing football semi-professionally while studying for a sports science degree, when he became interested in sociology and issues around pain and injury.

'I was interested in emotions and the way in which players presented themselves in the context of a football club under circumstances where their form was going in and out, they were injured, they were having success and failure but yet they were still having to look terribly keen – not just to coaches and team-mates but to fans as well,' he says.

At 26, while playing for Kettering Town, he was diagnosed with Hodgkin's lymphoma, which brought his playing career to an abrupt end. While being treated and recovering he studied for a PhD and realised that there had been very little written about football and the people that he knew – giving voice to the players who weren't being paid the top money, who weren't in the top leagues, who weren't soaking up the attention. His research covered around 50 professional footballers, from top-class players to those who had 'bumped along the bottom'.

'I started off talking to them solely about injuries and their experiences with injuries, as it had affected all players and they all feared it. While I was asking about injuries, most of them were telling me about what their injury meant. Depending on the time of the season or depending on their situation at the club, the biggest fear was securing another contract,' he reveals.

He travelled to meet a lot of footballers and, by chance, got to speak to a lot of their wives. Some of the experiences of the women were often more interesting than those of their spouses, he admits.

'I decided to move from injuries to transfers because I realised, for the most part – while in the newspapers a huge amount of attention was paid to key players who were moving to big clubs – most players left one club and joined another not because they were wanted and could negotiate huge fees, but because they were unwanted and they were trying to secure employment. In situations where they were realising that they had very few choices.

'Most of the players I spoke to were in the Bosman era when a lot of discussion had been around player power, agents, the choices, negotiations, this fee and that fee. However, the majority of the players I spoke to who weren't playing in the Premier League were on very short, very fragile contracts, where they had to make so many games in a season to secure another season,' continues Martin. 'Contracts of over one year were very limited unless the club really fancied a young player. The older players weren't on anywhere near the money people thought they were on and they were in very precarious situations, where a lot of them did have agents, but those agents didn't really care about them.'

He became aware that over 700 players every season were released in a total population of somewhere between 3,000 to 4,000. The short-term nature of most players' contracts was having a huge impact on family life.

'That's a huge number of people, relatively speaking, all of whom were scrapping for another club, another employment contract,' he says. 'I heard stories of players turning up for a trial and realising they were one of three or more players scrapping for one contract. In these circumstances, many players were not moving house, but were living in a family that was sort of in a commuting relationship, as the contract might only last one season. So I came across lots of wives who were saying, "Bugger this for a game of soldiers, I'm staying here. You can go off and do your thing and we'll manage." And some players coped better than others.'

Around the time of his research, the TV show *Footballers'* *Wives* was being broadcast and there was a huge amount of press around the notion of a WAG, which he found was debilitating for many of the women he encountered.

'The husband of one wife I met had played for a couple of big teams and he'd had a couple of big contracts, but not the kind of money that meant they could live in luxury for the rest of their lives,' he recalls. 'He had to earn money, and all he knew was football. When I arrived at their house, expecting to meet the player, it was the wife who welcomed me. There were loads of removal boxes dotted around the house and she said, "I'm really sorry. I've moved five times in two years and I'm not moving again. This is it. I don't care where he goes."

'They were struggling to establish relationships, they were constantly moving schools and doctors' surgeries, struggling to maintain friends. Some of them turned up to the school playground and were seen as the wife of the player that everybody had their eye on. They found themselves slightly unapproachable. I heard these slightly heartbreaking stories. The players did feel guilty about leaving their wives and families in these places, but to some extent, they were able to establish relationships quite quickly in clubs. However, even that was relatively tenuous as so many players are moving so often now that I think it's quite difficult to maintain a kind of team spirit.'

At one club Martin visited, a player told him that he was the only one in the squad who hadn't separated or been divorced.

'I felt really sorry for some of the wives, who were hearing stories about their husbands,' he points out. 'The level of strain that they were put under meant that if there was some crack in a relationship, it was incredibly hard for them to sustain it. I did come across plenty of players and their families who had survived or were surviving and had just managed to organise their lives in a way that meant they coped. I've done a lot of research with a range of athletes, not just with footballers, and these issues seem to be cropping up everywhere I look.'

One of the findings that Martin was struck by was the volume of players he spoke to that just didn't enjoy the career of being a footballer. They came to realise that what was once a childhood dream had become an uncertain route to earning a living, and quite often only a modest one.

'Yet they were in a world where everyone was telling them that it was a dream come true,' declares Martin. 'You never hear players talking about this kind of thing in an open way. I felt like there was a small boy inside all of them, who still liked to kick a ball around, but it had turned into a job and that had slowly crushed their spirit – that constant upheaval. No matter where they went in their lives, the only type of discussion they had was something related to their work.'

The human need to feel wanted meant that any transfer was welcomed, given that it meant a move away from a club where they felt unloved.

'One of the reasons I focused on transfers was because so many players found themselves in situations where they realised they weren't wanted, but had to exist at a club for a period of time until they could transfer,' concludes Martin. 'And that might be quite a long period of time, across a season, where they knew that they probably wouldn't start. So I was interested in scenarios where they would have to watch from the stands as somebody else took their place in the team, all the time having the problem of where they would end up next when they weren't regularly in the shop window. The precariousness of their work, the uncertainty of their work, meant that almost every move came as some kind of relief. It was a positive move for them. Even if it subsequently went badly, no player went from one club to another thinking, "This isn't really what I want, but I'm having to make-do."'

Quite often, players will have little or no say in the identity of their next employer. A change of manager, pressure from their current club or agent or financial reasons means that footballers are often the last to know that they're on the move again.

Liam Rosenior was aware of interest from other clubs throughout one transfer window but was shocked when a bid for him was accepted on deadline day.

'I didn't really even have time to weigh up the decision with my wife, "Is it a good move, is it not?" You just get down there and it's almost pressure,' he reveals. 'I've been pressured into moves before when I've not wanted to move but it represented a good financial deal for the club in question. And I was told that if I didn't go and speak to a club then I would never play for them again. I had been playing well for that club and got on well with everyone, but because it was a good financial deal for that club, I had to go and speak to another club, just so I had a chance to play for my parent club if I didn't go there.

'There is a lot of pressure on players when it comes to financial deals,' Liam continues. 'If you're lucky enough to have a good agent, that's great, but some agents will force a player into moves that they don't want to make because it's a better financial deal for that agent. It's a difficult situation to be in sometimes for players. We get paid a lot of money, live a great life and play a game we love but, at the same time, there are so many outside elements. Fans want loyalty but it's difficult at times when you've got to think of your family and what's right for them. It's a difficult situation to be in.'

Neill Collins was out of the side for a week or two at Leeds United and got a phone call when he returned home from training one Sunday with some unexpected news – his club had accepted a bid for him from Sheffield United.

'It was totally out of the blue,' recalls Neill. 'I was like, "Okay, so that means you want me to go?" It wasn't even the manager that rang me, it was his assistant. I didn't even speak to the manager prior to leaving. I thought about it, mulled it over, thought about fighting for my spot and staying. I finally decided to take the opportunity to move and play. Sheffield United were third from bottom of the league but I went and had five great years there. But it's a case of being rushed into a situation where you have to make a move. You could be somewhere that you don't feel really wanted, you don't know what's going to transpire and you might not get a club like Sheffield United in the summer window.'

Mark Roberts agrees that it's a tough situation to be in when it's obvious that your current employers no longer desire your services. 'I think sometimes if it's the player's choice then that's great,' he says. 'But often a club will decide that for you, whether you like it or not, and I've been in that situation before. I've been told I can leave a football club but managed to stick it out and the manager ended up playing me and changed his opinion of me. That is a difficult mental process to go through because if the door is shut it sometimes won't be reopened. There's only so much you can do in your power as a player, so that's a difficult situation to deal with.'

Premier League rules on tapping up are clear with a contracted player, or a person on his behalf, forbidden from directly or indirectly making contact with another club without having obtained the prior written consent of his current club. Chelsea received a £300,000 fine and a suspended three-points deduction when they were found guilty of tapping up Arsenal's Ashley Cole in 2005. However, it is naive to believe that this sort of contact does not take place in a large proportion of transfer deals.

'I've had an agent for the majority of my career but someone will always find a way of contacting you at the lower levels,' says Mark. 'Managers always find a way of speaking to a player whether that's directly or indirectly. It's kind of who you know not what you know, and that's how some of my transfers have transpired.

'When I was at Cambridge, I was told I was able to leave in the transfer window, certain clubs came forward but it was about choosing the right club for my family and me. So you're waiting for the phone to ring and sometimes in the transfer window that doesn't materialise. That can be a very stressful time because you're wondering why the phone's not ringing, should you chase your agent, could you be doing anything more and try and manufacture a move but that's not usually how it happens.'

Former Tunisia international defender Radhi Jaïdi played for Bolton Wanderers, Birmingham City and Southampton following a move from his homeland and accepts that constant moves are part and parcel of the game.

'It's the nature of football, I think, especially nowadays,' says Radhi, who is now a coach with The Saints. 'Since my era, a lot has changed. I didn't have to move a lot but I still moved to three clubs in England, but I spent at least three years at each club before I retired. It depends on the player. If the player wants to stay in one place then he needs to become one of the people who that club are reliant upon. I saw some foreigners become club captains in England and settled themselves and stayed forever in this country, which can be applicable for any player who proves themselves. It's difficult to stay for more than three years either way if you perform well or if you don't.'

Richie Ryan had only been at Jacksonville Armada for four months when his manager and technical director called at his apartment one night and told him they'd been negotiating his transfer to Miami FC, then managed by Italy legend Alessandro Nesta, for the previous three weeks. It came as a shock to Richie, who hadn't even unpacked all of the boxes he'd shipped from his previous move. A fee had been agreed, however, and he was wanted in Miami the following morning.

'I wasn't really left with any option but to move. I didn't know anything about it until I was told that they'd made an offer for me and that the club had accepted it and were quite happy for me to leave,' says Richie.

'The talks had been ongoing for weeks and I'd known nothing about it. I ended up playing four or five games for Jacksonville and signing for Miami one month into the season. I had no real choice but it was benefiting my family and I to move on to Miami as they were giving me a two-and-a-half-year contract, which was better financially. It worked out better for us, but I'd only been in Jacksonville for four months.'

Prior to that move, Richie had been settled in Canada but a lack of ambition at Ottawa Fury softened the blow of being suddenly traded to a club 1,265 miles away.

'A lot of times players don't have much of a say in things,' maintains Richie. 'When I left Ottawa over here, Jacksonville were willing to pay a fee for me and it was a new opportunity for me and was a chance to go and live in Florida. One of the main factors for me was a massive change of personnel at Ottawa. The manager had changed, the coaching staff had changed and, after the success we had in 2015, I was expecting the club to put a little bit more money into it. The organisation owned a soccer team, an American football team and an ice hockey team so most of the money was invested elsewhere.

'We were very happy in Ottawa and I was hoping that the club would invest a little more money to keep the squad of players and keep the coaching staff together to build something and have success moving forward. But that wasn't the case and I had an option to go elsewhere and challenge myself at another club. The clubs agreed on a fee and I was quite happy to take that move. There wasn't that ambition being shown that I wanted to see as a player.'

Middlesbrough striker Rudy Gestede argues that when it comes to the crunch, players should have the final say in a move. 'You have the choice whether to accept or not,' says the Benin international. 'You still decide on your move. Sometimes you feel the pressure that you have to go but you still have a choice when you have a contract.'

However, most players realise when they've outstayed their welcome and it's time to move on. Michael McGovern spent his formative years at Celtic, with his first call-up to the first-team squad for a UEFA Cup clash against Barcelona at the Camp Nou, but by the age of 24 had yet to play competitively for the first team.

'It was a wrench to leave Celtic as I loved my time there. It is an institution, as is Rangers, to be fair,' says the goalkeeper. 'People don't realise how big the two clubs are until they go there, and I loved every minute of it. However, from a football point of view, the manager didn't know if he could trust me and kept saying that I had no experience. It's difficult when you keep hearing that you've got no experience, yet nobody's willing to give you experience. You're caught in an awkward position. So I had to sort of take a step back to go and get games. I had to build myself up then over the years to get back to a decent level with Norwich City. It's taken time but, of course, as a goalkeeper you can play a bit longer.'

In Raffaele De Vita's experience, being cut loose from a club has never really come as a surprise. 'Most times you know what's coming when you go in to speak to the manager towards the end of the season,' says the midfielder. 'Sometimes it's because you've not played enough or sometimes you've played well and they want to extend your contract. You kind of know whether it's going to be positive or negative so you've got the time to prepare.'

Charlie Sheringham, who has spent much of his career in the lower leagues of English football, agrees that moves often have an inevitability about them.

'It's not quite as high profile as some of the Premier League moves. In the lower leagues, it's quite often a choice between renewing your contract, if you're offered a new deal, or considering a better offer from another club. It's not like the drama of a Pogba transfer that goes on all summer!' he laughs. 'During the season, you usually have an idea of whether you're playing, whether your manager likes you and if you're playing well. If you're not getting in the team or involved as much as you'd like to be you start to look and put the feelers out a little bit. You might have agents calling you or your own agent might be quietly putting your name out there. I think you definitely have an idea. Sometimes an unexpected bid or opportunity might come in that takes you off guard a little bit, but a lot of the time I think you know when you're going to move on. Or you're playing so well that people are interested in you.'

Sometimes it's difficult to prepare, though, when deals gain momentum on transfer deadline day. For football fans, it's an entertaining sideshow, but for players, it's a period of intense uncertainty and anxiety.

'It's horrible,' admits Liam Rosenior. 'I've moved on deadline day myself. I think I signed for Reading an hour before the deadline closed. That was literally a phone call at seven o'clock in the morning telling me that I was on my way to Reading and had to do a medical. It took the whole day to get everything done for the transfer to go through. It's the uncertainty. Players leave their phones off on purpose. I've seen players get calls at ten o'clock at night saying, "Can you get to the training ground to sign for a club that's absolutely miles away? We've had an offer come in for you."'

You would think players would have the inside track on potential moves but they're often as in the dark as the public when it comes to the machinations of deadline day.

'It's funny, when I speak to fans and they ask who the club are going to sign, you literally have no idea,' reveals Liam. 'You have no idea even about yourself. And it's just a call out of the blue and you're moving somewhere else. It is very uncertain, especially the last few days of a transfer window. It's uncertain for players who think they're going to move and are anxious to move. There's anxiety for players who are at a club and settled as their club may be signing a replacement. There are a lot of unseen things in the world of transfers that I think we need to look at and deal with in a different way.'

One former Premier League captain agrees that players are often oblivious to potential moves.

'It is a nervous time, in terms of waiting, as you don't really know what is going on,' he says. 'You're waiting for a move to happen, your agent is saying that this or that is going to happen and you just wait. It does unsettle you because your mind is wondering, "Are they going to put in a bid for me? Are the club going to let me go? What's the transfer fee? And, ultimately, do I actually want to move?" If your family is young enough it's not a problem but when they start school that's where the other side of it comes in. If you've only got a one- or two-year contract, do you uproot your whole family to move?'

It was 5pm on 31 January and Steven Caldwell was relaxing in his Sunderland home. He'd been watching the latest deadline-day deals on Sky Sports News when his phone rang. The club had accepted a bid from Burnley for him and had very little time to complete a deal. A last-minute scramble ensued and Steven was a Burnley player just hours later – and minutes before the deadline passed. The next day he was looking for a new home.

Unwanted by Roy Keane at The Black Cats, a possible move to The Clarets or Coventry City had been mooted earlier in the month before negotiations had come to a standstill. He hadn't wanted to leave Sunderland and was surprised at the late turn of events.

'The transfer window, and particularly deadline day, is a really emotional time,' says Steven. 'If you're comfortable at a club and you're not really thinking about moving, you're not really worried or concerned about it. But if you know you're kind of on the way, you can see it coming.'

Keane had given him permission a few weeks beforehand to speak to Burnley manager Steve Cotterill but Steven admits he was a 'bit nonplussed about the move and not really bothered about going.' The deal was reignited at the eleventh hour and Steven admits he had very little time to consider the ramifications.

'All of a sudden, as happens especially on January deadline day, things heat up really quickly,' he says. 'Steve Cotterill had been calling me every few days, but I didn't expect anything to happen. Then at 5pm it was beginning to pick up steam. Sunderland were moving with the things that Burnley needed them to move on and it started to become a reality. It was another learning experience because it was the first time that I was like, "Oh god, I am actually leaving here!" I was a wee bit like, "Do I want this?" Anyway, it happened and I decided it was better for my career to play again and it was probably going to be a miserable six months at Sunderland as Roy wanted me out of the club.'

A three-and-a-half year deal was agreed and Steven went on to captain the Lancashire side to promotion to the Premier League. 'I went and, again, I was a bit unsure about what to expect and what was going to happen but, lo and behold, it was the best thing I ever did in my career,' says the former Scotland international. 'I just love that football club and we had so much success. It was perfect. The experience just made me think that you should always go with your hunch, to go play somewhere and make the best of it. It can turn out to be amazing. You've got to be positive about a move. If you're still negative about it once you move then you won't succeed. Once it happens, you have to be positive about it and, if you are, good things happen.'

He had originally moved to Sunderland from north-east rivals Newcastle United and what could have been an acrimonious move was understood by Toon fans. In contrast, former Newcastle goalkeeper Steve Harper had to close his Twitter account in 2016 in the wake of abuse from some fans when he joined The Black Cats.

'I just wanted to play football,' explains Steven, of his move across the Tyne-Wear divide. 'I never really got that much stick, to be honest. I played against them a couple of times and I got my fair amount of stick during the game, which I understand, but I wasn't getting pelters when I was out and about or having a meal in the city or anything. I think they appreciated that I gave my best for their team and that I needed to play football at that point in my life.

'I was happy to stay in the north-east. I liked playing football there and my wife, my girlfriend at the time, is from there.

Sunderland is a great club and Mick McCarth
badly so that was nice. From being a kind of
Sir Bobby Robson never really saw me as a
having a guy who really wants you, you kinc
by that. I think the Newcastle fans realised
against the club or anything like that.'

Former Stoke City and Chelsea goalkeeper Asmir Begović has
moved a couple of times during transfer windows and concurs
that speculation can certainly affect players.

'You might have something brewing. There may be talk of you
getting a move somewhere bigger and better,' says the Bosnia and
Herzegovina international. 'Or, on the flip side, a guy in the same
position you play in is linked to your club. So, of course, there's
a bit of uncertainty there as it could affect your position. There's
definitely a sense of uncertainty during the transfer window for
many players.'

Mark Roberts agrees that deadline day, and the run-up to it,
can be a frustrating time for players for various reasons. Most
players I spoke to admitted they also keep track of transfer gossip,
which isn't particularly helpful if your club has been linked with
a player in your position. Imagine your own profession suddenly
introduced biannual occasions where you had to constantly read
about a potential replacement for your job, or the possibility of
being traded to another company in an unfamiliar city or country.

'The transfer window has changed the dynamics of things
since it's been introduced. If things aren't going so well on the
pitch then maybe you start having a look over your shoulder
while the window is open to see if any players are coming through
the door and wondering whether that competition will affect you,'
admits Mark. 'The flip side to not being in the team is it raises
the hope that the phone might just ring. You do check as a player
while the window's open, "Oh, he's moved there," and you see the
yellow ticker tape on Sky and you're thinking, "How's he got that
move?" A lot of players in the dressing room might comment,

ne's done well there!" and you're just hoping that person
you. But once the window closes you've got to then get your
head around the fact that you might be at a club who've told you
they don't want you for the foreseeable future. Sometimes that
can work for you as the manager can't bring any more bodies
in and has to work with what he's got. It depends where you see
yourself in the pecking order and if there's a realistic route back
into the first-team fold. Sometimes it's taken out of your control
and you've got to make the best of the situation. There's a lot of
things to consider that possibly the supporters in the street don't
always think about. There are issues that affect players from the
bottom level to the top.'

Michael McGovern has never moved on deadline day but
admits he's seen team-mates affected by the speculation about
a possible move.

'There is a funny atmosphere in January, probably more
than at the start of the season,' he reveals. 'I've found that with
certain players who might know something's happening in the
background. Maybe they want to go, the club want money for
them or the club are saying they're not able to go and that they
want to keep them. In training, sometimes, you do get some
players that don't exactly down tools but it's all about body
language.

'I think everyone's different, though. You have some players
who are model professionals. Nothing fazes them, they're like
machines, like robots, they just go out and play and train. But
everyone's human. If you've potentially got something lined up
where you really want to go and think it'll be better for you, then
it's almost hard to give your all – even if you want to give your
all. Maybe subconsciously it's hard to give everything,' he adds.

'It depends on the individual,' agrees Mark Roberts. 'If it's
a club from a higher level then certain players' heads will get
turned. I've always had a good relationship with my agent and
he'll ring me when it's something genuine that he needs to tell

me. I know that there are players who have people advising them, where you wonder if they've got their best interests at heart. A lot of it can be speculation and a lot of it can be hearsay but it does affect some players in a negative way. Don't get me wrong, though, sometimes a player may deserve their move. They've put in the performances where you think, "God, if they don't move now they never will."

'I've seen many times over the years where one club will be interested in a player then, all of a sudden, there are four or five clubs lined up – whether that's concrete interest or agents circulating someone's name I'm not certain, you're never totally sure,' he continues. 'I guess every club has a list of players as targets and you never know quite where you fit in that list. Sometimes your agent can possibly bump you up that list. He might have a connection with a club or an affinity with a club. You see it at the very top level where the super-agents move players to certain clubs and they negotiate better with some clubs than others. I'm sure that goes on at all levels of football and that does help certain players get certain moves. I think, though, you've got to be patient sometimes and just hope that that right move does come, that the phone does ring and that the right club that you would like to go to is the one that picks up the phone.'

Neill Collins agrees that it comes down to the individual player as to whether speculation affects them. He's seen both sides of it – players thriving on the fact that clubs are after them and coming to watch them. And players who'd been hoping for a move and then crumble under the pressure of clubs coming to scout them.

'I've seen people, when it comes to January, and their head's been turned in different directions and they do take their foot off the pedal,' he discloses. 'The club then fight to keep them and you wonder whether it'd be best to sell them because you're dealing with a human being at the end of the day. If they miss out on a move that was going to be life-changing for them and their family then you'll never get the best out of that person again. Some players are oblivious to that, they can turn it on and off and don't worry about speculation. Again, each individual reacts to these things differently.'

He's not a huge fan of the transfer window and believes unwanted players should not be forced to remain at a club who deem them surplus to requirements.

'In my opinion, the transfer window is ridiculous,' he argues. 'When I grew up players could move at any time. In some respects it made it much easier. When you set a deadline people tend to work to the deadline. If there was no deadline, it would either be happening or not happening. There would either be discussions or there wouldn't be. Whereas, right now, you've got all this will it, won't it and then, all of a sudden, the deadline's passed and everything goes back to normal but there's a lot of pieces to pick up. I don't particularly like the window and I think players should never be held to a club for five or six months if they're not playing. You should have the ability to leave that club. I don't think it's right that you can't do that.'

He's moved a couple of times during a transfer window and believes that changing clubs in January can be an even more difficult time than in the summer.

'I moved to Sheffield United from Leeds United on deadline day, very unexpectedly. That was a bit of a whirlwind. It was really quite strange, it happened so fast. And, all of a sudden, you have a few hours to make a decision on something that can impact the rest of your career, which is not easy,' he says. 'I signed for Preston North End from Wolves on deadline day, but that was expected. It had been coming a long time, they'd haggled for weeks over a price and it eventually happened on deadline day. That's another thing: clubs want you at the oddest times. Sometimes you can be playing great and you need a move and it's not really there. And then there are times when two clubs want you at the same time out of the blue.

'I think January's a really tough time to move,' Neill continues. 'You're in the middle of the season, you talk about the logistics, you talk about your family. People give footballers some bad press and we've got one of the best jobs in the world, if not the best. But in terms of playing professional sport, you imagine living in a hotel day in, day out. People think that'd be great. But when you're trying to play at your best on a Saturday, even things like food are a problem. You're stuck in a hotel all day; where do you eat? When you can prepare your food in the comfort of your own home, with your partner and kids – these are all the things that impact you on the field. You rush to the other end of the country, you're stuck in a hotel, you don't know your team-mates, you're trying to look for houses, and schools for your kids. All these things add up and it needs to be a really, really good move in January or it's best to leave it until the summer when you can get everything right.'

Raffaele De Vita hasn't experienced any last-minute moves but concedes that even speculation about a transfer can be worrying.

'I've always moved at the end of a season,' he says. 'I've left a club and not known where I was going to sign. Talking to my agent every day, new clubs popping up – it is a bit unsettling. Sometimes you can't really decide. When I left Swindon Town my agent told me I could be signing for Sheffield United. All of a sudden, in a minute, you have to think about living in the north of England. You're trying to picture everything and then, next minute, my agent mentions a Scottish club. All of a sudden, you have to change everything again and tell your partner, "Oh, we're actually going to live in Scotland now." Until you sign, every two minutes you have to change your life. You have to do it sometimes in a split second and it is very unsettling.'

Despite admitting to tuning in to deadline-day coverage, Leroy Lita isn't a fan either. 'I've had two proposed moves on deadline day – one I turned down and one Reading turned down. I didn't want to go to Sheffield United, and Reading turned down a bid from Bolton Wanderers,' recalls Leroy. 'They make too much of it now. Most of the transfers are already done and it is just Sky trying to make it exciting, which is understandable as a lot of people watch it – including myself.'

Liam Rosenior believes the closing of the window before the league season kicks off – which happened for the first time in August 2018 – will be beneficial for players, with conjecture around possible transfers no longer hindering performances on the pitch.

'I think it's logical now for the transfer window to close before the season begins,' he argues. 'From a player's point of view – and you have to be selfish as a player – you're playing for a club but you have a chance of moving to your dream club in two days, but you have to play a game on Saturday. Are you really going to be committed to a tackle or are you going to be thinking, "Am I going to get injured?" It's little things like that that affect players' performances.'

He is also in agreement that coverage has become over the top and just adds to the pressure on potential signings.

'It's due to the money involved,' he says. 'In the media, they speak about how much the transfer fee is and how much wages the players are getting paid, but the be-all and end-all is the performance on the pitch. I think the way that we look at transfers in this country is if you sign a player for £20m, £30m, £40m they're going to transform the whole club and the club are instantly going to be successful because they're at the club.

'In terms of the media's dealing with the transfer market – we have a special transfer deadline day and we're talking about deals going through – for me, it's not important. What's important is what happens on the pitch. The players are being put under so much pressure now. Going into the training ground with cameras following them and jumping out of cars with blankets over their head – it's gone to a completely different level. I think that increases the pressure on players when they first join a club,' he argues.

Liam says that he's often been called at the last-minute of a transfer window and asked if he'd consider joining a particular club, which he believes is characteristic of the lack of foresight clubs display, despite the vast financial resources in the modern-day game. English clubs were involved in 119 deals on the last day of August 2017, with over 30 per cent completed in the final two hours of the window. It does seem comparable to a desperate husband's Christmas Eve dash for a present for his wife. In contrast, clubs in England completed just 11 deals on the first day of that month.

'In terms of transfers, I'm amazed at how much business is done on the last day of a transfer window. I'm absolutely amazed with the money that is now in the game,' he says. 'It's not hard to plan who you are going to sign. There's a fundamental flaw, and not just in English football, but in football generally. There are not too many teams planning what they want to do. I think that's why you see so much business done. So I don't think it's to the detriment of English clubs that Spanish or German clubs can sign players later on, when the window closes earlier here. Obviously, it would be better if the transfer window closed on the same day for everyone. You hear the term 'panic buys', which a lot of signings are. They are absolute panic buys. I've been called on deadline day and asked, "Would you go here?" just because they needed to fill a position and they just came across my name. There's no real planning or structure to transfer deals that you would expect and I think that's something that really needs to change.'

Leroy Lita is a product of the youth system at Chelsea, who are often criticised for their loan policy and failure to blood youngsters in the first team. He's had several loan moves during his career and insists they are crucial to a young player's development. At the time of writing, The Blues had 37 players on loan, only eight of whom had ever started a league game for the club.

'Everyone moans about Chelsea sending their youngsters on loan but I think it's a good thing,' says Leroy. 'They're playing first-team football and they're getting experience, which is very important for a young player because you don't get experience by playing under-23s or sitting on a bench all the time. It may not be where you want it to be, but you're getting experience and getting used to life as a first-team regular. When I'm playing, I'm happy. When I'm sitting on a bench, I'm not happy.'

I watched Eamon Dunphy, a pundit on Ireland's state broadcaster, RTÉ, describe loan moves as 'embarrassing' during the 2018 World Cup, when discussing the volume of England players at the tournament who had spent time away from their parent clubs earlier in their careers. Gareth Southgate's 23-man squad had 46 loan spells under their collective belts, with Harry Kane declaring that his temporary spell at relegation-battling Millwall at 18, 'turned him into a man'.

Leroy's opinion was shared by the majority of players I spoke to who have had loan spells during their career, a period they often see as a rite of passage. They often give a player their first opportunity to play at a senior level, so are looked back on fondly by most. Sir Matt Busby once said, 'I aim to make footballers of my boys,' and that's the predominant purpose of the majority of loan moves.

'For me, my loan moves were great – they were always at the right time,' says Steven Caldwell. 'It's your choice. Obviously, a manager will suggest it but, at the end of the day, if you don't want to go to a certain place then you don't have to leave. I went to Blackpool for the first one for a month and played in League One. I did pretty well and it was great to know I was playing on a Saturday afternoon or a Tuesday night. I did really well at that level and it gave me the confidence to come back. I didn't think I was coming back to play for Newcastle, I just wanted to get experience as a professional player. I then went to Bradford City reasonably soon after that and it was a step up again. It was the Championship and it was difficult – Jim Jefferies who took me there got sacked after a couple of games. I got a new manager and I was a loan signing so it was going to be complicated. But I still played and the experience of going through that, being part of a team where a manager had lost his job, was a great learning experience.'

He got his first taste of regular top-flight action at Leeds United, where he went on loan in a swap deal with Michael Bridges.

'That one was another fantastic loan move,' he enthuses. 'So my loans were always progressive and improving me as a player. Leeds was amazing – I played every week in the Premier League for the first time. I was 23 years old so I was getting on a little bit and needed that opportunity. Of course, we got relegated, which was disappointing, but from a selfish point of view, it was a great experience to play games and know what it took to play at that level. I'd played in the Premier League with Newcastle but I'd never been a starter. Knowing on a Monday that you're playing on a Saturday is really different to coming off a bench or getting picked because of an injury to someone else. It was nice to prepare at the start of the week for a Saturday game knowing that I was in the starting XI.'

It was Steven Caldwell's presence in the first team at Sunderland that contributed to Neill Collins's first loan move away from the club. He feels the success of these temporary deals depends on what stage a player's career is at, but that some clubs have taken it to the extreme.

'I think the loan window has got a wee bit out of hand,' he stresses. 'I went on loan to Hartlepool United from Sunderland, which was pretty natural and what loan moves are all about. I wasn't going to play for Sunderland in the Premier League so I went to Hartlepool to get experience, to go there with the right intentions. I was a Hartlepool player for that time and was going to play hard and hope to do well for them.

'It's definitely a grey area as you get too many loan players and if things aren't going well you've always got that problem in, does it affect them at the end of the season, in terms of if the club get relegated they can swan off back to their own club and everything's fine. That comes down to the individual player. Clubs also don't really want loads of loanees because it produces too much uncertainty. I think Celtic, for example though, have done a good job with long-term loans for players like Patrick Roberts.'

Michael McGovern, who had a couple of loan spells in Scotland while starting out at Celtic, agrees that they are more beneficial to younger players – if they go well.

'I think it depends what position the player's in,' he maintains. 'If you're a young player and you're well thought of at the club, they'll send you on loan to try and get experience of playing first-team football. So when you come back to your parent club you're ready to kick on and challenge for a first-team place. You get the other side of the coin, though, where you get older players who are out of the picture and they're just going to get game time, which won't really enhance their status at their parent club no matter how well they do. It's often just so their parent club can get some of their wages off the wage bill.

'As a young player, they can go either way. You see some young players go out on loan and they do really well and the club looks at them in a different light when they return. Then you get the other side of things when you have a bad loan, and you think, "Well, my parent club's a big club and I can't even get a game at this smaller club." So, if you can't get a game for a lower-division team, how are you going to get into the first team at a bigger club?'

Early in his career, Mark Roberts enjoyed several loans with non-league clubs before making his Football League debut in the Championship with Crewe Alexandra. He concurs that their success depends on the circumstances of your career at that point.

'There was a purpose to it and a design to it in terms of me gaining experience,' he says. 'And a lot of young players that I played with or against during my career have been sent to places to toughen them up or to see if they're ready to progress. Later in my career, there have been options to go on loan, but uprooting my family for a month or three months has not been an option I've considered. I guess you have to weigh up the options at the current time and decide what's right for yourself, your career and also your family.'

It was four days before the 2018 summer transfer window closed and Jimmy Dunne was gearing himself up for a season as Burnley's fourth-choice central defender. The arrival of £15m signing Ben Gibson from Middlesbrough changed all that and pushed him further down the pecking order. Another loan move was imminent.

'The main priority for the club is that the first team are going to do well that season,' says the Irishman. 'And, if you're not getting into that squad it's down to you to try and find a club. They will help you, they will guide you, they will put a phone call in for you but this is kind of when you need your agent. The loan window stays open for a month after the permanent transfer window closes so I had a few weeks to get a loan. That's when I need my agent making phone calls to find the best place for me.'

Jimmy joined Manchester United when he was ten years old, moving across the Irish Sea to the Red Devils at 15. After about six weeks, the enormity of the move hit him. 'I started to realise, "Well, I'm not going home now. This is me for good." I did go through a little spell of struggling. The only problem is when you're not playing football. At 17, I had a double hip operation, which put me out of action for 13 months. That was at the beginning of my scholarship, so I was away from home and not even playing football. I thought, "What am I doing here?" It just didn't make any sense. I got through that but it never looked like it was going to work out at United. I still had a year left there but it made more sense for me to go somewhere that I might have an opportunity. Luckily, Burnley came in and I could do that,' says the 20-year-old.

He spent one season playing with The Clarets's under-23s side before embarking on a series of loans to aid his development.

'Their plan for me was to learn how to become a man and a defender as soon as possible,' says Jimmy. His first temporary move was at National League club Barrow, before he stepped up a division to help Accrington Stanley – with the lowest budget in the division – win an unlikely League Two title.

'The loan thing is difficult because you go from being in a comfortable environment with top facilities and top pros to learn from, to right down the bottom of the leagues where you have nothing,' admits Jimmy. 'You really have nothing. At Barrow, the club was great and made a great effort to try and give the players everything, but there's no money, there are no facilities. I always say, though, "This isn't where I want to be, but it's where I need to be to get to where I want to go."'

Lower-league football is often thought of as having a rough and tumble nature, but Jimmy believes it's the mental rather than physical side of such moves that often proves toughest.

'Going from being a boy to a man in football is definitely tough,' he says. 'Being able to tell yourself that you do have to move away, that you do have to fight for a place. No one's going to give it to me, that's the reality of football. It's going to be difficult and it's difficult everywhere you go. You have big squads everywhere, all looking to play in the first XI. It's always going to be competitive and I think that's what younger players, who are comfortable in academies, find difficult. When you're playing under-23s football, you might be rotated a little bit. It's not really competitive, no one really watches it and there's not much pressure. Whereas, when you're playing with men – and they're fighting for their lives, their careers, to pay for a daughter's birthday present – it's a whole new ball game. It is tough.'

In August 2018 Jimmy was given the security of a contract extension by Burnley, but Gibson's arrival at Turf Moor meant he would have to seek another loan move. The club did advise him on his next move but, ultimately, it was down to the player and his agent to find a new club.

'I had to weigh up my options and discuss things with my club and agent,' Jimmy explains. 'A step up for me would have been League One, where I could have gone, but I thought that, at 20, I wanted to play at the biggest stage possible, in front of the biggest crowds possible. Somewhere that I can put my name out there even more. It's a marathon, not a sprint. I don't need to scrap through the leagues frantically. I need to take my time and make the best decisions, which I think this one is.'

We spoke a couple of days after he signed a six-month deal with Heart of Midlothian, who topped an embryonic Scottish Premiership table when he joined. With an average home crowd of 18,429 at Tynecastle during the 2017/18 season, it was another step up for Jimmy following his spells at Barrow and Accrington Stanley. As for the long term, he's not ruling anything out.

'The Scottish Premiership is a massive opportunity and a massive step up. It's a massive, massive club. They've got everything up here. It's like Premier League facilities, with top coaches and it's a chance for me to play on a big stage and there are a lot of games televised so I'll be seen a lot more.

'With my attitude, I would never turn down an opportunity anywhere, I would never get too comfortable anywhere. I did get comfortable in Manchester, but I had to leave. I got comfortable in Burnley, but I had to leave. Edinburgh's a beautiful city but this is only a six-month loan, so I'll probably be going back to Burnley in January and who knows where I'll be going from there. I don't have a problem with that. I'm contracted at Burnley until 2020, which I am chuffed with. It keeps me at a fabulous club. But if I'm not going to get into the first team, then I need to go somewhere where I will. That's what these loans are about,' he concludes.

Despite famously being a one-club man, former Liverpool defender Jamie Carragher wrote in early 2018 that players consider three things before moving clubs – ambition, geography and finances. He wrote this in the context of a troubled Newcastle United's failure to attract big-name signings, but I wondered if it is true of all players and, if so, in what order they take these factors into consideration.

'I think everyone's different, it depends what position you're in,' contends Michael McGovern. 'I wouldn't say every player would have them in that order. Most of the time you're either moving because you're not playing or you're moving because you're doing really well. If you're not playing I'd imagine your options would be less than if you were setting heather on fire, doing really well and scoring goals.'

Neill Collins agrees. 'Everyone is different. I'll be honest and say that the size of the club is possibly the biggest thing as that generally goes hand in hand with finances and ambition. The biggest thing I've found when it comes to a move is that you almost need a crystal ball. There are so many things to weigh up and it's never as clear-cut as you'd like to think. For example, when I was leaving Preston North End I had the opportunity to go to Leeds United or Coventry City. Coventry were going to make me captain. Aidy Boothroyd, their manager at the time, was really impressive when I spoke to him. I really liked him.

'But the size of Leeds United, the history of the club, all these things – I couldn't turn it down, I couldn't miss this opportunity to go there. I'd played under Simon Grayson and wasn't entirely convinced it was the right match for me but I just felt that I couldn't turn down the chance to go to Leeds. It didn't really last as long as it could, or should, have done but I don't regret the decision I made at the time. I don't know how things would have worked out if I'd gone to Coventry. It's not like some players are choosing between Manchester United or Arsenal, but the principles are the same.

'If I was giving anyone advice I would always take into account the club because that never changes. The managers might change but if the club is a big club it's generally always going to be a big club. The manager is the one that impacts your life the most. If you feel that they have a certain amount of security in their job, that's the man that's going to impinge upon your life the most and the biggest reason for going to the club. I haven't even talked about finances, but they generally take care of themselves if you're doing things right.'

When Michael McGovern joined Norwich City, he was reunited with his former manager at Hamilton Academical, Alex Neill. However, this wasn't a major factor in his decision to join The Canaries, amid interest from several other clubs.

'From a personal point of view, I would never join a club just because I was friendly with people already there,' says the Northern Irishman. 'That would be a secondary bonus point, it would never be a major factor in my decision. First and foremost, you're a footballer and you want to go to the best club where you've the best chance of playing and where you think you'll do well. Maybe other people are different. It's different if it's the manager because he picks the team. If it's a manager you worked with before and you know what you're going to get with him then that's completely different. But players come and go, that's what happens. Even this season, at Norwich, some of my friends have left. It's sad but it is just part of the game.'

Jamie Carragher's considerations when choosing a club are true for many players, believes Mark Roberts. 'You want to be signing for a club heading in an upward direction or that do things maybe a bit differently. At different stages of your career, the boxes that you need to tick before you make a move alter. I've seen it from a number of different ways. I didn't move away until I was 25. I'd always played for local clubs and been around that support network of family and friends. When I moved to Stevenage at 25 it was very much, I would probably say, a last-chance saloon situation for me and my professional career, but I was playing for my local club and they'd gone into administration. We weren't getting paid and I was worrying how I was going to pay the mortgage and then an opportunity came up that I felt was too good to miss.

'It was a decision that changed my life and changed my career,' he continues. 'From then on it took an upward curve. I was quite fortunate that the manager who was at Northwich with me became assistant manager at Stevenage. He had also played for the club so he was aware of the area. When I first signed I was staying in a hotel two or three nights a week before moving down there permanently. The place I chose on his recommendation, I stayed for close to five years, and I would have chosen the same place to live if I had chosen the last day of being there. It was the perfect location for me and it was one of the most enjoyable stages of my career. I loved where I lived and I loved playing for the club that I'd signed for. So, that worked out fantastically well.'

As his career progressed, he admits geography played as much a factor as ambition when it came to choosing his next club.

'I met my now wife while I was at Stevenage. She is from Wigan and I'm from the north-west as well so when the time was right for me to leave Stevenage and I felt I was ready for a new challenge, there was an opportunity to move closer to home,' says Mark. 'Fleetwood were a club who matched my ambition on and off the pitch. They were on a journey themselves as a football club and that was very important to me. I wanted to sign for someone who had a vision that I could buy into. They were selling me the complete package as a player. The chairman, Andy Pilley, was very ambitious and he'd had multiple promotions already, but they'd identified me as a player that could help them to continue that rise up the football pyramid. I signed there as captain and was able to help them to win promotion in my first season. So, that worked out great. It was brilliant having been away from family and friends – them having to travel down maybe three hours just to see you for five seconds after a game if they were lucky. You'd give them a handshake or a hug on the side of the pitch and then they'd get back in their car and drive three hours back up the motorway. To be closer to family and friends was very important to me. They've always been very supportive to me but you realise when you move away that that support network is no longer there.'

Former England midfielder David Bentley once mentioned to me that one of the reasons he retired early from the game was due to feeling like a commodity or, in his words, 'being owned like a piece of meat'.

Most players agree that they often feel more like an asset than a human as soon as they enter the professional game. As far back as 1936, Peter Doherty was sold to Manchester City by Blackpool against his wishes – having just bought a house in the area – commenting, 'My personal feelings counted for next to nothing in the transaction. I might as well have been a bale of merchandise.'

'Definitely,' agrees Liam Rosenior. 'You feel that from the moment you sign for a football club. You know that you have a financial value for that football club, who will look after you and do anything for you. But if the club doesn't want you or you're not in the team or squad, you're made to feel like you don't exist. That's natural, it's a competitive industry we're in. And it's amazing when you're at a club and doing well, how well you're treated and how important they make you feel. As opposed to when you're injured, for example, when you don't have that value on the pitch. A lot of players struggle to deal with that.'

Neill Collins is of the same opinion. 'You definitely feel like a commodity,' he says. 'There are times when you sign that piece of paper that you can feel like they've got you and can do what they like with you. There are times when they should protect their investment a lot better than they do. Some clubs are quite happy to throw money out there and forget that these players are assets. I have seen players definitely struggle with the weight of a transfer fee. It's not just the fee, though, it's the whole pressure of the fans and signing itself. It's not the fact that they paid £10m or £50m but it's the fact that there's such a big furore around the signing and the pressure on the field. It's not the money, specifically, it's the whole pressure of coming in and having to produce.'

Leroy Lita fully understands Bentley's point of view but admits he's never let it get to him. 'I don't really think about it, to be honest, I just see it as another challenge or opportunity and try and do my job and be as professional as possible.'

He's had a couple of seven-figure transfers during his career but has shrugged them off to concentrate on matters on the pitch. 'Not one bit did it affect me,' says Leroy. 'I didn't put the price on my head, it was nothing to do with me! I knew my focus. My focus was to get to the Premier League. I didn't care what price tag was on my head, I don't deal with all that. There's going to be a lot more pressure on young lads though. I don't think the young lads now, no disrespect to them, are strong enough characters. I look at the England team and I remember when I used to watch the likes of Shearer, Beckham, Gerrard and Scholes and you saw men. Now when I watch England it looks like the youth team.'

Fellow striker Rudy Gestede has been involved in transfers totalling over £14m so far in his career but, similarly, hasn't allowed them to weigh him down. 'I had transfer fees when I moved to Blackburn and then to Villa and then to Boro,' says the 29-year-old. 'It has never been a huge amount of money so, for me, there wasn't any pressure.'

When one player I interviewed moved between Premier League clubs in 2006, he was just one of several seven-figure signings for his ambitious new club. Others had joined for larger fees, which took the pressure off him somewhat.

'So, for me, it was no real big pressure,' says the defender. 'It depends on your debut and it depends on how the manager treats you. I've seen other players come in, with a big price tag, who just can't deal with it as everyone's expecting them to be this amazing player from the very first game. If the team is not playing the way you're used to, or you don't know anyone, or the manager is playing you out of position, or you're not even that manager's signing, it's quite hard to fit into the system that the manager wants and to perform at your best. You might also be living in a hotel for three months, like I once did before I actually got into a house.

'Sometimes it's easy to settle, sometimes it's more difficult,' he continues. 'I had a friend who kept going back to London whenever we had a day off to see his family and friends. He didn't really settle up north. And you have others that fly abroad at any opportunity they can to see their families. It is a difficult settling-in process. It's a good life but there are bits of it that you have to deal with that don't come easily to certain people.'

Asmir Begović believes it comes down to the individual player. 'The more money a club spends on you, the more pressure and more expectation of a return,' says the keeper, who's moved for a number of seven-figure sums. 'You either take that as a negative or go the other way and just embrace it as a challenge.'

Despite the last-minute, unexpected transfers, despite the constant upheaval and effects on family life, despite the unwanted relocations to a strange town, city or country, players seem to look back on the majority of their moves with a certain fondness. Michael McGovern encapsulates many footballers' thoughts on the transfer market when he concludes, 'I'm not one for regrets but whatever's meant to be will be. I never really look back and wish I'd done things differently. You get ups and downs. You go to some places and enjoy it and other places not so much. A football career is like a rollercoaster, but it's never boring. And, to be honest, that's the thing I love about it.'

The Media

MASAL Bugduv was no ordinary teenager. The 16-year-old attacker was labelled as 'Moldova's finest' by *The Times* in their 2009 rundown of the 'Top 50 rising stars', making 30th on the list which stated he'd been 'strongly linked with Arsenal ... and plenty of other top clubs'.

Except that Bugduv wasn't a teenager. He wasn't even Moldovan. In fact, he didn't exist. *The Times*, and other British media outlets, had been duped by an elaborate hoax that consisted of a series of blog postings, Wikipedia entries and fabricated *Associated Press* reports.

The source of the ruse was not initially located but there was a strong suspicion that it was a lampoon of the transfer market that had been generated in Ireland.

Masal Bugduv is pronounced similarly to *M'asal Beag Dubh,* Irish for 'my little black donkey, or ass'. Indeed, the 20th century Irish writer Pádraic Ó Conaire wrote a story called *M'asal Beag Dubh,* about a man who is tricked into overpaying for a useless donkey – which is certainly analogous to large swathes of transfer deals in the football world. Furthermore, a blog post about the player came from a fictitious Moldovan newspaper – *Diario Mo Thon. Mo thóin* is Irish for 'my arse'.

The suspected location of Bugduv's creator was one transfer-related rumour that was true. Declan Varley, the man eventually unveiled as being behind the fictional Moldovan's creation, is

Group Editor of the *Galway Advertiser* newspaper and felt the football transfer market was ripe for lampooning.

'Fake news has now become a big thing. But this was not malicious, it was just a bit of *craic*. It was really just a social experiment,' says Declan. 'I've been a journalist for almost 30 years covering sport, so I knew that a lot of sports writing involves giving people what they want. When you're writing a match report, you map it out in a certain way so it's easier for the readers to follow along. I felt a lot of the media were just leading readers along in a merry-go-round of hope, in a sense that their club would actually sign a player. So I wondered how far it would fly if you had a fake player.'

Ó Conaire was a revered writer in Galway, where a statue of him was unveiled in 1935 before it was decapitated in the late 1990s. The sculpture's head was later found on a bus and the statue transferred to Galway City Museum. Declan confirms that one of Ó Conaire's stories was the inspiration for the elaborate ruse.

'It's about bringing a useless donkey to the market and trying to flog him for a lot more than he's actually worth. So there's a lot of similarities there to when you're trying to flog, for example, Philippe Senderos or selling John Stones for £50m,' he explains.

'Rather than make him a superstar straight away, I gave him potential as people were big into buying potential back then. I went on to the Moldovan national team's Wikipedia page and I added him to the squad. I also added him to the squad of a team called Olimpia Bălți, as a 16-year-old. Coincidentally, there is a player who plays for Moldova called Bugaiov at the moment, who scored against the Republic of Ireland in a 2018 World Cup qualifier,' he continues.

Declan modelled his creation on Wayne Rooney – 'built like a tank, with a powerful shot' – and, rather than give him a spectacular debut goal, credited him with an outrageous assist on his Moldovan 'debut'.

Bugduv even got his own representation, based on Borat's sleazy agent in the Sacha Baron Cohen film which was popular at the time.

'At one stage I wanted to base Bugduv on Borat, in the sense that he was a legend in his own mind,' recalls Declan. 'I noticed Moldova were due to play Luxembourg in 2008 in a World Cup qualifier and I wrote a story in the style of an *Associated Press* report, as I did with all the stories. I made sure I wasn't going to put this in any papers I was involved with, but just wanted to plant a seed out there. I put it out there on message boards along the lines of, "Hey, have you seen this?" and then copied and pasted the story.'

The seed grew. A story where Bugduv was quoted as stating that he 'would destroy Luxembourg and then join Arsenal' took off. Declan was soon watching his creation on Sky Sports News in a list of players that Arsenal had been linked with. Mark Hughes, Manchester City's manager at the time, was asked about the wonderkid in a press conference and replied that he wasn't ruling out any signings.

'People didn't want to say they'd never heard of him, people wanted to be in the know and he just got into popular conversation,' laughs Declan.

At one stage Harry Redknapp, then Tottenham Hotspur's manager, had said, 'We're not going to spend money on a nobody from Lithuania or Moldova or something.'

'This was an opportunity for Bugduv to be slighted, so he responded to that. If you Googled his name at the time you'd get a couple of thousand mentions.'

Then came the tipping point. In January 2009, Declan's friend rang him and told him to switch on Irish sports radio show *Off the Ball*.

They were discussing *The Times's* article that had compiled a list of the Top 50 most promising players in the world. In at number 30 – ahead of Robert Lewandowski and Mesut Özil – was

Masal Bugduv, a player who didn't exist. Even the official FIFA website mentioned the fictitious player in a discussion about Moldova. 'The country was riven by political turmoil at the time and it said the only bright hope was this young footballer,' says Declan. 'Bugduv was getting a life of his own.'

The prank was unveiled when a Russian journalist, who covered Moldovan football, realised, 'Hang on, this guy doesn't exist.' After a couple of days, *The Times* corrected its error, replacing Bugduv at number 30 in the list with a young Arsenal striker called Jay Simpson, rather than bumping everyone up one place.

However, the original Top 50 had been syndicated worldwide and, all of a sudden, Bugduv had 106 million mentions when you Googled him.

'It went everywhere, it went viral, it went crazy. It was just a good old yarn. It's easier to share things now with social media but it's hard to know if you could get away with something similar now,' says Declan.

He had experience of this, supplementing his journalism income by selling Irish yarns to English newspapers. He knew that 'there was an appetite there for this sort of bullshit story'.

Masal Bugduv has gone on to become the subject of 'The Role of Truth in Digital Journalism' coursework at an American university. There's also a pub in Connemara in County Galway – where the aforementioned poet Pádraic Ó Conaire used to drink – that was so fascinated by the story that it set up a shrine to Masal Bugduv in the corner, including a mannequin wearing a Moldovan number 10 shirt.

I had a similar experience with internet users taking stories or headlines at face value. A couple of years ago, I felt there was a niche for satirical football news in the style of Ireland's *Waterford Whispers News* or the *Daily Mash* in the UK.

Under the pseudonym Midfield Generals, I posted a few articles and shared them on social media. They got some traction but were obviously a piss-take. Headlines such as 'Calendar Suggests It's Only Two Leeds United Managers Until Christmas', 'Brendan Rodgers Forgets to Use Word "Outstanding" in Press Conference' and 'Paul Scholes' Family Never Heard Him Speak Until Retirement' were all clearly parodies.

Then, after an unusually effective performance from the Belgian midfielder about two years after joining Manchester United, I posted one headlined, 'United Club Shop Finally Sell First Fellaini Shirt'.

The article got thousands of shares, a lot more than click-throughs to the actual piece, where lines like 'the anonymous customer becomes only the second person to wear the Fellaini name on the back of his shirt, the first being Fellaini himself' and 'the bespoke shirt comes equipped with elbow pads and a marsupial-type pouch on the chest to capture long balls' clearly portrayed that it was meant to be satirical. But a large percentage of those who just saw the headline took it at face value, with many tagging their mates and wondering had they not bought one when they visited Manchester United's Megastore.

I ponder with Declan over why football fans, including both of us, are so enamoured with transfer gossip, when the majority of it seems to be untrue.

'The transfer window is the fantasy element of football. A lot of it is speculation and you need that. A lot of people believe it all though, they can't see how there can be any mistruth. It's an enjoyable part of the season. You still check after midnight on transfer deadline day. The public don't really fully understand what goes on, though,' he concludes.

A few years earlier, French under-21 international Didier Baptiste was a man in demand. The defender had been heavily linked with a move to Gérard Houllier's Liverpool by the British press, including the *News of the World*, *The Times*, *The Observer* and the club's own ClubCall service. Except he also didn't exist.

It transpired that the Frenchman was a character on Sky One's *Dream Team*, who revealed on the now-defunct show that he would sign 'for an English club who have a French manager'. A spokesperson for the drama stated, 'We can only assume someone saw the show and thought it was genuine.'

In this era of post-truth, fake news and ubiquitous social media, it comes as no surprise that media outlets are still duped by bogus transfer stories. As recently as January 2017, Sky Sports reported that Aberdeen had signed a Turkish midfielder called Yerdäs Selzavön. The 'news' had originally been broken by a fake Twitter account, which resembled the Dons's official handle. It transpired that the player's name was a play on a Scottish insult 'your da sells Avon' – defined by UrbanDictionary.com as, 'Your father is a representative of the Avon company', and described as, 'The peak, the maximum, the be-all and end-all of humiliation. The ultimate insult of one's self, one's family and one's dignity.'

How difficult is it in these times of social media to pull off a similar transfer hoax? I turned to George Weah's cousin, or rather @WeahsCousin to find out. This Twitter user has built up a reputation on the social media site for hoodwinking the media and some respected online accounts with fake quotes from footballers and, indeed, the press themselves. It's no surprise that his Twitter handle is inspired by the greatest transfer hoax of all time.

Aly Dia was allegedly the legendary George Weah's cousin, once removed. And that removal came during a dismal display for Southampton in a 1996 league clash with Leeds United. The story goes that The Saints's boss Graeme Souness had signed Dia after a phone call, supposedly from Weah, claiming that 'his cousin' was a Senegalese international who could be of use to the club. Souness, allegedly with no questions asked, gave him a month's contract and threw him on for Matt Le Tissier after 32 minutes against Leeds. He lasted 53 minutes and was withdrawn by Souness when it became apparent that he had been duped.

Le Tissier commented that Dia 'ran around the pitch like Bambi on ice, it was very embarrassing.' Dia was immediately released and made eight appearances for Gateshead before hanging up his boots.

@WeahsCousin will typically accompany a fictional quote from a footballer or media outlet with an official looking image, a formula that's fooled a surprising number of celebrities and media outlets. It reached its peak when a fake Sky Sports quote about Gibraltar's Lincoln Red Imps was picked up and broadcast by Sky Sports themselves.

The Gibraltese part-timers had beaten Celtic in a Champions League qualifier, after which @WeahsCousin tweeted an image with 'facts' about the club including that their 'average home crowd is 28', that their manager had been hired after 'winning a competition' and that they couldn't train 'on Tuesdays as a local Metal Detecting Society use their pitch'. The Wigan Athletic fan behind the account admits he was shocked himself at the reach of some of his deceptions.

'The Celtic one was the most surprising hoax of the lot due to it duping Sky Sports News,' he says. 'Using the Sky Sports style, image and graphic was meant to make it look realistic to a social media audience, but in turn it ended up duping Sky Sports themselves.'

The mischief-maker believes it is the rush to be first with breaking news online that has led to many of his fake rumours and quotes being shared by celebrities and national media outlets.

'In this day and age with social media and 24-hour news, it should be more difficult to create a fake transfer rumour or news story, as it's a lot easier for people to verify the authenticity when you've got Google and thousands of websites at your disposal,' he argues. 'Almost all of my hoaxes could've been easily proved as false within minutes. But social media is also of benefit for hoaxers. I think it's encouraged both media outlets and consumers to become slightly lazy at times. Why verify a news story when it's got a thousand retweets? "That's a lot so it must be true," seems to be the way people go with it. News outlets often put out stories that aren't right on the money, in order to be first and to get those vital clicks. The whole online news industry is awash with fake news because of the desire to be first with a story, which makes it easier to get things to slip through the net.'

As a teenager, I had a guilty little secret. Indeed, I still do. Late at night, when my parents and brothers were in bed, I'd grab the TV's remote control and nervously key in three numbers. Nowadays, I lie awake in bed about midnight as my wife lies asleep beside me and grab my mobile phone, visiting a page I've bookmarked.

Those three numbers. 3-3-8. Ceefax was a wealth of information, from news to entertainment gossip to weather forecasts. But there was only one page I was interested in.

Page 312, a previous favourite, covered the football news in brief but page 338 gathered all that day's tabloid transfer gossip in one place, a service that has been superseded by the football gossip page on the BBC's website. The page first appeared in 2002 and is consistently one of the most-viewed pages on the Beeb's site, regularly attracting over one million daily browsers during a transfer window.

So, just how accurate is the media's transfer gossip? I delved back 11 years, picking 26 May 2007 at random, to find out. The BBC gossip column that day included over two dozen transfer stories as the season drew to a close.

It opened with a story from the *Daily Express*, which stated that Juventus were preparing a £17m bid for Chelsea's Frank Lampard. *The Times* reported that 'The Old Lady' were also interested in Liverpool's Xabi Alonso and Mohamed Sissoko. The latter did move to Turin, but a year later.

The Mirror disagreed, claiming Alonso could be heading to Barcelona as part of a £30m deal involving Samuel Eto'o going to Anfield. The paper also reported that Sevilla's Dani Alves and Zaragoza's Gabriel Milito would sign for Liverpool 'within the next few days', and claimed that Arsenal were closing in on Sporting Lisbon's gossip column perennial João Moutinho for a fee of £15m. *The Mirror* was certainly busy that day, reporting that Tottenham were set to challenge Manchester United for a young winger named Nani, while the *Daily Express* reckoned Spurs were looking to bring Michael Owen to White Hart Lane.

The Times linked Sunderland midfielder Dean Whitehead with three clubs, while *The Star* mooted a move to Reading for Liverpool's Sami Hyypiä. *The Mirror* claimed Portsmouth were also 'in the mix' for the Finnish defender. Luke Young was linked with a transfer to Portsmouth or Everton by *The Sun*. He would join Middlesbrough two months later.

Former Portsmouth striker Yakubu was linked with a return to the club by the *Daily Mail*, along with Mark Viduka. Neither transfer transpired. *The Times* felt Pompey were instead after Marlon Harewood and Bonaventure Kalou – again, neither deal took place.

However, *The Times* also stated that Harewood was attracting the attention of Aston Villa and Wigan. He would join the former a few weeks later.

Viduka was also linked with a move to West Ham by *The Times*, who had more success predicting Scott Parker's £7m move to The Hammers.

The *Daily Mail* were on the ball by correctly including West Ham in a list of clubs looking to sign Liverpool's Craig Bellamy. He moved to Upton Park a few weeks later, but for considerably less than the paper had suggested. The Hammers were making room in their squad by allowing Nigel Reo-Coker to leave, according to *The Sun*, which is exactly what transpired later that summer.

There were a few more deals touted that failed to materialise. Matt Taylor was linked to Aston Villa, Chelsea's Paulo Ferreira with a switch to Lyon and David Nugent to Sunderland.

However, the *Daily Record* accurately predicted Chelsea keeper Yves Ma-Kalambay's move north of the border to Hibernian, while the *Daily Star's* story linking Sheffield United's Phil Jagielka to Everton was also on the ball.

So, out of 28 potential deals featured on that random date, just six – or 21 per cent – were correctly predicted. However, my research was plucked from a random day and may not be a fair reflection of the accuracy of newspapers' transfer rumours.

FootballTransferLeague.co.uk can do that, though. The website has compiled exhaustive stats behind all the rumours that newspapers produce, to determine the accuracy of each publication's transfer tittle-tattle. Its data stretches back to the start of the 2006 summer transfer window, giving us over 12 years' worth of research into the accuracy behind the back-page gossip.

The Guardian comes out on top, with 37.9 per cent of their 1,071 transfer stories proving accurate. Bottom of the table is *Caught Offside*, with just over seven per cent of their 357 stories resulting in a confirmed transfer. At the time of writing, the site had compiled data on 45,326 transfer stories, with 9,938 – or just under 22 per cent – actually coming to fruition. The people behind the site admit their stats aren't very scientific but they give a decent overview of the accuracy behind the stories you read and are similar to my random research of one particular date. The BBC itself delved back through over 800 stories they had reported during the 2016 summer window and found that just over one-third developed into an actual transfer.

When José Mourinho took over at Manchester United in May 2016 he insisted that he would make four signings in his first transfer window. Three of these deals – for Eric Bailly, Zlatan Ibrahimović and Henrikh Mkhitaryan – were completed quite quickly. His final target was Paul Pogba, whom he eventually acquired following an interminable saga that lasted the summer.

However, this didn't stop the British media linking United with dozens of players between 1 June and 31 August. A cursory glance through transfer rumours from summer 2016 suggests that the Red Devils's squad could now also contain the likes of Luan, Fabinho, Gabriel Barbosa, José Fonte, Jordan Pickford, Gareth Bale, Cristiano Ronaldo, Karim Benzema, Reece Oxford, Mauro Icardi, Álvaro Morata, Gonzalo Higuaín, Romelu Lukaku (who they did sign the following summer), Paulo Dybala, Pierre-Emerick Aubameyang, Antoine Griezmann, Neymar, Alex Oxlade-Chamberlain, Isco, Riyad Mahrez, Sadio Mané, Rafa Silva, John Stones, Nicolás Gaitán, André Carrillo, Willian, Adam Ounas, Arda Turan, James Rodríguez, Toni Kroos, Óscar de Marcos, William Carvalho, Lucas Biglia, N'Golo Kanté, Nemanja Matic (who they also signed a year later), Lassana Diarra, João Mário, André Gomes, Radja Nainggolan, Saúl Ñíguez, Grzegorz Krychowiak, Andrew Robertson, Dani Alves, Naldo, Kostas Manolas, Kalidou Koulibaly, Sergio Ramos, Raphaël Varane, Victor Lindelöf (a third who signed in summer 2017), Javier Mascherano, Ezequiel Garay, Thiago Silva, Marquinhos and Blaise Matuidi. This is not a definitive list – there were countless others – but the above players are enough to fill five teams.

During a two-week period in November 2016 alone, FootballTransferLeague.co.uk noted that 11 players had been linked with a move to Old Trafford in the UK press.

So, where do these stories emanate from? The imaginations of bored tabloid journalists? Agents using clubs like United for leverage in their clients' contract negotiations? Clubs themselves? Or is there a sliver of truth in some of these rumours? Why do only 22 per cent of rumours prove accurate? And, why do we even bother reading them when over three-quarters of mooted deals will never occur? I decided to investigate.

In August 2008 Mikaël Silvestre was undergoing a medical at the City of Manchester Stadium. The French defender had enjoyed nine trophy-laden years at Manchester United but his final season at Old Trafford was marred by a knee injury. A move to France had been considered but he decided to make the journey across Manchester to a Mark Hughes-led City, who were about to be taken over by Sheikh Mansour bin Zayed Al Nahyan's Abu Dhabi United Group.

Halfway through the medical, Silvestre's phone rang. Arsène Wenger's name appeared on the screen. He was wanted at Arsenal. United hadn't sold a player to their north London rivals for 34 years, but Silvestre's decision was made. He apologised to City, claiming he couldn't turn down the opportunity to work for his compatriot, and signed a two-year deal with The Gunners.

Tom Hopkinson, Chief Sports Reporter with the *Sunday Mirror* and the *Sunday People*, cites Silvestre's U-turn as an example of how newspapers can sometimes get a story wrong despite having the correct information.

'I wrote on the Sunday morning that Silvestre was on his way to join Manchester City. But then he joined Arsenal. So, of course, you get the usual stick, which you develop a thick skin to because you know you did all the right checks. But he got a phone call from Arsenal saying, "We're keen to talk to you, will you come down?"' recalls Tom. 'That's quite common, particularly on transfer deadline day, where a player will be driving to one club and then he'll get a call from another one, spin the car around and head back in the other direction.'

I query the enduring appeal of transfer gossip, when such a large percentage of rumours do not materialise into an actual transfer. 'It's an interesting question,' replies Tom. 'I think it's because fans are so desperate; they're avaricious, almost, for what is going on behind the scenes at their clubs. And with the transfer stories, it's almost a day-to-day way of looking into their clubs when there's no game action going on. I remember travelling in a taxi from Liverpool Lime Street Station to Anfield and as soon as I told the driver I worked for the *Sunday People* the first thing he said was that he loved our Hotline transfer column. I think what's fascinating for me was that, for him, it wasn't about whoever our columnist was at the time or the back page splash stories that we write, it was about those transfer stories. They really interest supporters, I think, because not all of them come true. We get a lot of abuse on social media, like, "Oh, you're just making it up again," or, "You've just pulled that one out of the bag because you've nothing else to write," and I presume some people actually do believe that. But I believe that a lot of people are open-minded enough to step back from it and say, "We don't believe this person would risk their credibility by writing a story they hadn't sourced and don't believe to be true."'

I must admit that prior to researching and writing this book I'd presumed the majority of rumours were figments of journalists' imaginations. The more I spoke to players, agents and others within the game the more I realised there was some truth, or spin, to most of them.

'Rumours can come from anywhere,' admits Tom. 'You can speak to a player directly, you can speak to an agent, you can speak to a chief executive or a chairman or a manager. Maybe a taxi driver has had a player in his car, who has been a little bit more open and honest about what's going on than, perhaps, he should have been. It can be anyone. We all have friends who are friends with a manager or a player or an agent, or you might know them directly and they can be the ones ringing you.

'There are some people who I speak to and I know what they're telling me is absolutely gospel,' he continues. 'I know how well connected they are or I know they are involved in the deal themselves and I can just trust them. There are other people who we speak to and I know that we'll have to check the story out in as many ways as possible – we'll have to go to the potential buying club, the selling club, the agent. If it doesn't come back that all three parties say, "Yes, it's right", then we won't run the story. It just depends on how confident you are in your original source.

Only then will you ring your sports editor and tell him you're about to file a story on such-and-such.'

The rise of social media and the decline in the traditional newspaper industry has led to gossip columns being reined in a little, though. 'In years gone by, there was probably even more of an appetite for it,' admits Tom. 'We would often run a transfer page throughout the season when the transfer window wasn't open. It could, invariably, go up to a double page spread during the transfer window. In the last few windows, I know a lot more money has been spent than ever before but I don't know whether as many transfers have gone through. To be honest, this is probably also to do with newspapers scaling down the number of pages they've got. We tend to run a double column in the *Sunday Mirror* called the Football Spy and in the *Sunday People* it's Hotline. It tends to be a double column in September, October and November. I speak to one or two agents and they've been saying, "Nothing's going on," but recently they've begun to notice phones starting to ring a little bit. I think during the upcoming international break phones will start ringing more – "Can this happen?", "Would he be interested?", "Would they let him go?" So, come December we'll probably go back up to a page and then there'll be more of an appetite for it from the sports editor.'

The advent of social media has meant that journalists have had to develop thick skins. Previously, where transfer gossip columns would become the following day's fish and chips wrappers, they now leave digital footprints with fans online who are only too eager to jump on any mistakes.

'Why people don't believe a lot of transfer stories is because it's taken them a little while to realise that every manager will identify a position for which he needs to sign a player in and he'll have a shortlist of five or six players,' Tom explains. 'I might only know the name of one of those players on that list because I happen to know the camp or the player who told me about it. So, I might write that a team is interested in a particular left-back, which they are, but he may be number three or number four on a list. They may get their number-one target and it's very rare that someone comes out and says, "Yes, he was on my list but he was a long way down it", or, "Yes, he was on my list, he was my number-one choice but we couldn't do the deal so we had to look elsewhere." So, of course, some fans automatically think, "Well, you've just made it up." That hasn't been the case. You'll have been given the information, you'd have spoken to as many people you know who are at one of the clubs involved.

'It depends on the situation. This is football, and people in football lie all the time. But often, they lie for a reason. I'm not saying I condone it because it drives us mad. There have been times I've been told, "That's definitely not going to happen" and then you see a deal has gone through. They might have been told by a club, "If this gets out, then the deal is off" and with so much money riding on it they don't want to risk it.'

Agent Gary Mellor backs up Tom's point that clubs' shortlists for each position they need to strengthen in often leads to multiple rumours in the press. 'I was dealing with Manchester United in the summer of 2017 and they had three players on a list for every position they needed,' Gary says. 'They were quite open about that but weren't, perhaps, as open about where you stood on that list. Their transfer team, for want of a better term, would go and do due diligence on the three players to see what their cost would be, their suitability to the style of play and so on.'

I questioned Tom as to where a recent story he wrote about a fringe player at Liverpool came from, but he won't divulge his sources.

'I can't! We speak to fellow journalists, we speak to agents, we speak to players, we speak to chief executives, we speak to chairmen, we speak to press officers, we speak to friends of players,' he reveals. 'As a journalist you build relationships with as many people as you can. Clubs do this, too. Fans shouldn't be misguided that clubs don't occasionally – whether it's a press officer, chief executive or head of scouting – ring the journalist and say, "Can you get this out there? We are interested in this player but we're having a few problems with their club. They don't want to sell but he wants to come to us. We believe that by getting this out there, it can help the transfer." You want to be that journalist that they call. That comes through years and years of building the kind of relationships that make you the person they think of first. That goes for agents and players too. There might be times when they tell a couple of journalists with whom they're friendly. They could even brief everybody in the pack or maybe the Sunday newspapers might all get a phone call. There's a multitude of different ways in how it works and I think that adds to the excitement of transfers.'

The more people I speak to, the more agents have come to the fore regarding transfer rumours. They want the best for their clients, ergo themselves, and are not backward about floating stories out there to achieve their goals.

'There are agents who, let's say they've got a player who wants to go somewhere and they'll also know the club is not 100 per cent convinced,' adds Tom. 'The camp, or the player himself, might leak out that another club is interested to try and generate that final push of interest from the club they want to go to. I think that's why there's a real fascination in it and also why some supporters don't believe everything they read, which is a shame. I think, hand on heart, that just about every journalist I respect and know well will never just write a story for the sake of it.

'If anyone rings me, I ask them, "Where are you coming at this from? Just be honest with me so I'm going into this with my eyes completely open. Are you angling for a new deal at your current club? Is it correct that there is interest from the club you are telling me about?" I'll then try, where possible, when I've been given all the correct information, to ensure that that is represented in the story – whether he's open to a move if the offer of a new deal isn't forthcoming from the club he's with at the moment. There's a hell of a lot of that goes on. Journalists have to protect their contacts and if they give you a story, they'll often say to you, "Can you do me a favour in return and get this out there?" If it was something that just wasn't going to happen, I'd just say, "I'm not doing that one, come back to me with one that will help you, but one that's also true.'"

Jon Smith represented the likes of Diego Maradona and Ruud Gullit during his 30-year career as an agent and had no qualms about using the media to progress a transfer. 'You'd do the same if you were my client and I wanted to get you out of your contract because you wanted to leave – if it was difficult and you had an awkward manager or a sporting director who didn't want you to go,' explains Jon. 'So, yeah, the media is an option. Of course, today, we've got more options than just putting it on the back pages of the *Sunday People*. We've got social media. ArsenalFanTV has got as many viewers now as Arsenal TV. There are some major platforms out there. It works for the clubs as well. They quietly do the same thing.'

Rob Shield, an agent based in the north-west of England, suggests that transfer stories were planted in the media in the past but that this practice is gradually becoming less common.

'Previously, a lot of rumours would be planted,' says Rob. 'Sometimes the newspapers are involved to try and engineer a move or pressure a club to try and give the player a new deal. A lot of clubs have wised up now to gossip columns and don't pay much attention to it. Good agents don't use that route any more, putting things in gossip columns, I think it's frowned upon.'

Newspapers have had to adapt to the rise of social media, through which anyone can break a transfer story. 'You only have to look at sales figures for newspapers,' says Tom. 'The industry is constricting across the board. And I've absolutely no doubt that a contribution to that comes from the fact that sports lovers don't always have to go to a newspaper these days to get their information. Everyone's a journalist, aren't they, on Twitter and on social media? Anyone can break a story. There is a pressure but I'd like to think that when you're at a certain level, your professional standards remain such that people trust you. I'm not saying that everyone who sees my name says, "Oh yes, I believe everything that man writes," because I'm sure there are people who are out there who don't, unfortunately! That seems to be par for the course when you're a red-top journalist. But, you hope you've got yourself to a level where the majority of your readership says, "I believe that story will be correct if his name is on it."'

There is more and more pressure to secure transfer stories and Tom thinks that this will continue to evolve. 'You're seeing that Sunday papers are less standalone than ever before because the media world is now so instantaneous. For example, I think Rob Beasley picked up the Roman Abramovich takeover story on the Monday and had six days sweating over it, that it would hold for the *News of the World*. I just cannot see that happening these days. To have a little transfer story, of three or four paragraphs, is difficult to keep for more than a couple of days but to have a story of that magnitude would be nigh on impossible to sit on. I think that's why you now see newspapers reacting in terms of getting stories online as quickly as possible to try and combat the growth of social media.

'Sometimes, however, a media leak cannot only hinder a deal but drive up the price. This is not confined to traditional media,' he concludes.

Indeed it's not. When Liverpool fan Sean Cummins created an online character called Duncan Jenkins, there was no grand plan to create an in-the-know transfer guru. It just sort of happened – up to the point where he was accused of costing Liverpool £300,000 when the club signed Fabio Borini from Roma.

'Duncan was just a comedy character I initially launched on a Liverpool FC forum, where I knew everyone quite well,' recalls Sean. 'One night, extremely bored as a new dad, I created this idiotic character who had some very bad opinions – and I did this simply to wind up the lads on that forum. He went down quite well and a couple of the lads who knew I was behind it suggested I launch him on Facebook, which I did. It wasn't a football thing, it was simply this vacuous airhead who thought the world was waiting to hear his opinion on everything and the internet gave him the kind of platform he wanted.'

By 2011, Sean had become immersed on Twitter and noticed a proliferation of young lads who would set themselves up as football writers but didn't appear to work for anybody.

'I thought that this was the perfect vehicle for Duncan – an aspirant journalist. There was still no grand plan. He would comment on matches or football events on Twitter. It was just all about his ineptitude and the fact that he wanted to be a journalist but clearly didn't have the tools to get anywhere near football journalism. He lived with his mum, so he'd commentate on a game but he'd have to finish as his mum wanted to watch *A Place in the Sun* on TV,' laughs Sean.

Typically, clubs will announce their line-ups an hour before league games commence. Sean noticed that someone was posting Liverpool team news on the aforementioned forum a few hours before kick-off – and it was always correct. He felt it was an ideal development to enhance Duncan's reputation.

'Duncan had a human avatar and people thought he was a real guy living with his mum. So, for somebody who wanted to become a journalist, it was a natural progression for him to be seen as having an "in" and breaking exclusives. So, for a month or so he tweeted the team news and it was always right,' says Sean. 'That led to an exponential rise in the number of followers he had and, at that point, the buzz began. That led into the January transfer window so I thought I needed to keep up this façade and momentum that he had an "in". The fact that he was breaking the team news pulled the wool over everybody's eyes.'

It became apparent that the team news had been posted on the forum by a friend of a Liverpool player. He wasn't on Twitter so Duncan was the only one announcing it there. Anyone else could have found it on that forum if they'd looked hard enough. 'But nobody did,' says Sean.

With a burgeoning reputation as being an in-the-know, Duncan began circulating transfer rumours, most of which Sean admits were educated punts. 'It was about separating the wheat from the chaff,' he says. 'The first punt Duncan took was on Joe Allen. I'm a glutton for all this transfer stuff, I voraciously hoover it all up. So I'd remembered a footnote in an *Independent* article a few months before about Liverpool scouting Joe Allen. After that January transfer window had passed, Brendan Rodgers got the job and they'd worked with each other at Swansea City. Duncan went big on that. It didn't take a genius to think that it may well happen. And Joe Allen, at the time, was pretty well in demand. Duncan really staked his reputation on that one.'

Borini was the next guess, as he had been mentioned by Rodgers in an interview with the *Liverpool Echo*. The manager had also worked with the Italian at Chelsea and Swansea City.

'They were both complete punts that anyone could have made educated guesses about. But Duncan went for them and they came off. Duncan's reputation went through the roof at that point,' says Sean.

The rest of that summer he was just taking pot-shots. Some, like Gylfi Sigurðsson, didn't come off but people didn't care. Duncan had called enough right for his followers to be hanging on his every word.

'I'd also gone big on Twitter on Rodgers becoming manager, but I'd also gone big on André Villas-Boas,' admits Sean. 'That proved to be wrong but it still gave Duncan additional kudos as respected journalists subsequently reported that Liverpool did have talks with him. Followers didn't seem to care if it was right or wrong, they just cared that he seemed to have an in with the inner workings at the club and that someone at Liverpool was telling him secrets.'

In May 2012 Liverpool appointed Jen Chang as corporate relations and communications director. He wanted the club to be more inclusive of fans' sites and bloggers.

'He contacted a load of bloggers like The Anfield Wrap and Redmen TV and Duncan was one of them,' recalls Sean. 'He asked for an email address and a telephone number and I gave them, staying in character hoping that I'd get invited to a press conference or something. I had absolutely no idea how I would pull it off because Duncan's avatar was a completely different human being's face to mine. But, at the time, I didn't think about that. I just thought it was an amazing potential development for the character.'

Meanwhile, Sean's creation had become incredibly time-consuming. Duncan secured a regular column with *Goal.com* during Euro 2012 and at one point that summer did a live webchat with the Delhi branch of the Liverpool Fan Club. They were 'rabid for transfer gossip' and it was at this point that Sean began wrestling with his conscience.

'There were hundreds and hundreds of them. Ten minutes into it my heart sort of sank and I thought, "I'm taking these lads for a ride here." At that point I started to wonder whether it was morally right or not. I did become increasingly bored of it. After the Euros, a journalist told me that Jen Chang was after me in a big way. And, at that point, it started to become a real pain in the arse. Being a Liverpool supporter, I didn't want to fall out with anybody at the club or get into any type of war with the club. And then all the stuff with Jen Chang happened, which was completely insane.'

The 'Jen Chang stuff' all blew up over the season-long loan deal from Real Madrid of Nuri Şahin, who had looked on the verge of joining Arsenal.

'In line with me becoming sick of it, Duncan had staked his entire journalistic career, if you like, on Şahin joining Liverpool,' says Sean. 'I was quietly hoping it wasn't going to happen. Duncan said that if he went anywhere but Liverpool he'd quit his dream of becoming a journalist and quit Twitter. Personally I was hoping he'd go to Arsenal so I could knock all this on the head.'

He actually closed the account when a move to The Gunners looked imminent for the Turkish midfielder but then reopened it when several fake Duncan Jenkins accounts immediately cropped up.

'And then I, personally, received a direct message on Twitter from Jen Chang which said, "Back so soon after your sabbatical?" I was aware he knew the person behind the character's Christian name was Sean so I thought, "How does he know it's me?"'

Sean was eager to nip things in the bud so he emailed Chang at the club and offered an olive branch. A meeting was arranged in a Manchester restaurant the following week, which Sean turned up to apprehensively.

'He met me and was very passive-aggressive, not a shred of humour about him. We met for just under two hours and it was awful,' says Sean.

The main sore points were that Duncan was costing the club money, including in the aforementioned Borini deal, and that he was reliant on a mole in the club.

'It wasn't true, he'd made that up to emotionally guilt trip me,' states Sean. 'That I'm a supporter and was costing my own club money. And that I would then "fess up" to having this mole. There were other emotional guilt trips too. He claimed he had hired a private investigator to find me, which at the time I'd believed. It was the only thing that had come out of his mouth at the meeting that I thought was true because he knew so much about me. As it turns out, somebody had grassed me up and given him my full name. He could type my name into Google and find out all sorts about me, which he did.

'He also tried to emotionally guilt trip me by saying that the money for the people he'd hired to find me – who compiled the dossier on me – had come out of his own budget, which had previously been earmarked to spend on charitable projects with, in his own words, handicapped kids in Toxteth. At the time, I had to just sit there nodding along, playing along. I didn't want to cause a big scene, for a start, and it was a very fast-moving conversation. His bone of contention was that I was a so-called Liverpool fan who was wilfully damaging the club and costing it money, and that I should, "Pack it in, I should cease straight away, go home and tweet as Duncan that the whole thing has been a big ruse and apologise for it all." If I did then all of the threats he'd made against me would be off the table.'

These threats included the immediate revocation of Sean's season ticket and a ban for life from Anfield.

'He also said that Duncan's mere existence had infuriated and embarrassed a lot of journalists because it was perceived that Duncan was out-performing them in terms of exclusives. So there were lots of embittered journalists out there who were ready to write smear stories about me in the press if I didn't comply with his requests. He'd whip up the Liverpool fanbase into such a frenzy that I would have to take down my Facebook page, that I would have to move house, that they would come around to my house and post dog shit through my letterbox.'

A shocked Sean was given a deadline – 'It was like it was in *Goodfellas*' – of Thursday at 8.30pm to comply with the demands. The time limit passed and it was announced that Nuri Şahin was, in fact, going to sign for Liverpool.

'That was a great chance for Duncan to come back on to Twitter, lording it,' admits Sean. 'When he did that, within minutes Chang got in touch again and said, "I've seen your latest tweet. Are you reneging?" He spent the remainder of that day and night phoning me, which I ignored because I wasn't sure how I was going to play it. I knew it was going to get messy and I wanted to fight back. I wanted to reveal the story through a respectable newspaper but it never came to fruition. I spent a month trying to make it happen and it was really frustrating.'

Instead, he decided to write a blog about the saga, which eventually led to an apology from the club. 'His behaviour was completely appalling and I thought that there was no way he should get away with it. If I had just been a normal fan and I'd heard about it, I'd be demanding action. I was personally aggrieved as he'd not only made threats against me, he'd threatened my parents' business,' he reveals.

After the blog was published a couple of people got in touch with Sean and told him that the club were aware of it and that there was a possibility of him meeting Ian Ayre, the managing director of Liverpool at the time.

'I was staggered, I didn't think it would even register on the club's radar,' admits Sean. 'Although Chang was a representative of the club, I was pretty sure the whole thing was a solo mission on his behalf. I met with Ian Ayre and about a week or two later I was called back. He had a letter, which was a bit of a fudge. It basically said they accepted that some of the things I detailed were totally unacceptable, but it was a full apology. He said I could do whatever I liked with the letter, so I left the meeting and rang a couple of journalists.

'By the time I got home an hour or so later it was already all over the internet. Ayre had explicitly asked me what I wanted out of it all and all I wanted was to be vindicated. It sounds callous but at the time I wanted Chang to lose his job. I look back on it and it was the bloke's dream job, he was a Liverpool supporter, he'd only been there five minutes and I think that it really shouldn't have happened.'

At the time, though, Sean doesn't mind admitting he punched the air when he heard Chang had been removed from his role.

'It emerged that this wasn't the only issue that the club had with him. His practices were very unusual,' says Sean. 'He was a journalist and had come barrelling in there with very aggressive American business techniques, which are completely alien to how we operate over here, particularly in football.'

One of the things that struck me about the whole story was the futility of the transfer market. None of the three transfers associated with the drama – Borini, Allen and Şahin – had much impact at Anfield, with the latter's loan agreement terminated after an unsuccessful five months.

'It is completely futile and, yet, you're not deterred,' Sean agrees. 'You plough on regardless reading all this stuff. It allows you to fantasise that, "We may sign him," but, deep down, you know damn well that you're not going to sign him. If you sign a player, particularly one from another league, there is almost limitless potential. I wish I knew why people are obsessed with transfer rumours. I'm every bit as infatuated with transfer gossip as Duncan's followers were. I don't know why. There's some sort of crazy value attached with being the first to find something out. You're dying to find out before it actually happens. It's like with Naby Keïta. I'd never seen him play and I'd never been more desperate for us to sign a player! If it was someone like Morgan Schneiderlin, I know he's mediocre so I'm never going to get excited.'

'Duncan Jenkins' has long since given up his ambition of becoming a journalist, but what of the other protagonist whose dream job also fell by the wayside?

'I'd like to meet Jen Chang now and shake hands to bury the hatchet because it was a complete farce. Now it's all subsided I feel pretty bad about it,' concludes Sean.

On 2 January 2003, I can almost guarantee that the first thing I did was check page 338 on Ceefax (RIP). Of course, I had been addicted to the transfer gossip page for years, but the new-fangled January transfer window had just been introduced so it was a bumper crop of rumours with more short-lived hearsay than that found in that era's *Popstars* show.

Spurs misfit Sergei Rebrov was linked with a move to Fenerbahçe, Leeds United's Jonathan Woodgate to Newcastle United and, tucked away down the bottom, World Cup winner Christophe Dugarry with a loan move to Birmingham City.

'Ludicrous,' I no doubt thought to myself before checking the TV Guide on page 606. But the latter deal became the first-ever move in the English January transfer window. The Blues shocked the football world, and me, on that second day of 2003 when they secured the loan signing of the former AC Milan, Barcelona and Olympique de Marseille striker.

Dugarry had an immediate impact in the Midlands, notching five goals in five matches to help save the club from relegation. It seemed that the Frenchman's survival instincts played a part in his initial success – he signed a permanent deal that summer but his second season at St Andrews was a comparative failure.

He left the following March as his family had failed to settle in England, but made such an impact in his short time at City that he has since been inducted into the club's hall of fame.

Dugarry may have lasted less than 18 months in England but the transfer window has endured. Deadline day, in particular, has almost become a national event with Sky Sports presenter Jim White synonymous with proceedings. If you Google 'transfer deadline day', you won't find many images of players holding a scarf aloft at their new club or nervously signing their new contract next to some bloke in a suit. The majority of images are of Jim White, wearing a yellow tie, looking like he's about to break the biggest transfer story of the decade. As José Mourinho once said, 'Even if nothing is happening, Jim White makes it sound exciting.' The Scotsman quickly realised that deadline day was a phenomenon, after the channel first broadcast the extravaganza during the 2002/03 season.

'I recognised that the impact it made was huge. Everybody was talking to me about it,' says Jim. 'I think that Sky Sports News understood that this was the perfect vehicle for it because of the immediacy of it and the reach that the channel has. They knew then that they had something that was different – you're not talking about tactics, you're not talking about a flat back four or attacking wing-backs – you're talking about names and you're talking about clubs. And those are the two key ingredients to any transfer deadline day. After the first or second one I did, we realised, "Oh my god, this is something massive." In the final hour of deadline day they would get their audience figures and everybody was pleasantly knocked out by the reach that it was getting. I believe the viewing figures are among the best of the year. If two clubs in the lower half of the Premier League play each other the audience figure will be pretty healthy. But when Manchester United play Liverpool the audience figure will be colossal. When deadline day comes along the audience figure is colossal. It's enormous.'

Jim began his broadcasting career as a sports reporter in his native Scotland and believes people have always been fascinated with the transfer area of the game. 'From my point of view it goes back to when Graeme Souness became manager of Rangers,' he recalls. 'Souness quite early on proceeded on a campaign to change the face of Scottish football. All of a sudden he was introducing people to the Scottish game that we could never have imagined would come north. It was straight after the Mexico 1986 World Cup and he presented us with England internationals Terry Butcher and Chris Woods. Everyone became fascinated by that, not least myself, and I was right in the middle of it all. Celtic did their bit as well by bringing up some big-name players at the time like Mick McCarthy, but Rangers dominated it. And it was intriguing to see who Souness was going to produce next. I always remember being at the forefront of that because Souness was very generous with his information towards me. I was getting it out there on Scottish TV and the reaction was unbelievable.'

Jim suddenly found himself at the centre of it all again when he moved across the border to Sky Sports and the transfer window became an increasingly significant part of the game. 'People are absolutely infatuated by it, they love it,' says Jim. 'I think it's to do with the expectation and anticipation. Everybody talks about it to me – in the office, in the street, in the dentist's surgery. Everybody's talking about who might go where and, to me, it's become an enormous part of the game. I think it's the, "Who might Queens Park Rangers be getting? Who might West Brom be getting?"'

We spoke during the 2018 January window, when Borussia Dortmund's André Schürrle had been linked with a move back to the Premier League with The Baggies.

'He's only won the World Cup with Germany, only scored twice in the 7–1 rout of Brazil. And then I see this week that West Brom are interested in him,' says Jim. 'To me, I look at that, I know Schürrle, I texted him and he texted me straight back and said, "No disrespect to West Brom but no truth whatsoever."' Schürrle did not leave Germany at the time, but from where did the rumour – which was heavily reported in UK newspapers – emerge?

'In this day and age, the story probably started life on social media and grew arms and legs. West Brom fans buy into it and, before you know where you are, it's appearing on Sky Sports News,' concedes Jim. 'It's who you know in this business and all it needs is one text or one phone call to either stand it up or knock it down. And I always go to the source, the key person involved – in other words the player. These guys spreading fake stories don't exactly help. It's a real hindrance and quite obstructive, doing something like that. There are plenty of people out there who want to do that. There's a lot of misinformation.'

It wasn't exactly a 'JFK moment' but I can certainly remember where I was when Andy Cole signed for Manchester United. I and a few mates usually lunched in a commons room in Dublin City University's campus residences, despite none of us residing there. We'd while away the hour watching Harold Bishop become exasperated with a thieving cat on *Neighbours* and making cult figures out of some of the strange characters who competed on Henry Kelly's *Going for Gold*. Before returning to our studies, we'd stick on Sky for 'the football news'.

On 10 January 1995 we, and the football world, were stunned. Manchester United had pulled off the out-of-the-blue transfer of Cole from Newcastle United in a deal worth around £7m, with £1m-rated winger Keith Gillespie moving to St James' Park as part of the deal. Newcastle manager Kevin Keegan had to placate irate fans who'd converged at the stadium, while one fan who had just had a full-length tattoo of Cole inked on his thigh subsequently had it reworked into an image of Les Ferdinand. It was certainly a quicker deal than Cole's earlier move to Newcastle from Bristol City. Keegan rang the striker, mistakenly calling him Adrian, and asked him to meet him the following day. 'I can't come tomorrow,' Cole replied. 'I have to finish my laundry. I can come the day after, though.'

Cole's transfer to Old Trafford was the kind of unexpected move that doesn't tend to happen any more, in an age of 24-hour media coverage and online ruminations. There are still the exceptions to the rule – in May 2018 rumours surfaced on Twitter at around 8pm linking the Brazilian Fabinho with Liverpool. An hour later, the deal was done and dusted with the official club account tweeting a short video of their signing in his new kit. I ponder with Jim whether this lack of spontaneity in the transfer market has arrested the excitement somewhat.

'I recall the Andy Cole situation, I was left open-mouthed by it,' he replies. 'I always think that there's a chance that anything can still happen. The main thing about this area of work is that you can expect the unexpected. I always remember being left absolutely open-mouthed, too, when Roy Keane went to Celtic, following an incredible career at Manchester United. It's always that moment that catches you off guard and you think, "What?! What did I just hear? Is he really going there?"

'That's what this transfer area of the business has – it's the shock element, the surprise element that I find is just irreplaceable. What I always find is that if a player is a) certain to move, and b) doesn't move to the club you expect him to go to and goes to another club, then there's a twist in the tale and people lock into it and stay with that story right to its conclusion. Robinho was absolutely nailed on to go to Chelsea and then, the next thing, Mark Hughes unveils him at Manchester City. A more recent example is Moussa Sissoko at Newcastle United, who looked certain to sign for Everton. That night, I was being told he was on his way and would be pitching up at Everton's training ground at any moment. And then, the next thing, Tottenham announce that he's joined them. The Everton fans were going off their heads. Now, in view of the complete let-down that Sissoko has proven to be, Everton fans are relieved that Tottenham's gain was also their loss. Willian was also a case in point in that. He was having a medical at Tottenham and then he and his agent got the call, "Get right out of there, pull out now and go to Cobham because Chelsea want to sign you and they'll give you better terms than Tottenham." And he literally got up and walked out.'

'According to Sky sources' has become one of the many catchphrases associated with the transfer window. Jim confirms that rumours, although he's loathe to use that word, can come from various parties. 'A mixture of players, agents and clubs,' he states. 'You've got everyone working on that day to further their own ends, not least the agents. They're at it big time, they're working on behalf of their client to get the best deal possible for their client, and if that means taking that client or player out of a certain situation or club late on in the day, they will do that. All these people – agents, club owners, managers and players – are never straying too far away from Sky Sports News to make sure they are locked into what is going on. As an aside, the word rumour is one I never use. Rumours is a weak word in our language. Transfer talk, transfer decisions, all that kind of thing, I go with that.'

He admits that deadline day can be chaotic but believes closing the summer window before the Premier League season commences will be beneficial for English clubs. The move, however, carries the risk of foreign clubs poaching talent in the last few weeks of August with no opportunity for English clubs to find replacements until the following January's window.

'There's a huge feeling of anticipation about deadline day itself, everybody's up to speed on what might be going on and, of course, most of us have been working in the preceding weeks so we know what's coming,' says Jim. 'We know who the key players, the runners and riders, will be. We're pretty much all singing from the same hymn sheet as to what may, or may not, happen. It's a great feeling, it's like no other to be honest. It's like heading towards a World Cup final with your nation being in it. The sense of anticipation is huge and you hope that it lives up to the billing. Sometimes it doesn't, but most of the time it does.

'There could be more desperation with the earlier deadline. It makes a lot of sense to me and I can see where the managers are coming from. They all want to start on a level playing field before a ball is kicked. I totally understand that. They don't want the complication of having to do transfer business just a few weeks into a new season. It just means that they have got to get their business done in a way that satisfies them a lot sooner than they have done in the past. But they're the ones who've been shouting about it so it's up to them to deliver on behalf of their clubs.'

He's had many memorable deadline-day moments, including Mesut Özil's move to Arsenal from Real Madrid and Fernando Torres's switch from Liverpool to Chelsea, but his highlight involves another man inextricably linked with deadline day.

'The one that stands out for me was a call I got from Harry Redknapp during a commercial break to tell me that Robbie Keane was in a vehicle on his way to Celtic Park to sign there on loan. The next thing there was something like 3,000 Celtic fans outside Celtic Park waiting for Robbie. The reaction to that was just colossal. Things like that give me a huge amount of satisfaction and happiness when something like that works out,' he says.

And the deals that fell through? 'There have been a few. Nothing really that stands out where you thought, "Damn it, I wish that had happened." I must say most of them always go through, even ones I was sceptical about. I remember thinking, "What? Danny Welbeck to Arsenal? I can't see that happening." And Arsenal very much talked that down that night. But then, sure as day, Danny Welbeck joined them. The rule of thumb is that they usually go through in the end. Even Andrey Arshavin to Arsenal – it was a day late but it still happened.'

Before we go, I can't help but ask about one of the biggest deals of deadline day – the infamous yellow tie. Jim laughs. 'Sky wondered how they could make the most impact with breaking transfer news. So they started running a yellow ticker across the bottom of the screen saying, "Jim White has signed for whoever." And they thought, "Well, how can we match that up? Jim could wear a yellow tie and his female co-presenter could wear a yellow dress." The colour yellow is now just synonymous with breaking news on transfer deadline day. I'm driven demented, everywhere I go – especially in the run-up to deadline day – I'm asked dozens of times where my yellow tie is!'

Jim White may not like the term 'transfer rumours' but Simon Chadwick is a self-confessed sucker for them. A Professor of Sports Enterprise at the University of Salford, he's written about the socio-cultural and psychological dimensions to transfer rumours, driven mainly by his own fascination with them.

'The first thing I do every day, when I visit the BBC website, is go into the gossip page and read what the rumours are,' admits Simon. 'They are stories created to fill an information vacuum. The papers on a Saturday tend not to have any stories about transfers.

'That, to me, is an illustration of the above. People working in the media have to pay their mortgages so they have to fill their pages with something. In an ideal world they get the scoop and they are accurate in reporting the story.

'The information vacuum is when there are no games taking place, when there's nothing particular happening, when the season is finished. Rumours are a very engaging way of filling that vacuum. This is all built upon, psychologically and behaviourally, the nature of fandom, which is a group of people who are highly engaged with a club, a league, a sport. Research we have done in various contexts has found that people like to talk about their clubs. These are high-engagement brands.'

It's clear that there are certain times of the year when there's nothing to talk about in football so rumours help to fill that gap. But why do fans have such a voracious appetite for them? 'If rumours are stories created to fill an information vacuum, the question is, where are those stories coming from? What are the origins of those stories?' asks Simon. 'Clearly fans are one source of these stories. I think fans do this because they are highly engaged, because they want to feel close to their club, because they want the best players. There's something about fans' psychological projection of themselves. If they can get a story first, if they can be seen as having an interesting view, if they can say something on social media that gets retweeted lots of times, that then confers a particular image and status upon them.'

He has recent experience himself in this regard. While teaching a cohort of students earlier this year, Simon began discussing the fortunes of FC Sochaux-Montbéliard with a French member of the class. The club has struggled following Chinese investment in 2015.

'One of the things that really interests me is China and football,' Simon reveals. 'Sochaux used to be the Peugeot workers' club but was sold to the Chinese and it's been an unmitigated disaster. This French guy told me that in French football chat rooms there was a very strong rumour going around that the Chinese investors were going to sell Sochaux.'

So Simon tweeted it.

'I was overwhelmed with tweets from Sochaux fans asking, "What do you know? What's going on?" Straight away I took it down and asked myself, "What have I done?" Normally I don't spread rumours, particularly professionally, as the strength of an academic's brand is in their ability to remain impartial. In this case I thought I'd make an exception and I was genuinely taken aback by the response. I took it down because, firstly, I didn't like the way I felt, but I felt uncomfortable with the way in which people responded to it.'

Why tweet this one then? For the same reason, he believes, that others spread and consume transfer rumours.

'For me, I wanted to get the scoop,' he admits. 'I wanted to be the first to share this information. I wanted to reassert my position as somebody who knows something about Chinese football. So, what's that all about? I think it's about image and identity. And I think, fundamentally, it's about ego. There is something genetically programmed into us where we want to win, we want to be first and that plays out through your ego. If you get the "Arsène Wenger to resign from Arsenal" story this morning first then it plays into that fundamental part of the human condition where we want to compete and win. Ultimately rumours come out of that. Once you filter it through ego, self-image and self-identity, you then start getting into, "Well, I'm just going to start making up rumours." You filter it again through social media and what you get are wild rumours that are fake news.'

Simon likens the spread of transfer rumours to market signalling, an economics term which basically involves somebody somewhere signalling to the market that they want something to happen.

'Arguably the most interesting part of this is around the concept of signalling. For example, you've got a football club who want to get rid of Aleksandar Kolarov or Joe Hart,' explains Simon. 'Clubs will signal, somehow, that they are receptive to an offer for this particular player, that they are receptive to disposing of their asset. By the same token, obviously, you're going to have players and their agents who equally want to let it be known that they're unhappy, that their contract is coming to an end, that they're looking for a bigger and better club, that they want regular first-team football. Signalling is a very important aspect of this. If you're signalling, who are the signallers on your behalf? Players and agents, for example, have got preferred members of the media that they will talk to. Equally, they will know that if they tell a story to someone – it may be a member of the media, but it could be a relative, it could be someone working inside a club – this type of information will get leaked to media and fans. So they become the signallers.

'There are certain fans who are signallers, too. I'm thinking about Liverpool, for example. There are several really influential Liverpool fans, Liverpool Twitter accounts and Liverpool websites that, effectively, service signallers.'

I mention that the phrase most players and agents expressed to me is 'floating stuff out there'. He doesn't see much distinction between the two terms.

'I know an agent and I was with this guy during the last transfer window. My idea of signalling and his idea of floating was the predominant characteristic of our conversation that day,' he contends.

Simon believes that this political manoeuvring behind the scenes of football transfers has always been the case but has increased exponentially due to online networks. 'What social media has done is it has democratised it – anyone can do it now. Anybody can pass themselves off now as a football agent, anybody can pass themselves off as an international superstar,' he asserts. 'What social media has done is to more readily enable it to happen. Let's be very honest and direct about this: football transfer rumours, in the vernacular of Donald Trump, are fake news. All of those concerns and insecurities we feel about fake news in a broader socio-political context are equally applicable in terms of transfer rumours. A lot of this is fake news. Essentially, what agents, players, fans and others are doing is that they are generators of content and they are propagators of fake news.'

He also believes that another aspect to this is the extent that rival agents, rival clubs and even rival players might use rumours as an instrument to destabilise or gain some competitive advantage over their rivals.

'So, if you're Pep Guardiola and you're trying to wind up José Mourinho, you start mentioning that you could have bought Pogba in the last transfer window,' he muses. 'Who knows whether that story was true or not? I don't know whether that story was true or not. And I'm not suggesting that Pep Guardiola goes out of his way to do this kind of thing. But knowing what I know about football and the people involved in football, you can well imagine that what some people will do is to use this as a competitive, strategic, psychological tool for undermining or destabilising rivals.

'So, if you're constantly saying, "I think Eden Hazard's going to leave Chelsea," then suddenly people are saying, "Oh my god, Hazard's going to leave Chelsea."

'Eden Hazard is not immune to reading this kind of stuff. Once your head has been turned you then start to lose form and start to think, "Well, maybe I should leave," and say to your agent, "Can you check if Real Madrid are interested or not? And who has been spreading these rumours?" It takes on a life of its own and, potentially, there's something self-fulfilling about all of this.'

Simon's correct: players are not immune to reading this kind of stuff. The majority of footballers I spoke to admitted that professionals do pay attention to it, although it affects some more than others. Norwich City goalkeeper Michael McGovern has been linked with clubs in the past but has no idea where the speculation originated.

'There will be some clubs who will ask your agent about you but you'd never consider going there,' admits the Northern Ireland keeper. 'That would be more them wanting you than you wanting them.

'I think, nowadays, it's far easier for rumours to start with social media and things like that. It's so easy. Years ago you could maybe go and meet a manager or meet an agent but nowadays, with people taking pictures of you, it's more difficult. For instance, I recently saw a picture on Twitter of the Millwall manager meeting Jason Shackell for lunch. A couple of days later they'd signed him on loan from Derby County. It's hard to keep things quiet now; everyone talks.'

Michael's another who mentions the 'floating things out there' phrase and has seen it at close quarters. 'There's a bit of politics with that. There's a player I worked with in the past and I knew the club wanted to get rid of him. Things kept getting leaked to the press, that there was some talk between his agent and different clubs. The parent club were maybe leaking that to drum up interest from elsewhere and get him off the books.'

Neill Collins, the former Sunderland and Sheffield United defender agrees, 'A lot of it comes from agents and a lot of it comes from clubs who want to move players on. You can generally tell when it's purely fabricated or the reason that it's in there. There are certain agents that spin their players to hopefully generate interest for a move. Even clubs know that so it's such a farce, really, the whole gossip thing.'

He admits to previously being a regular visitor to the BBC transfer gossip page but, as he's experienced more within the game, he's come to view it quite differently.

'In the past four or five years I've seen or heard a few things and, if anything now, I go on it for a laugh as it's nonsense,' he states. 'It can actually put people off, if agents want to agitate for moves. I can understand why fans love it, I used to love it, but now with social media I think it's outrageous. I think when you're young you're more inclined to pay attention to transfer gossip. When I was playing for Dumbarton in Scotland I was getting linked to clubs left, right and centre and it boosted my confidence and gave me more belief in myself. But as you get older, you realise these gossip pages are nonsense.'

Former Hull City and Brighton & Hove Albion full-back Liam Rosenior is also under no illusion as to the background of transfer gossip. 'It's 100 per cent true that there is always an agenda behind a transfer rumour. It might be an agent trying to get a move for his player and making other clubs aware that he is available. It might even be a club putting it out there that a bid has come in for a player, in the hope of getting another bid. That's where journalists get their information from. The role of the media is huge. The media really sensationalise transfers because, at the end of the day, it's a guy, a player, that another club want to sign. It's so funny, whenever we get to the end of a transfer window now we see clubs getting graded on the transfers that they've done without even seeing these players play. It's incredible. "We'll give this fellow a C but we haven't seen him play in the team yet or whether they actually fit into the way the team play." There's always an agenda behind those rumours.'

Often for footballers, job security comes into play. An accountant doesn't lift up a newspaper or read a tweet linking his or her practice with a direct replacement for them, but a footballer often does.

Benin striker Frédéric Gounongbe concedes that it's part of the game. 'There are different types of players. When you are a striker and you hear your club is looking for a new striker in the transfer window, of course you are a bit worried and wondering, "Why do they want a new striker if I am performing and scoring goals?" It is a very competitive business. I like to compare it to the business world where companies want good employees. But, of course, it affects you. It affected me when I was in Belgium. When I was performing well with Westerlo I was a top striker in the league. Just before the winter break I had an injury so I was already down because of that. And I saw on Twitter that my club was linked with a move for another good striker. I was like, "Okay, yesterday I just got badly injured and they're already looking for a new striker? Like, I'm done now, you know!"

'A football player is very sensitive. They are human beings like everyone else and trying to protect ourselves from everybody around us is difficult.'

It's almost midnight as I finish this chapter and, with the 2018 summer transfer window in full flow, I can't help checking what nuggets the BBC's gossip page has in store. Arsenal are apparently in talks with Sampdoria's Lucas Torreira, while Tottenham have joined the race for Barcelona midfielder Rafinha. José Mourinho could reignite a move for Tottenham's Toby Alderweireld but has no plans to sign Juventus left-back Alex Sandro. CSKA Moscow are willing to do a deal on Arsenal target Aleksandr Golovin, while Wolves are reportedly closing in on a loan deal to sign Benfica's Raúl Jiménez and are also interested in Sunderland's Paddy McNair. Meanwhile, Norwich City's James Maddison is in demand, with Everton expected to make an opening offer.

By the time this book is published we will know whether any of these deals went through. I suspect it might be around 21 or 22 per cent of them. What we can be sure of is that there is some spin to the rumours, some 'floating stuff out there', some market signalling – whether they emanated from the machinations of an agent, a club, fans or players themselves. We'll probably see the names, the clubs, the figures and forget that they're stories about 'human beings like everyone else'. And, I, like countless others, will continue to lap it all up.

The Agents

GOT a spare 500 quid handy? No unspent criminal record? Not bankrupt? If so, you could become a football agent later today. Actually, that's not entirely accurate – the correct term these days is football intermediary, but we'll use them interchangeably. The vast sums swirling around the game in recent years, however, has led me, and many football fans, to wonder how one goes about becoming an agent, regardless of what we call them.

It certainly appears to be a lucrative business. The general consensus seems to be that an elite player's agent can pick up millions for a few minutes' work on deadline day, having spent months unsettling the player and aggravating his existing club. Indeed, the figures seem to back this up. Between 1 February 2017 and 31 January 2018, Premier League clubs paid a net total of £211,011,187 to intermediaries, more than the GDP of several of the world's smallest national economies.

FIFA's deregulation of the industry in April 2015 has led to an explosion in the number of licensed intermediaries. Prior to this, there were between 500 and 600 licensed agents operating in the UK. By June 2018, the number of individuals registered with the Football Association (FA) had rocketed to 1,897. Those who had previously failed an exam now had access to the industry, along with family members of players, who had previously been barred from benefiting financially from deals involving their relatives.

Others have seen it as a lucrative earner, perhaps encouraged by press reports about the gargantuan sums involved in transfer deals.

In October 2016, for example, Juventus director Giuseppe Marotta claimed that Paul Pogba's agent Mino Raiola earned €27m from the deal that took the French midfielder back to Manchester United earlier that year. However, while Raiola represents stellar names like Pogba, Zlatan Ibrahimović, Romelu Lukaku and Mario Balotelli, the majority of intermediaries in the UK are plying their trade on a much smaller scale.

Rob Shield, of Evolve Sports Management, is typical of those who've been representing players since before FIFA's deregulation of the industry. Fed up with a career in IT, he hooked up with an established agent in 2006 and began shadowing him. Rob had worked with a few former players and quickly began building contacts within the game. He soon realised he could forge a career in this new world.

'I'd been doing it for a couple of months and I probably had more contacts than the agent I was following. I set up a couple of trials for one of his players and, eventually, that player signed for Blackpool,' recalls Rob.

Prior to deregulation, aspiring agents had to undergo an exam before being issued with a five-year licence by their national association. The exam comprised 20 multiple choice questions, with 14 correct answers required to pass. Sounds easy, right? Well, not really. Here are two sample questions. The answers are provided below.

Question One:

The Greek player Angelo Patsouris, born on 1 March 1990, was registered with and trained by the Greek club FC Anthropos, a category 3 club, as from 1 January 2002. The football season in Greece runs from 1 July until 30 June of the following year. On 1 January 2004, the player signed a two-year scholarship agreement with FC Anthropos, according to which the club agreed to pay all expenses incurred through his football activity, plus an additional monthly amount of €80. During the following two years, Angelo remained registered as an amateur. On 1 January 2006, Angelo signed a professional contract with FC Anthropos, valid until 31 December 2008.

On 1 January 2008, Angelo and FC Anthropos agreed to terminate their employment relationship and simultaneously signed an agreement that both parties had no further financial obligations towards each other. On 2 January 2008, Angelo was registered as an amateur with the Belarus club FC Bensko, a category 2 club. On 1 January 2010, Angelo signed a professional contract with FC Bensko and was consequently registered with the Belarus Football Federation as a professional one day later.

On 28 September 2011, FC Anthropos lodged a claim against FC Bensko in front of FIFA's Dispute Resolution Chamber, asking for training compensation. How much training compensation is FC Anthropos entitled to receive from FC Bensko for the training of Angelo, if at all?

NB: Greece is a member of the European Union (EU) and Belarus is not a member of the EU.

€0.

€110,000.

€185,000.

Question Two:

Raj is currently a 24-year-old football player of Indian nationality who has continuously lived since the age of two with his family in Cape Town (South Africa) where he currently plays for a local football club. Raj was called by the All India Football Federation to play with the Indian Under-19 representative team in an official team competition. Raj was unfortunately injured ten minutes into his first official match which took place on 2 May 2007 and did not subsequently take part in any other matches with the representative teams of India. In August 2007, Raj obtained South African nationality on a permanent basis. He now wishes to play for the "A" national team of South Africa.

In this context, which of the following statements is correct?

a. Since Raj has lived continuously in South Africa for more than five years after reaching the age of 18, he is immediately eligible to play for the South African Football Association.

b. Raj is no longer eligible to play for the representative teams of South Africa.

c. In order for Raj to be eligible to play for the representative teams of South Africa, a request for change of association will have to be submitted to the FIFA general secretariat and be accepted by the latter.

The answer to Question One is C, while the answer to Question Two is B.

Pass rates for this exam were notoriously low – as little as six per cent in some years. In order to become a licensed agent you had to pass the exam and, if you passed the other criteria and had professional indemnity insurance, you would then be licensed by your national association. Rob Shield took the exam in 2008. He was one of two that day who passed the test – out of the 70 who sat it.

'It was like two big ring binders, about 2,000 pages of FIFA, FA, Premier League and Football League regulations,' recalls Rob. 'It was tough to pass. When I did it there were only 250 licensed agents in England. That increased gradually but since deregulation happened in 2015 it's gone mad.'

Dan Lowen, a partner and specialist sports lawyer at LEVEL, was involved in transfers worth over £100m during the 2016 summer transfer window alone. He also successfully tutored over 120 aspiring agents for FIFA's exam so is well placed to comment on its difficulty.

'Prior to April 2015, FIFA governed the regulation and practice of agents on a worldwide basis,' explains Dan. 'In order to become a licensed agent you had to pass what was a very difficult exam, you had to have professional indemnity insurance and there were various criteria you had to meet, such as not having a criminal record. The exam itself – a 20-question multiple choice paper – was extremely difficult. The pass rate between 2008 and 2014, when the last exam was set, fluctuated in this country between 6 per cent and 35 per cent. In some countries around the world, no one would pass in a particular sitting.'

There was a misconception that the exam was relatively straightforward as it was multiple choice, but Dan explains that the questions were designed to trip up candidates.

'If they didn't know the regulatory provision which held the key to a question, then the common-sense approach would generally yield the wrong answer,' he says. 'The syllabus was huge, comprising lengthy and, in some cases, complex international and domestic regulations. FIFA would set 15 questions and the national association the other five. The questions were scenario-based, involving practical problems which needed solving, so it wasn't just a question of learning the materials, but really understanding them and being able to apply that detailed knowledge to the complex practical scenarios.

'There was never such a thing as a FIFA agent's licence, however, even though many agents called themselves FIFA licensed agents. While FIFA oversaw the licensing system, licences were actually granted by the relevant national association. The licence had worldwide application. What it allowed the licensed individual to do was conduct player and club representation domestically and internationally, which of course is very important in football, as the player representation business, by its very nature, is very international. Then, in early 2015, FIFA decided to essentially pull out of the regulation of agents, establishing a loose framework for intermediaries but devolving responsibility for regulating intermediaries to each national association. FIFA's rationale was that, apparently, only 25 to 30 per cent of international transfers were conducted by licensed agents, the corollary being that 70 to 75 per cent of international transfers involved unlicensed individuals. In FIFA's mind, the system wasn't working, but rather than double its efforts in an attempt to fix it, the world governing body effectively relinquished its regulatory responsibilities.'

Gary Mellor, Director of Beswicks Sports – whose clients include England goalkeeper Jack Butland – agrees that FIFA 'just gave up', with much of the work conducted with unlicensed agents driven by clubs.

Clubs using any means necessary to get their transfer targets is hardly a new occurrence. In 1908, a transfer limit of £350 was placed on players by the Football League, which clubs quickly found a way around. Larger fees were agreed between clubs for the transfer of several players in one deal, of which all but one were makeweights. The ruling was abolished within months.

'It has opened it up to anyone with a mobile phone and £500 in their pocket. Clubs will work with whoever they need to work with to get a deal done,' says Gary. 'It doesn't necessarily make it right but I understand that they've got to look after themselves. They want the player and they do what they can to get the player. For 90 per cent of players, clubs don't want to deal with any agent, because the player is desperate to get a move or desperate to get a new club. The top ten per cent, who make all the headlines, will be chased by numerous clubs and the clubs that have got them probably want to keep them. So, people use whoever they possibly can to keep the player, move the player or convince the player that their club is the best possible place for him.'

FIFA decided to regulate the industry in a different way, focusing on the actual transfer taking place rather than who could conduct the transfer. The responsibility for administering the agent system was delegated to national associations, such as the FA in England, and the barrier to entry that was the exam was removed.

'They required national associations to put in place a registration system pursuant to which any intermediary would register on a transaction by transaction basis each time with the national association,' explains Dan.

'FIFA permitted national associations to go beyond that and implement more thorough or more prescriptive rules and regulations than FIFA's regulatory position. FIFA's regulations amounted to the minimum terms. And many associations have indeed done that. In England, the FA implemented its own version of the Regulations on Working with Intermediaries, which are more prescriptive than FIFA's regulations. They provide for an annual registration system, rather than a per transaction registration system.'

These changes made it a lot easier to get involved in agency or intermediary work. Aspiring agents are now required to register with the FA and are charged £500 plus VAT for their initial one-year registration. No exams are sat, no professional qualifications are required. Almost anyone can do it.

'You have to have what's termed an impeccable reputation by FIFA, and there's the FA's test of good character,' continues Dan. 'But, ultimately, the vast majority of people can decide to become an intermediary, register and that day become entitled to represent players – there's no need for professional indemnity insurance or to pass an exam. Provided the applicant doesn't have a criminal record that's not spent, is not bankrupt etc., then the applicant should have no issue meeting the requirements of the test of good character.'

With an almost 300 per cent increase in the number of agents since 2015 competition is rampant, leading to some adverse decisions on behalf of players.

'A lot of agents are worried now that if they don't find a deal for their client, someone else will, and could be giving their players the wrong deals because of that,' stresses Rob Shield. 'There's a lot of poor deals being handed out because of that, as agents are getting worried about losing their clients. A lot of people say it's like the wild west, but it's probably worse than that. I'm lucky in that I've got a bit of a niche, working with English players in the Scottish Premiership. That's kept me going, it's my bread and butter. I've got seven or eight players playing there. I've had some good successes with players up there. I've got 12 lads signed up and have dabbled in the women's game with some England internationals.'

Clifford Bloxham has over 30 years' experience in the agency business, where he is senior vice president of Octagon. He agrees that FIFA's decision to deregulate has been detrimental to the industry, but feels that the players themselves should shoulder some of the responsibility.

'Ultimately, it can only come from the player,' says Clifford. 'They don't have to sign with these agents. They need to set the parameters for what a good agent is. Is it watching every training session and coming to every game? No, it isn't. Some agents are mentors and that's not a bad thing. What's their job? Is it to be a mentor? Is it to do their commercial deals, their PR, their press? The majority of these new agents are practising as they go along because there are not enough players.'

He uses the example of England's 2018 World Cup squad to illustrate his point that experience is key.

'England brought 23 players to the World Cup so you're already dividing roughly 1,900 agents by 23,' begins Clifford. 'In essence only 23 of those 1,900 have the experience of working with a current England international. That means of the other 1,877, if they get one, they're practising. They've not done it. Out of those 23, you're going to have – at best – two or three superstars. So that means of the 1,900, there's only two or three of them who are working with a superstar. If you're an agent who comes along and comes across a great young superstar or, maybe your son or nephew is a young superstar, you're going to be practising with their career. Would you have your wisdom tooth taken out by a dentist who's never taken a wisdom tooth out before? No. Would you have your heart operated on by a surgeon who'd never done it before? No. Why would a player allow someone to manage their career when they're practising?'

He is quick to point out that agents should never be judged as one homogenous group and that a company like Octagon – with a 35-year history that began with clients likes John McEnroe, Steffi Graf and Dan Marino on their books – should not make mistakes.

'If we did, we should be crucified as we have no excuse. We're not practising, we've done it before. We've represented the best sportspeople in the world. Our expectations for the way we do things are completely different to a young agent starting out who has no experience. They're going to make mistakes, they're going to learn.'

Mention the industry to many football fans and it conjures up images of super-agents such as Raiola, Jorge Mendes, Pini Zahavi and Jonathan Barnett. However, scroll through the list of almost 2,000 FA licensed intermediaries and very few household names jump out.

Several well-known former players' names appear, such as Pierre van Hooijdonk, Mikaël Silvestre, Celestine Babayaro, Ian Harte, Antoine Sibierski and Francis Benali. Abedi Ayew aka Abedi Pele, the three-time African Footballer of the Year and father of loaned-out Swansea City strikers Jordan and André Ayew, is also among them.

It's certainly an enticing avenue for remaining in the game for some retired players and several footballers I spoke to have admitted it's a path that they have considered pursuing when they hang up their boots.

'It's a business that I like and I don't like,' says Irish midfielder Richie Ryan. 'I like to try and look after younger players and, when I retire, agency work is something that I've thought about. I've had plenty throughout my career. Some good, but I've definitely had more bad. The thing is with agents, if you're doing well and performing on the pitch it's a lot easier for them to get you moves. And if you're getting moves, he's getting paid for it. Then he's your best friend. In my younger years when my career went sort of downhill a bit, I ended up having three or four agents as they all just seem to go missing on me. It becomes a very lonely place as a player then. You're not in a good run of form, you're not in the team or you might want a new challenge elsewhere. Your agent notes all this but he just doesn't pick up the phone or he doesn't give you a call to see how you are. A lot of this comes down to agents having too many players on their books.'

However, it's not just retired players getting in on the act, according to Rob Shield. 'A lot of players playing in the lower leagues are now doing it, at Conference North level, for example. They're playing and acting as agents as I think that's the lowest level of football you can play at and act as an agent. Before, players couldn't do it, for obvious reasons. They're all getting in on it, realising they no longer have to do the exam. There's nothing holding them back now,' says Rob.

What's probably more striking from the list is the number of familiar surnames – Christopher Welbeck, Dane Rashford, Daniel Arnautović, George Shelvey and Pierre François Aubameyang, to name but a few.

Dan Lowen explains that the changes to FIFA's regulations in 2015 opened up the market to players' relatives. 'Under the old agents' licensing system, parents and close relatives were permitted to represent players but could not be remunerated for doing so. Now relatives can be registered as intermediaries and/ or be paid commission by another intermediary in relation to the player, provided that the relative is registered as an intermediary.'

It's not that surprising that professional footballers should want a loved one looking out for them and their career. Bournemouth's Jordon Ibe has stated in the past that he doesn't see what an agent could do for him that his parents couldn't. Scottish defender Neill Collins has had several agents throughout his career but regrets not having his father more involved in his transfer and contract negotiations.

'One of the best deals I've ever had, my dad did it,' says Neill. 'At the end of the day he only has one person's interests at heart, and that's mine. Agents, even the best ones, will still have to work with these clubs in the future so they always have to play both sides. The agent I've had for the past six, seven or eight years I wish I'd had longer. I'd one bad experience with an agent. It wasn't that he was a bad person, he just didn't do a very good job. It is important to have someone to look after you.'

There were a couple of particularly contentious changes in the new regulations, notes Dan Lowen. 'The most controversial change, which was the subject of a challenge to the European Commission by the Association of Football Agents, was a three per cent recommended commission rate. The second controversial aspect was the prohibition on an intermediary earning commission in relation to a minor [i.e. a player under 18 years of age]. So hypothetically, if a 17-year-old signs his first three-year pro contract on £10,000 a week – making it a contract worth over £1.5m to the player, the intermediary is prohibited by FIFA's regulations from receiving commission.

'The other big problem is that the international licensing system has been replaced by a new system where each national association has its own registration rules which differ wildly from association to association – in terms of who is allowed to register, how they go about registering and how they conduct their business,' continues Dan. 'The problem is that a national registration is not recognised in other countries around the world. So, an English intermediary who wants to take a player from England to Germany will have to register in Germany, pay their registration fee, comply with the requirements of the German-specific regulations and so on. Many intermediaries' business is very international so they may be facing thousands of pounds' worth of registration fees on an annual basis and, each time, need to comply with the various regulations of each association, which will often necessitate legal advice from experts in each relevant country.'

I comment that it seems a total mess. 'I wouldn't dispute that,' replies Dan.

So, just how lucrative is the industry? The 1990s super-agent Eric Hall once quipped, 'The terrible thing about my job is that players get 80 per cent of my earnings.' But Dan explains that agents' fees can be extremely variable.

'In England, the standard commission rate that an agent will charge is five per cent,' he says. 'The agent's earnings are nothing to do with the transfer fee in 90 to 95 per cent of cases. When an intermediary is acting for a player the commission is calculated with reference to the player's gross guaranteed remuneration under the deal, i.e. five per cent of the player's salary and any signing-on fee that he earns under his employment contract with the club, not five per cent of the transfer fee.

'For example, if a player earns a salary of £1m per year throughout a four-year contract, then the five per cent will be £50,000 per year and that will generally be paid on an annual basis. It depends on what the player and the intermediary have agreed and, subsequently, what the club and the intermediary have agreed – as it's ultimately the club that pays the intermediary their commission on behalf of the player. It tends to be in annual instalments but it's open for them to agree to pay in a lump sum or fewer annual instalments than the number of years for which the contract will last.'

Of course, there are exceptions to this. If an intermediary is acting for a club on a transfer then they are permitted to frame their commission with reference to the transfer fee on that deal.

'It is open to an intermediary to earn money from different parties in a deal,' continues Dan. 'Under the old English system you could undertake what's called dual representation, which is where the intermediary acted for a player but, when it comes to the deal, he would also act for the club in recognition of the fact that he helped bring the player to and/or negotiated the player's contract with the club. So, essentially, he could be paid by both parties to the deal. Under the new system the intermediary can be paid by multiple parties in the deal – so he can be paid by the buying club, selling club and the player.'

This duality can obviously lead to a conflict of interest. If you're a player and your agent is also representing the buying and/or the selling club, can he or she really have your best interests at heart?

'It is a requirement of the regulations that there is complete transparency and disclosure of conflicts of interest,' says Dan. 'What is certainly not permitted, for example, is an intermediary acting for the selling club but not disclosing that fact to the buying club. All parties to a transaction need to be fully aware of who the intermediary is acting for.'

FIFPro, the world players' union, has been negotiating with FIFA for some time on tougher regulation around this problem area. FIFPro Europe's Secretary General, Jonas Baer-Hoffmann, believes that it is probably the most fundamental conflict of interest imaginable.

'Today, most of those agents are either exclusively or almost predominantly paid for their services by the club,' says Jonas. 'So they are a player agent but a club is paying their fees. Which means their interest can be conflicted. They're also often paid, not based on the salary that they negotiate but on the transfer fee. It's in their interest to get the highest possible share of the transfer fee. In many cases we find that these agents don't truly represent the best interests of the players and, now, we've had clubs complaining about the agents having more power over the market than the clubs themselves. What happened was when FIFA changed their agent regulations and made them intermediaries, they legalised the conflict of interest as long as it's disclosed to all parties.

'So you now have transfers in which the agent is paid by every single party involved in the transfer – from the player, the current club and the new club. That brought the public's attention to it but, in fact, it's also led to the agents making even more disproportionate amounts of money from transfers. I actually don't call them agents any longer, I call them brokers as they're sitting between the parties and brokering the deal.'

FIFPro is of the opinion that intermediaries should be exclusively player agents and is striving to regulate the market more robustly.

'In the football industry, at least internationally, almost everybody agrees that the free-for-all we have right now is not helpful for anybody,' continues Jonas. 'At the moment you have agents working on both sides – you can't control this market. We need to talk about a way in which we can cap their fees. The size of the money flow doesn't make sense compared, for example, with the solidarity payments among clubs.'

Simon Chadwick, Professor of Sports Enterprise at the University of Salford, mentioned an agent acquaintance in the previous chapter, who he believes is increasingly characteristic of agents in general.

'It's clearly in an agent's best interests for their players to move. This is their bread and butter. This particular guy is not unique,' says Simon. 'He works for a large, global corporation. And these large, global corporations are typically run out of, for example, New York boardrooms. The people who sit in these New York boardrooms don't take prisoners. They want a constant turnover of business and shareholder returns every year. So I think there is an aggressive commercial imperative here for agents to be cutting the best possible deals for their players. Whether that's in terms of getting increased salary or improved terms and conditions.'

Gary Mellor had several clubs interested in some of his players during the 2018 summer window. He insists that the onus was on making the best choices for their careers rather than their bank balances.

'It should always be all about the player,' maintains Gary. 'I understand why dual representation is there, and not just because it saves the player benefit-in-kind tax. If you go to the right place, you can soon make that money up. Sometimes we would advise players to go backwards in order to go forward.'

As an American-owned company, Octagon have a global perspective across many sports and Clifford Bloxham explains that, when it comes to representation, football is unique compared to any other sport.

'The football world is completely different to when we move an NBA or NFL player,' he says. 'I'm not going to bash agents but one thing they've done over the years very well is created a myth of complexity. Clubs use agents to help get players, which wouldn't happen in any of those other sports. The concept of an American football team using an agent to recruit players just doesn't happen. In those other major team sports worldwide, it takes away one layer of complexity because the agents are always working for the player, they're never working for the club. There are different levels of agents, which allows agents to have different standards. Again, this doesn't happen as often in other sports. In football, there is lots of room for agents who work to different standards to interpret the situation in different ways.

'Prior to deregulation, agents could work for the club so it's always been there,' Clifford continues. 'The single biggest myth is also that the agent's fee comes from this mystical, separate pot of money but it doesn't. Any club can only spend their money once, whether they spend it on the player's salary, the transfer fee, or the agent's fee. In the player's mind, historically, the agent's fee has never come out of their personal money, it's always been this separate, mystical pot of money that doesn't impact them. But the truth is, it does. In other sports the players realise exactly how much money their agents are making. In the NFL, NBA and NHL the agents' fees are regulated, it's a fixed percentage.'

Clifford acknowledges that something similar will probably happen in football, but that the status quo suits all parties.

'If a club are very desperate for a player, they won't mind paying the agent a higher fee. One of the areas that will need looking at is that there should legally be a relationship between what the player's representation contract says and what the agents receive – it should always be the same number,' he reasons.

Agents aren't in the business for the love of the game; they have to make money from their clients to pay their bills. And then there's the moral dilemma: are they willing to put their player's career ahead of their personal financial gain when it comes to a possible lucrative transfer or contract negotiation?

'That's a really tough question and that's down to each individual agent,' Clifford accepts. 'Some of the good ones will always put their client's long-term future over their personal short-term gain.

'Part of the problem is whether the player can see that an agent is pushing their financial well-being first. Can they see that if they are going to be a great player, it may not make sense to go to this particular club at this particular moment, even though you're going to triple your salary and buy everything you've ever wanted? It's the players who look at it purely from a football perspective who are going to make it. If money is ahead of career development, then they're probably never going to get to where they want to get to. If they're great they'll know that eventually they're going to be making the money that they deserve. When we worked with Andy Murray there was no doubt in his mind that he was going to be Wimbledon champion. It's harder for the football guys as it's a team sport but it makes it hard on the agent too. Is it the agent's job to help make the player the best player they can possibly be or to make them the most money they can earn?'

I suggest that it's up to the individual player. Clifford agrees, but maintains that it's sometimes difficult to ascertain a footballer's true motivations.

'The most important thing is that you've got to really know the player. How well do you know that mindset? Do they want to be the best they can be or do they want to make a lot of money? Do they want to be comfortable and look after their wife and kids? You have to really know the person and that's not always easy to do,' he contends.

'They need to be honest, it's a two-way street. It has to be a team, working together. If he says, "I've had enough. I've two or three years left and just want to make as much money as I can," then that's fair enough. As long as you know that then we can do our best job. Ninety-nine per cent of players, though, believe that their agent is unbelievable at negotiating deals in the boardroom, even if everything else about them is a disaster. And that doesn't happen in any other walk of life. You have to be competent in every facet of your discipline, you can't get away with just being great at one thing and rubbish at everything else. Now, that one thing makes the most money, but how can they feel so comfortable that that guy's going to be amazing in the boardroom when they're not amazing at everything else they're doing?

'The other misconception is that you can separate team contracts from commercial deals, PR and brand management,' Clifford continues. 'Everything is interlinked. Some agents say, "Oh, I only do the team deal. I don't give a damn about the marketing side, the press, PR or social media."

'Well, in this day and age, everything is linked. When a club buys a player, the player's image, brand and reputation all count for something. Their social media presence counts for something. The way they conduct their day-to-day life and business counts for something. A lot of leading agents use different companies for PR, for social media or commercial work or don't even bother with it.'

Former Tunisia international Radhi Jaïdi was involved in transfers to Bolton Wanderers, Birmingham City and Southampton during his career and has seen at first hand players who have chased money rather than career advancement.

'Sometimes players follow the money and think they will succeed in a certain environment but it doesn't always work out. So they need to be careful of that,' he says. 'I don't think the players are the main subjects in this. The agents are the main subjects of transfer gossip. I think the agents have the most impact in players' movements from one club to another, due to the financial benefits of a player moving – but the players engage with this. You can have one good game and the agent can work around that game and benefit from that. The players can control all this though.

'The media are engaged in that game, where there is already a buzz two or three months before the transfer window opens. The agents have a lot more power than before. The agencies now are big companies that have control of journalists, they have control of clubs and directors and have a lot of contacts and links. That's the nature of agents. That's their business. At the end of the day, though, the players are in control of that. There needs to be some law that can manage things better for players moving from club to club. I saw some players who just signed a five-year contract but then, six months later, they wanted to move and got that move. They put pressure on the club and it's not fair on the clubs. I don't think the law is good enough now.'

While most players I spoke to didn't go as far as to call agents a necessary evil, they did acknowledge that they can be of benefit – even after mixed experiences throughout their careers.

'They are obviously people that are needed because they know how to speak to clubs. I honestly couldn't do it myself,' admits Raffaele De Vita. 'I know why a lot of players, including myself, get frustrated with them because sometimes they tell you what you want to hear and sometimes they don't tell you the exact truth. Sometimes they don't understand how much it means to you. There's always going to be conflict between the player and agent but they are needed because they have the knowledge and skills to speak to clubs, which most players don't have.'

He stresses that he is not a confrontational person but concedes that the only arguments he has had in his life have been with agents. 'You're always pushing them and always want more from them,' continues Raffaele. 'Sometimes you have to understand that it's out of their hands. They do their best but, occasionally, you think that it's not enough and they can do more. So there's always going to be arguments and heated discussions.'

Liam Rosenior agrees that agents are an essential part of the modern-day game, despite some bad experiences earlier in his career.

'I think with the way that clubs are operating you need an agent to represent you,' he says. 'You need the right agent, someone you can trust. In my career I've had some good agents and bad agents. I've had agents who have tried to force me to a club that I didn't want to go to because it was a better financial deal for them, which is unethical, more than anything else, but that's the way some agents will operate. And when you've got the amounts of money that are involved now in football, you are going to have people like that who are looking to capitalise financially from any deal. It's really important that you choose the right agent, one you get on well with and who puts your interest above theirs.

'It also comes down to the relationship between clubs and agents. Some clubs will have a better relationship with a certain agent's company and you will have more chance of moving to that club because they like dealing with that agent. It can sometimes be quite political. One agent might have a better chance of getting you the move that you want than another. And that's where the lack of trust comes into it. It's a really difficult thing for a player to make the decision on what agent to go with, and clubs make the most of that as well.'

Mark Roberts agrees that players need to be careful about who they choose. 'I had one when I was younger when I was coming through at Crewe Alexandra as a youngster. I felt, though, that I was equipped or able, or at a level of football, where I was able to represent myself. I was quite comfortable in those negotiations in terms of sitting across from the manager or the chairman and speaking about a move. In my mid-twenties, and towards the end of my time at Stevenage, I felt it was the right time for me to get an agent.

'You have to be careful about who you choose,' Mark continues. 'Someone advised once me that you should always be happy that an agent will go into a room and represent you and say something that you would be comfortable with saying. There are agents out there who are quite brash with a kick-the-door-down approach and that certainly works for some players, don't get me wrong. But, for me, I felt that I wanted someone representing me that I was comfortable in knowing he would speak and act in a way that I would if I was in that room myself.'

Former Portsmouth midfielder Martin Roderick did not have an agent during his career but admits he'd probably have one if he was still playing. 'Agents are terribly important in some respects and for other players they're a hindrance,' says the academic. 'I still visit a lot of academies and the agents are hanging around watching under-14s and under-16s games and it's heartbreaking to see. I came across players who had agents who would simply not pay them any attention because they wouldn't make them any money. And yet they were tied to this agent, so no matter what move they made the agent would take money and it was exploitative, really. I also came across players who need agents to protect them in some ways from clubs, who would pressure the players to sign under certain circumstances. The more people who are wrapped around players, the more distant the players are from understanding the kind of deals they're entering into.'

Charlie Sheringham's form at non-league Dartford in 2010/11, where he scored 30 goals in 46 appearances, helped attract interest from Football League clubs and he credits his agent with helping him get a move to Bournemouth.

'I think agents have been helpful throughout my career,' says the striker. 'When I was 23, I got a move to Bournemouth from the Conference and my agent was certainly useful then. There were a few clubs interested, four or five different league teams, so he was helpful then. Sometimes it's good to have somebody to talk to.'

The majority of the players I spoke to disclosed that they'd had a mixture of good and bad agents throughout their careers. Some who helped advance their careers and others who wouldn't even pick up the phone. But what makes a good agent?

'When you want to move and your agent doesn't get you a move, then he's a bad agent. If he gets you a move out of the blue, then he's a good agent!' laughs one former Premier League star. 'Agents are there to make money. Whether we like it or not, that's their job. A lot of the time it's the player that gets the move in the first place. It's the legal side of it that the player doesn't understand. The older you get you start to understand how negotiations go, and that depends on how much money is at stake. It's good that agents have to declare how much money they've made from deals these days, whereas in the past there may have been back-handers going on and players didn't really know how much agents were earning from deals.'

A combination of hard work and honesty sets a good agent apart, believes Gary Mellor. 'Some players don't have the careers they should have because they'll sign with one of these agents that don't have any connections and don't, therefore, get the right loan moves or clubs. People won't know them. We're fortunate as we've got over 170 players, so if we pick up a phone to a club they'll normally speak to us because we have a number of options. If you are a new agent you might have two or three players, and you're less likely to have your calls taken. There have been instances where very good players have fallen by the wayside because their agents haven't kept them in the game. We have players like Jack Butland, for instance, who's been with us since the age of 17. He went to Cheltenham Town at a young age on loan from Birmingham City because of our connections. When he moved to Stoke City, he was loaned out to the likes of Barnsley, Leeds United and Derby County. We kept him playing because we had relationships with these clubs. You need to play to pick up experience – to have a career.'

Loan moves are a large part of Gary's job, especially for younger players. As we saw earlier for the likes of Harry Kane, they can be crucial in developing a path into senior-level football.

'You've got to get them experience,' Gary emphasises. 'We did a lot of loan deals when Mark Robins was the manager of Barnsley and when Simon Grayson was at Blackpool because when we sent players to them, they worked. A lot of it is about character. I've been doing this for nearly 20 years and clubs know me and know I'm honest about the character of my players. So they're probably more likely to take your player over someone they see as just as good, but they don't know their agent well enough.'

Gary and I spoke the day after the 2018 summer transfer deadline passed for Premier League clubs and he'd had a busy few months – in no small part down to the fact that the window had closed for the first time before the league season kicked off. There had been fears that the move would be detrimental for clubs in England's top tier, allowing European rivals a few weeks to poach their players. However, Gary believes it's a positive move and that other leagues across the continent should fall into line.

'It's like a turkey voting for Christmas, though,' he concedes. 'The window closing before the season starts is good for football. But it's not good for football when all the European teams can pick off players or get better deals as they've got nowhere else to go. From the Championship clubs' point of view, they can still do loans with a view to permanent deals, which needs to be sorted out. If there's going to be a deadline day, there needs to be clarity on all sides.'

Clifford Bloxham wholeheartedly agrees with Gary's sentiments. 'There are positives and negatives. There's a very good playing reason why you want your team on day one. That's a real positive. The negative is that the European clubs have an advantage in terms of a longer window. Will they all come into line, which it could do? The Premier League has the biggest buying power and has the power to bring all the other European markets into the same time frame.

'Someone smart out there might work out that it is an advantage to buy early. You probably get the players cheaper. When a European club wants them after the English window has closed they'll probably pay a premium, as the Premier League club won't be able to replace that player like-for-like. But, again, that's a mystical phrase because if you're talking about superstars, there isn't a replacement. I was reading earlier about the Chelsea goalkeeper leaving for Real Madrid and whether they have time to replace him. When you're at that level you might get someone who is of a similar quality, but you'll never replace these sort of guys. They're obviously the best in their business, they're geniuses really. And these guys are one-offs, there's not five of them out there.'

Everyone from Sir Alex Ferguson to José Mourinho have blamed agents for 'ruining football', but do those in the profession feel that they get bad press due to the conduct of the minority?

'Yes,' replies Gary Mellor, 'The stories aren't told about the players who are in their early thirties, with families, who have been released and are who you probably work the hardest on. They're the deals that probably mean the most to you. I'm not trying to paint the profession as being Mother Teresa-like but, if you do the job properly, that's where you earn your money. You really have to work hard to move a player who has been in League One or League Two and has been released and has got a family to feed and a mortgage to pay, to a club like Yeovil Town or to a Scottish team. They haven't been paid the money that the fans see floated around for the top players.'

However, Clifford Bloxham believes the industry has a long way to go to reach the standards of other sports worldwide.

'I don't think agents get a bad rep,' he says. 'I'm not saying all agents are bad. The problem with any sport is that you're judged on the lowest common denominator, that's the reality. Even if 95 per cent of agents are great, the five per cent of agents who are bad will make the headlines, and that will be the public perception. The only way you can change that is to have unbelievably tight regulation. In the American team sports, the salaries are published, the agents' fees are mandated and the agents aren't involved in the club moves. It's much cleaner and much more transparent.

'Is the whole transfer business and the process and environment for representing a player conducive to the highest standards? The answer is no, it isn't. It's very hard for any agent to have a good reputation based on that environment and context. How good an agent are they at representing their clients' best interests? There's a percentage that do a good job and there's a small percentage that do a great job. The majority, compared to other sports, are not in the same league.'

Kevin Harris-James, a partner at Harrison Clark Rickerbys, has been involved in the legal side of numerous transfers, and believes it's easy to demonise agents in these transactions.

'When a club are buying, they hate the agent as the agent is there driving the price up,' says Kevin. 'But when they are selling, they love an agent! This idea of tapping up, for example, has been going on for years, at arm's length. It's ridiculous to pretend it doesn't happen. It's been like that forever. And the worst offenders, in my experience, are the clubs and not the agents.'

Jon Smith played a pivotal role in helping create the Premier League during a 30-year career as an agent for the likes of Diego Maradona. He believes that agents are soft targets. 'There are some very good agents. I've brought tens, maybe hundreds, of millions of pounds into the game,' says Jon, who sold his First Artist agency in 2010. 'I'd argue that Rupert Murdoch, a bunch of other people and I created the greatest league in the world. How bad a guy am I? I think I'm recognised as someone who has done quite a lot and, off the back of that, there's been quite a few acceptances of good agents. It's just the ones who pop up in the media like Mino Raiola – who's actually quite a good guy, who I like – bags a huge amount of money and people cast black eyes across at him.'

Naively, perhaps, I've always had the perception that agents come alive during transfer windows and don't do a whole lot in between. Jon refutes this, stating that agents are busy 24/7. 'It's not true,' he says. 'My sons look after several players and there's not a day goes past that they don't speak to them.'

Gary Mellor would certainly agree. His agency carries out a lot of work in the American market so his days are long. 'We try and speak to managers and coaches before training begins,' says Gary. 'When they are training you'll speak to the sporting directors, the directors of football and scouts and keep an eye on what the market is up to. Trying to find out who's got money, what positions people are looking to fill, what types of players you've got that might suit a style of play.

'If you're speaking to the manager and technical director you need to make sure they're on the same page, as sometimes it is difficult to understand who has the power, particularly when managers and head coaches change, like they've done at Chelsea and Arsenal this summer,' he adds. 'The biggest part of the job is about information and making sure you're ahead of the game, because quite a lot of the transfer window can be like a house of cards. You need to know if someone's going to move from a club, because they'll probably want to find a replacement.'

Rob Shield reveals that a good agent will have an inkling around March or April that their player is going to get released, so proactivity is key.

'That's probably when an agent is most useful,' he declares. 'You get a DVD together, you get stats together of the player from the past few seasons and pass it on to suitable clubs. You always try and avoid the lottery of trials in pre-season. I do enjoy it but it's hard work. I enjoy the satisfaction of getting a player into a new club early doors, if they've been released. It helps their family and gives them stability for another year at least.'

When Sunderland signed midfielder Stefan Schwarz, they probably hoped his movement would help find some space on the pitch. What they didn't expect was intergalactic travel. Concerned at an interview where the player expressed a desire to fly on the first commercial flight to space, The Black Cats added a clause banning him from any space travel until his contract expired.

Football clubs are often terrified of their players suffering injuries during extracurricular activities, and Liverpool were no different when they signed Stig Inge Bjørnebye in 1992. The defender's father was an Olympic ski jumper for Norway and Stig had inherited a passion for the sport. Liverpool were having none of it, however, banning the player from going within 200 yards of a ski slope.

Following Alex Oxlade-Chamberlain's move to Arsenal in 2011, Gunners fans became increasingly frustrated with the midfielder's lack of playing time. He was predominantly used as a substitute, often at around the 71-minute mark. After his contract details emerged, it all became clear: Arsenal were obliged to pay Southampton £10,000 every time he played 20 minutes or more.

When you're negotiating a contract, it's best to ensure you're 100 per cent clear about your demands. As Giuseppe Reina found out the hard way. Upon signing for Arminia Bielefeld, the German striker demanded the club build him a house for every year of his contract. Unfortunately for him he forgot to specify the size, enabling the club to build him a Lego house for the next three years.

These are just some examples of peculiar clauses inserted in the contracts of footballers. Dan Lowen explains, however, that in England the vast majority of players' contracts take the form of a standard-form document.

'The starting point is that the player is paid a salary as an employee of the club,' says the sports lawyer. 'Their playing contract is their employment contact. So much of Mo Salah's contract at Liverpool is the same as a young player signing his first pro contract with a Championship club. That's the front-end of the document, which has been developed over the years through negotiations with the PFA and other stakeholders in the game.

'It's in schedule two of the document that the commercial terms and the specifics of the individual player's deal are inserted,' Dan continues. 'Players will earn a wage, which is often expressed on a weekly basis. It's open for them to receive signing-on fees and/or loyalty fees when they've been at a club for a particular period of time. It's open to the club to pay bonuses based on all manner of things – appearances, scoring goals, assists, keeping clean sheets, national team appearances, etc. Their salary may ramp up or down depending on how many appearances they make or goals they score or whether the club is promoted or relegated.

'In addition to that, some players will set up an image rights structure, under which their image rights are assigned or licensed to a company. The standard employment contract between a club and player grants various promotional rights to the club in relation to the player and his image. The player must commit a certain number of hours per week to promotional activities for club partners, club charities and things like that. However, where a player has a valuable image, a club may be interested in acquiring enhanced commercial rights. So, for example, the club can acquire far greater control over the player's commercial portfolio and require that it is aligned with the club's commercial portfolio.'

Image rights payments have caused some controversy in recent years and raised the ire of HM Revenue & Customs (HMRC). Dan adds that they have been around since a case involving Dennis Bergkamp and David Platt in 2000, where HMRC claimed Arsenal were paying the players for image rights as a way of avoiding tax. The duo won their seminal case and image rights contracts have been used from time to time ever since.

'The courts have not ruled against image rights – they're recognised as a legitimate business arrangement,' he says. 'The reality is that where a player has a valuable and marketable image, that image is an asset in itself, and if it's transferred to a separate company, it's entirely proper for that company to then contract with clubs to grant enhanced services over and above what a club would ordinarily acquire through its employment contract with the player.'

Dan gets involved in a transfer at different stages, depending on whether he's acting for an intermediary or a club. Both the buying and selling clubs will do their due diligence before a transfer commences. The buying club will want to do due diligence on the player and his intermediary, and on the selling club and their treatment and development of the player. The selling club will want to do its due diligence on the buying club, particularly with a view to checking its credit-worthiness and its ability to pay in accordance with the transfer agreement.

'I can be brought in at various stages of the transfer process,' explains Dan. 'Potentially, it's very early on in the process with a view to advising parties on their options. Sometimes I'll act for an intermediary who knows that his player has been made available by his current club and there may be four or five different clubs that are interested and in dialogue with the selling club. The intermediary may want me involved from the outset to negotiate with a club with a view to structuring the deal in the best way possible and looking at the different options. At the other end of

Richie Ryan (above, left) in action for Miami FC. The Irishman has played for 11 clubs during his career.

Fleetwood captain Mark Roberts lifts the trophy after their League Two Play-off Final victory against Burton Albion at Wembley.

Liam Rosenior celebrates a Premier League victory for Brighton & Hove Albion. He admits to being pressured into moves earlier in his career.

Neill Collins in action for Sheffield United. Negotiations for his loan deal to Wolves was the first time Roy Keane and Mick McCarthy spoke after their infamous falling out at the 2002 World Cup.

Burnley captain Steven Caldwell holds the Championship trophy aloft after beating Sheffield United at Wembley. He joined the club on transfer deadline day and says it's difficult to put down roots as a footballer.

Italian midfielder Raffaele De Vita (right) in action for Swindon Town. He says that life as a footballer sometimes gets him down.

Leroy Lita celebrates scoring for Swansea City. His have-boots-will-travel attitude led to a move to Thailand.

Asmir Begović left Canada at 16 to join Portsmouth, where issues like homesickness challenged his mental strength.

Northern Ireland goalkeeper Michael McGovern saves from Germany's Mario Gómez during Euro 2016. His performances at the tournament helped earn him a move to Norwich City.

Charlie Sheringham in action for Ipswich Town. He's spent much of his career in the English lower leagues, before venturing to a club in Bangladesh.

Tunisian defender Radhi Jaïdi celebrates scoring at the 2006 World Cup. He credits Sam Allardyce with helping him and his family settle in England, following his move to Bolton Wanderers.

Rudy Gestede celebrates scoring against Liverpool in the Premier League.

Benin international Frédéric Gounongbe struggled to settle at Cardiff City due to off-the-field issues.

Cameroon international Benoît Assou-Ekotto celebrates a Tottenham goal with Gareth Bale.

Niall Quinn saw several overseas signings struggle to settle in England during his time as Sunderland chairman.

Jimmy Glass in action for Bournemouth, where he is now a player liaison officer.

Hugo Colace (left) captained Argentina at the 2003 FIFA World Youth Championship. He moved to Barnsley five years later, where he says he enjoyed the best form of his career.

Rohan Ricketts clears from Cristiano Ronaldo during a Premier League clash between Tottenham and Manchester United. Ricketts has gone on to play in 11 countries across four continents.

Viv Anderson was Sir Alex Ferguson's first signing at Manchester United.

Syd Puddefoot's 1922 world record transfer from West Ham to Falkirk for £5,000 prompted the media to question how 'any club could pay such an astonishing price'.

David Low (centre) with former Cameroon international Emmanuel Maboang.

the spectrum, I get a call at the eleventh hour and I'm asked to look at the playing contract and the intermediary arrangements literally at the very close of the deal.

'My job can be split into the legal work, in reviewing the documentation and ensuring it's as beneficial as possible for our client, the commercial work which entails constructing and negotiating the commercials of a deal and, thirdly, the regulatory and compliance side, as domestic and international regulations can have an impact on the transfer,' he continues. 'By way of an example, if a player's contract is due to expire on 30 June 2019 and he's at Liverpool, his intermediary is not going to be able to speak with other English clubs until the third Saturday in May 2019 at the very earliest. If he intends to go overseas, however, his intermediary can speak to overseas clubs in the final six months of his contract. So, it's important to have a handle on not just the domestic rules, but also the international position.'

I've always been intrigued by the mysterious transfer or compensation tribunal and wondered how it works. Dan Lowen was involved in Danny Ings's protracted 2015 move from Burnley to Liverpool. Ings's transfer was one that came under the remit of the compensation tribunal: even though the striker's contract was up at Burnley, the club was entitled to compensation when he signed for Liverpool but the two clubs in question were unable to agree the level of compensation for the striker.

'As a result of the Bosman case in the mid-1990s and several other decisions since then, a player who comes to the end of their contract at a club is free to move without being shackled by the imposition of a transfer fee by his current club,' begins Dan. 'However, both the international and domestic regulations recognise that it's important to reward clubs who have trained young players. Not only to reward them for their investment in training those players but also to incentivise clubs to train players.

'So the training compensation system is one of the bedrocks of the football system. In England if a player is not under contract and leaves a club before the age of 24, the club that trained him is entitled to compensation for the player. For players who are under 16, there is a fixed compensation system, called the Elite Player Performance Plan. This provides for a fixed remuneration based on the number of the years that the player has been trained by the club. There are then further contingent payments based on the extent to which the player makes first-team appearances for his new club, for example another £100,000 may be payable after ten first-team appearances, and so on.'

However, for players over the age of 16 and for those aged 16 and under who have been offered a scholarship by their club, there is no fixed compensation methodology. Instead it is left to the Professional Football Compensation Committee (PFCC), to give the transfer tribunal its correct name, to determine the compensation that is payable.

'There is a range of factors considered when coming up with the compensation award – including how long the player has been at the club, his playing record, whether the training club spent any money to acquire his registration, whether there has been any substantiated interest from other clubs, the costs incurred in training players,' Dan continues.

The ad hoc panel consists of a chairman, who is usually a lawyer, representatives of each of the leagues of which the clubs involved in the deal are members, and representatives of the PFA and the League Managers Association.

Dan acted for Burnley in the Danny Ings hearing, at which the Lancashire club were awarded a record £6.5m in guaranteed compensation, with an additional £1.5m in contingent compensation based on appearances. A 20 per cent sell-on fee was also included for the player, who is now on loan at Southampton.

'The clubs are given the opportunity to try and agree on the level of compensation first, before it goes to the PFCC – whose determination is final,' explains Dan. 'The reality is that it is a very complicated business. Both clubs make detailed submissions on the training of the player, the value of the player, the prospects of the player and the level at which they say the compensation should be set. And that is a lengthy process, which culminates in a hearing at which both sides present their arguments and the PFCC make their award shortly afterwards.'

Another aspect of the transfer market, which has fascinated me, is the term 'undisclosed fee'. It's become increasingly common when a transfer is announced to bandy this term about rather than divulge the actual finances behind the deal – often to the frustration of fans. However, even the subjects of these transfers are at a loss to explain why clubs are reticent about releasing the actual fee.

'I think pretty much every move I've had has had an undisclosed fee,' says Neill Collins. 'The deals have so many different layers to them. Let's say, for instance, I moved to Sheffield United for £400,000. There'd be £30,000 paid after a certain amount of appearances, for example. I think undisclosed fees are just to keep things simple. I've never really even asked about the transfer fees. I think it was around half a million pounds when I went from Preston North End to Leeds United but I don't know what the final figure was.'

So, how exactly do transfers come to fruition? A mixture of both clubs and agents being proactive, suggests Gary Mellor.

'There are ten of us in this office and we're talking to every single person that we can to try and find out what's going on, what the market's up to and what's likely to happen,' he says. 'Clubs will, quite rightly, have a Plan A, a Plan B and a Plan C and you've got to try and be honest and hope they're honest with you.'

Chelsea's interest in his client, Stoke City keeper Jack Butland, was well-publicised during the 2018 summer window. However, The Blues ended up shelling out a world-record fee for a goalkeeper when they paid £71.6m to Athletic Bilbao for Kepa Arrizabalaga as a replacement for Thibaut Courtois.

'While Antonio Conte was there, I think Jack was their number-one choice,' reveals Gary. 'When they had a change of head coach, that may well have changed. And that cost us. There was another situation where we took a player from Manchester City to a club where we knew, because they were honest with us, that he was third on their list. We felt that their first two options wouldn't happen and we got the deal over the line. We never told the player he was third-choice because you don't want him to feel like he wasn't their top target.'

Even when a transfer has been agreed in principle, there are often last-minute stumbling blocks. 'There are certain chief executives at football clubs who are renowned for changing the terms at the last minute,' says Kevin Harris-James. 'Jeremy Peace at West Brom was a shrewd negotiator. You'd think you'd agreed something and then, literally hours before, he'd change the terms, drop the buying price or something, forcing the hand of the other club in a deal. Of course, he would act in the best interests of West Brom but that would be little consolation if you were on the other side of the deal!'

The industry has certainly moved on since Jon Smith's first deal as a football agent – with the England national team in the late 1980s. He helped pioneer product placement in the game, encouraging substitutes to tie their laces as they entered the fray to allow camera close-ups of their branded boots.

'Today – and I'd like to think that I was the first to do this – it's a complete management service from beginning to end,' he says. 'From theatre tickets in the evening to multi-million-pound contracts. You are that person's lifestyle management, but you also have to have a very good intelligence network. You have to know where your player is likely to be and which clubs are likely to want him. You need to know the payments structures of those clubs, you need to know the tax regulations of how to configure a player's contract. The contracts in some of the cases are very, very complicated. They are multi-million-pound contracts, which have many working parts. That's what riles me about some of these people who just turn up and say, "I'm a football agent."

'It's kind of like a one-stop shop, really. If you look at some of the big movie stars, it's exactly the same sort of office arrangement with lawyers, accountants, advisors, tax advisors and personal managers. Someone who knows how to get hold of Quintessentially [the members-only luxury lifestyle management and concierge service] and the best flights for their families. It's an all-embracing office now.'

Players' contracts with agents are restricted to two years, although Jon is lobbying for an increase to three years. 'Four- or five-year contracts tend to refigure themselves after three years. Two years is still in that twilight zone before people are talking about new deals,' he explains.

I wonder whether agents can empathise with clubs when they lose a player as a client. 'Of course, absolutely,' he replies. 'It's their meal tickets. But there will be a situation where the agents will keep the reward for the contract they've negotiated. They currently lose that when they lose the player.'

Now an advisor to several agents, as well as helping to organise The Best FIFA Football Awards, Jon can look back on hundreds of deals, but one stands out as his proudest moment.

'There have been lots but there is one in particular,' he recalls. 'My brother and I took Kevin Phillips out of Watford. It wasn't working for him there and he was going to leave and play part-time football with Baldock Town and join his father's building company in Essex. We gave him one last shot by twisting Peter Reid's arm at Sunderland. And Peter said, "Yeah, go on, bring him up here for a couple of days and we'll have a look at him." He did well in those two days, so they signed him and he became an absolute hero. In their eyes, he's probably up there with the greatest players Sunderland have ever had. He's a demigod up in the north-east. Moments like that rank more to me than the days I had with Maradona.'

For Clifford Bloxham, his fondest memories are of helping young players make a difference.

'We were able to help Daniel Sturridge go the Brazil World Cup training camp in Switzerland when he was 16,' he says. 'He spent a week watching them train and seeing how it was done and watching them conduct interviews and so on. Eight years later he was playing at the World Cup in Brazil and it was familiar. We always start on the premise that whoever we represent, in the worlds of sport and entertainment, are going to be the very best in the world ever. They are going to be the best tennis player, the best golfer or the best American football player there has ever been.

'In that case, you work backwards. If you're going to be the best ever you better have done this, this, this and this. And, if they end up not being the very best, then it's easy to level out at their best level. So, if they become a decent Premier League player then it's easy to level out if that's where their talent takes them. What you can't do is make up ground if someone turns out to be a superstar and you were expecting them to be average. You haven't put the building blocks in. Daniel was a massive talent and it made sense for him to have that sort of experience at that age.'

Octagon give each client a blank book when they join to represent their autobiography, and ask them to think about how they will feel when their grandchildren read it in future years.

'From the very first second, they appear in the public domain – whatever they do is part of that book, good, bad or indifferent,' says Clifford. 'And even more so now with social media. They're dragging up things now that players said when they were 17 or 18 that were silly or childish, but they're still out there. The great ones in most sports don't have things that they're not comfortable about having in that book. Most of them do it the right way. Not everyone's perfect but they're always wanting to get better.'

At the outset of this book, I had toyed with the idea of registering as an agent. I have no criminal record, am not bankrupt and have a mobile phone. The 500-quid registration fee equates to a whole lot of book sales, but I could have gathered it together. But what would have been the point? It might have meant that I could have written it from the perspective of a current football agent, someone learning on the job with no actual clients or knowledge of the business. I couldn't have written it from the perspective of someone who could organise a loan move to kickstart a future international player's career. I couldn't have written it from the perspective of someone who could rescue a failing career and help turn a player on the scrapheap into a hero at a top club. I couldn't have written it from the perspective of someone who could organise a trip to a World Cup training camp for a young talent with the world at his feet.

The last thing professional footballers need is another rookie in a saturated market hoping to earn a fortune from their talents. Let's hope the regulators can regulate to the standards of other sports and ensure that the lowest common denominator do not have the conditions to thrive.

Let's leave it to the professionals, those with ethics, those with a long-term plan for their young players, those who strive for integrity in the face of negative publicity around the industry.

Those who can feel comfortable with the contents of their own blank book at the end of their career.

The Imports

WHEN Frédéric Gounongbe landed in South Wales it didn't take him long to realise that his school-level English wasn't going to get him far. However, that was the least of the Belgian-born Benin international's problems. The striker was Cardiff City's first signing of the summer 2016 transfer window, with fans of The Bluebirds hoping that he would follow in the footsteps of international team-mate Rudy Gestede.

Gestede won the Championship in the 2012/13 season with the club before moving on to Blackburn Rovers and there were high hopes that Gounongbe could repeat the feat and fire Cardiff back to the Premier League.

'Rudy is one of my best mates as we've played together for the Benin national team,' explains Frédéric. 'We're maybe not the same type of player but because of the link there were great expectations for me.'

There is often huge pressure placed on new signings to hit the ground running, disregarding any personal issues that players may be facing off the pitch. Danny Rose's admission before the 2018 World Cup that he had been suffering from depression following a family tragedy, among other things, was a potent reminder that professional footballers, however well paid, are human beings first and foremost.

'You can't blame the fans for not knowing,' reasons Frédéric. 'That's part of the game. Fans are fans. They just want you to perform on the pitch and you are not supposed to be affected by your personal life. That's the difficult part of the job.'

It was his first move away from Belgium and his first time away from his family, including his daughter. His contract had expired at Belgian side Westerlo and he was eager to ply his trade abroad. A relative latecomer to the professional game, at 24, Frédéric's student background had instilled in him a desire to learn English, which influenced his decision.

'When I got to Cardiff I realised that my English was about as much use to me as my Chinese!' he jokes. 'In day-to-day life, it's quite frustrating when you can't express something quite specific. We had a player liaison officer who spoke French and he helped a lot with all the French-speaking players because I was not the only one. But, of course, you can't really express your feelings. But that was not my main issue when I came here.'

Frédéric had always harboured an ambition to play in English football but other options were tempting. He had finished his final season in Belgium near the top of the goalscoring charts and was in demand, particularly as he was available on a Bosman transfer. 'I had a lot of competition from clubs in Belgium and abroad,' he recalls.

Frédéric has eschewed an agent throughout his career, relying instead on a friend he played with in the lower leagues in Belgium.

'I've stuck with him since the beginning until now,' he explains. 'Because I don't like agent people. I don't trust them. I've met lots of agents and I have had some bad experiences. So I stuck with my friend and we did all the deals together, which is a good thing but can also be a bad thing.'

Frédéric asked his friend not to contact him until a concrete offer was forthcoming. 'I didn't want to hear any speculation from him as there was already some on the internet,' he recalls. 'I told him just to ring me when there was something serious. I was on holidays in Lille and he called me and said, "Okay, there are three serious opportunities. One in Germany, one in England and another one in China."'

The Chinese offer was particularly tempting but family issues played a huge part in Frédéric's decision.

'China came with a big offer and I was like, "Wow! What am I supposed to do now?"' he laughs. 'I was no longer with my daughter's mother so I couldn't say, "Let's all go to China together." The offer was huge but I decided to stay in Europe because of my daughter. So I had to choose between my relationship with my daughter and money, which is quite odd. I had other options but I wanted to come to English football.

'Even though I am not with her mother any more, I was seeing my daughter quite regularly in Belgium, one week out of two,' explains Frédéric. 'So the first difficult thing was to find the balance with her. It was very, very, very difficult moving to the UK. It was my first move to another country. I was 28 and I started playing football quite late as I went to university first. So, I didn't know anything about the football world, which is not common. The problem in football is that you can't rely on the schedule. At the beginning of the month you receive your monthly schedule but it always changes. It's up to the gaffer. If he wants to give you a day off, he will. If he doesn't want to, he'll just change the schedule. You can't trust a schedule so you can't plan anything. If I want to see my daughter or get her on a flight to Cardiff it takes, like, a day. So it was the organisation which was one of the major problems in the beginning.

'The first year I had some personal problems,' he continues. 'During the first month at Cardiff, my mother was very sick,' he recalls. 'So, I was dealing with trying to be successful on the pitch with this going on. Any days off I had, for example, I flew back to Belgium to see her and look after her. And then flew back to Cardiff. When we had a game on Saturday, we would have Sunday off so I would fly back to be with her straight after the game and come back on Monday morning just before training. It was very difficult.'

138

No one at the club was aware of his difficulties until Neil Warnock arrived as manager, following Paul Trollope's dismissal. Warnock's first speech to the players was, 'Look guys, football is not that important. Your life and your family are much more important than football. So, if you want to go back home and see your family, just go. If you miss training, that's alright.'

Warnock has his critics, as he knows all too well – once joking that he wants a minute's booing at football grounds when he dies – but Frédéric credits the manager with helping him a lot and felt confident enough to call in to his office to discuss his situation. 'I'm not really the kind of person to complain, but I never spoke to anyone about what was happening to me until then,' he says. 'I had a discussion with him for about half an hour and explained the problem. It was much easier for me then. But he is like that with every player. And that's why I think he's a good gaffer to talk with. And I think that's why he is also so successful, because he is very close to us. His arrival was a good thing for me.'

Frédéric's mother sadly lost her battle with cancer in April 2017.

While he was dealing with these off-the-field issues, life on the pitch was also tough. His previous season in Belgium had finished in March and he didn't play again until pre-season with Cardiff in mid-July. 'Of course, nobody knows that,' he says. 'You just have to perform straight away. I was a striker and was the first transfer in that window for the club, who wanted promotion from the Championship. Of course, there were a lot of expectations around my transfer.'

The comparisons with Gestede, who himself had an easier time acclimatising to life in the UK, didn't help. Rudy had always dreamed of playing in English football and signed for The Bluebirds after a successful two-week trial, having spent his early career in French football.

'I came with my wife so that helped a lot when I was feeling down sometimes,' he says. 'But, in general, I was feeling good.

The food was a bit difficult at the start. France is a great country for food, whereas English quality is not the best! Of course, you live away from your friends and your family. When you have kids, there is no weekend when you can drop the kids to their grandparents. You are literally together every day.'

Frédéric feels the fact that he was an unknown quantity put even more pressure on his shoulders. 'If people don't know you they don't give you the time to prove your own value,' he says. 'When I was in Belgium, for example, people knew me and if I was not scoring for five games they knew that I would eventually, as I've already scored there. I'm known there. But, in Cardiff, no one knew me so I needed to prove my value straight away. So, I was putting more pressure on my shoulders and, of course, the fans and everything around it were putting a lot of pressure on me.'

The advent of social media hasn't aided players' confidence, with Frédéric stating that the first thing that footballers do after a game is check Twitter to see what people are saying about their performances.

'The thing that doesn't help is social media,' he explains. 'When you have a bad game, you already know you had a bad game. But when you go to the dressing room and take your phone out, you just see hundreds of people on Twitter hammering you.

'Of course, the players pay attention to that. You try not to but when it comes straight to your phone it's hard not to,' he continues. 'Supporters now have direct access to you, which was not the case before. The game has changed. They can say whatever they want, which could be good when you are playing well. But when you are in a bad period it's difficult. But you have to get used to it as it is part of the game. You just have to avoid going on your social networks.'

After his first week in Cardiff, he deleted his Twitter and Instagram accounts to focus on his on-field performances. He had used his Twitter account to follow the news and was taken aback at the immediacy of the platform, with strangers suddenly commenting on family photos of his daughter when he made his moves.

'I was like, "Woah, what's happening here?" If you are doing bad, it can affect you and your family as well so I felt it was better to get rid of my personal accounts. In England, everyone's on Twitter, in Belgium less so. That's the new aspect of the game and it plays a big role. It puts more pressure on you than it should. Maybe I'm a bit more sensitive to it as I'm not from the football world, so I'm not used to that. Even when I signed for Westerlo, I suddenly had people contacting me and I was like, "Wow, this is not the Twitter that I know."'

It took Frédéric a while to get used to changes on the pitch, too. He found the English Championship much harder and more physical, and was allowed much less time on the ball. 'You have to get used to a new style of playing. There was a huge difference between the top division in Belgium and the Championship in England. So, there is that aspect as well.

'In the beginning, it was all right, the preparation, the pre-season. The first competitive games were a bit more difficult,' he says. 'We were then in a down period when the sporting effect was not good. Of course, on a daily basis, I also had to get used to my new life. And I had my private problems, with my daughter, for example. The fact that I was now living on my own and had to learn a new language. And, at the same time, perform on the pitch when the team was not doing well. The pressure was on me because I was the main striker and they wanted me to score goals, which at the beginning is not always the case.'

He is another to mention the uncertainty of life as a professional footballer. 'It is difficult to put down roots. The good side of football is that you are well paid and you are in good shape but that's pretty much it,' he argues. 'For example, our summer break is in May and June. When you have a family you can't plan anything. My daughter is now in school and I can't take a holiday with her because her summer holidays from school are in July. That's the first thing.

'I had a bad season last year because I had played five or six games and then got an injury, which I am still struggling with. So, during the last summer break, I didn't know if Neil Warnock wanted me to stay or not. During the whole break, I was behind my phone waiting for a signal from Cardiff as to whether they wanted to sell me or to loan me. It was challenging mentally. That is a bad side of football.'

He is conscious, though, of his privileged position, playing a game he loves, but this latecomer to football is adamant that the life of a footballer is not all it's cracked up to be. 'You can't complain, though, because when you complain to someone they just say to you, "Oh, but you are a footballer, you're lucky." You can't complain to anyone, even your family because they're like, "Oh, come on, you just play football. I'm waking up every morning at 7am to go to work."'

The future is uncertain for Frédéric Gounongbe. His contract at Cardiff is up in the summer of 2018 and, with promotion to the Premier League secured, it is unlikely he will remain at the club. Or even move to another.

'I've been injured for 18 months now so I'm thinking it might be the moment for me to transition away from football,' he concedes. 'I just turned 30 but last year I had a big injury in a friendly game. I had two surgeries and I'm still struggling, so I'm taking a couple of months to think about it. Due to the injury, it will be more difficult to find a club. But I said to my friend last week that I do not want him to talk to teams as long as I am still injured. There is a club that wants to sign me even though I'm injured. But, the thing is, I'm not ready as the last two years were very difficult for me so maybe it's not worth it to sign somewhere and keep being injured like this and not be part of the team.'

When he signed for Cardiff in July 2016 he told the media 'Coming to the UK and playing my football here is a big challenge and I'm excited about performing in front of The Bluebirds' fans.' I get the sense that he laments not being able to show his full potential in English football. He wholeheartedly agrees but has no regrets.

'I am very frustrated because when I came to Cardiff I was not in a good period of my life. And then Neil Warnock came, just before my injury, and started playing me,' he says. 'He trusted me a lot and saw some qualities in my football. My biggest frustration is that I injured myself in, I think, the second game under him. So I didn't show anything in England and that's a big frustration. But you can't fight against injury, it just happens. On the other hand, I don't regret my choice at all. It's changed my life. I've met many people. It's been the most difficult period of my life but, on the other hand, I learned a lot about myself. It's been very interesting and if I had to do it again I would.'

Definitely?

'Definitely.'

A 2017 study co-authored by Khatija Bahdur and Dr Ricard Pruna titled *The Impact of Homesickness on Elite Footballers* looked at how moving to a new country or city impacted elite footballers. Its findings certainly tally with particular aspects of Frédéric's experiences. At a football level, the vast majority of participants cited difficulties adjusting to a new style of football, fitting into their new team and even adjusting to the new media culture.

Off the field, almost all admitted to missing friends and family back home while the majority suffered from the stress of moving, loneliness and the feeling that others didn't understand their culture. Concerns about a new language and dialect, weather and diet were also highly prevalent while many reported sleep disturbances, lack of appetite, self-doubt and susceptibility to illness in relation to their move abroad.

The research also found that experience of moving also made subsequent transfers easier for players. Timm Klose was 27 when he moved to Norwich City in the 2016 January transfer window and believes his previous moves in Germany helped in the transition.

'The move wasn't a surprise for me as I was talking to several clubs, including Norwich, in our winter period. It was only down to me which road I was going to take,' says the Switzerland international. 'My plan was definitely to play in England one day. I'd been in Germany for almost six years and it was time for a change. The move itself was quite similar to when I moved to Germany, little things were different but nothing major. The club helped me settle in and it didn't have a big impact on family life in my case – it depends on the woman you have to spend the rest of your life with. Of course, there was a bit of pressure, but football is a sport I love very much and I try to enjoy it every day. Sometimes you are a hero really quickly, sometimes you need more time to settle in. Every player is different. I was just happy to play football in a new country, facing a new challenge. Things like that push me, they never hold me back. Transfer fees are no problem for the players, I think they're more of a problem for the fans. If you buy a player for a lot of money and he doesn't work from the start they all think it's a waste of money, but you sometimes have to see what they can bring in the long term. The best example of this is David de Gea.'

When a 15-year-old Italian arrived in Lancashire he presumed it would be for just a few days. Something to brag about to his mates back home in Rome. He'd never even heard of Blackburn. England, to a teenage Raffaele De Vita, meant London.

'I'd never even been to England before,' laughs Raffaele. 'I remember when they mentioned Blackburn I didn't have a clue. I didn't even know they were in the Premier League. I didn't know where Blackburn was. I didn't even know where to travel to.'

Despite being a Lazio fan, Raffaele spent his early teenage years playing for a club run by some big-name former Roma stars. Blackburn scout Richard Glass was invited over to Italy by one of them and he saw enough to convince one of the directors of the academy at Rovers to have a look for himself. A couple of days later the 15-year-old midfielder was offered a five-day trial.

'It was surreal,' recalls Raffaele. 'I didn't really have time to think about it. For me, I wasn't even thinking about signing then. I thought I'd just go there, enjoy it and return to real life.'

He made his maiden trip to England with his uncle and a coach, training for five days 'without knowing what was going on'. He recalls his surprise at seeing a grass pitch for the first time but was in for an even bigger shock.

'All of a sudden, on the last day, they asked me if I wanted to sign. I thought it would just be a good experience in England, being away from home for five days, but suddenly they put a four- or five-year contract in my face. As you can imagine, I was just happy but for my family, it was something too big to think about at the time. After that, though, it just escalated so quickly, as six months later I was basically there full time.'

His parents were obviously anxious about the move but were conscious of standing in the way of their son's expeditious opportunity. He'd always done well at school, which had been a priority as his mother was a teacher, and a career in football hadn't previously been considered.

'It had never even crossed my mind at that age to leave Italy, absolutely not,' says Raffaele. 'The first thing has always been study and going to university. No one in my family has ever done anything else. It was always finish high school, go to university and get a job. So, for me, it was a bit surreal.'

It's difficult to imagine his parents' emotions when he finally left, to a place he'd never even heard of weeks before. They remained in Italy with his brother, who was 12 years old at the time.

'None of my family joined me in England. I think my mum and dad didn't really have the courage to say they didn't want me to go as it was a big opportunity for me,' he says. 'I remember my dad dropping me off in June, when I started my first pre-season, and when we got to Blackburn it was very different to Rome and he said, "I'm not leaving you here." It was just too far away from home.'

Raffaele told his father to get back on the plane and let him get on with it. 'For me, it was unbelievable. For them, it must have been a horrible time. They stayed in Rome with my brother.' Since then Raffaele has lived in the UK on his own.

Upon arriving at the club he was overwhelmed at the facilities but, like many young footballers, may have been mollycoddled a little too much. 'As soon as I went to Blackburn I realised what kind of club I had signed for. It was just unbelievable,' he remembers. 'The attention to every young player they signed was unbelievable. They just made sure that you were 100 per cent looked after and you never had a problem and that all you had to do was concentrate on football. I think, in a way, it was probably too much. I realised when I got my first place of my own that I didn't know how to do anything. I didn't know how to make a phone call in England. I didn't know how to set up a direct debit or pay my bills. They do everything for you. All you have to do is go to your house parents with a problem and they just go to the club and sort it out for you. In a way, they just make you live in a bubble sometimes. It's not really real life.'

Despite their new club's support, young overseas players can find even the most mundane tasks difficult. Niall Quinn recounts a story, from his time as Sunderland chairman, about a new foreign signing who the club was helping to settle in.

'There was one guy, who was single, and we got him a lovely apartment,' recalls Niall. 'He rang our liaison officer in the middle of the night to say, "There's something wrong with the washing machine, it's all going crazy here." So our liaison officer went over there at about 11pm at night and he had put his clothes in the dishwasher.

'That will give you some idea of the lack of real-life education that the young, up-and-coming sportsman has,' continues Niall.

'We didn't realise when we put him into that apartment that someone should have shown him how things worked. We had another player who couldn't come into training because his electricity was down and the gates wouldn't open in his mansion. So we said to him, "Okay, we'll have a taxi there for you in five minutes, can you climb over the wall?" And he replied, "Oh, yeah, yeah. I never thought of that." And he was in training 15 minutes later. I've also seen the mess that these issues can bring about post-retirement, such as divorce, bankruptcy and depression, and that's when it's not funny any more.'

At the age of 18, Benoît Assou-Ekotto became fascinated by the Premier League and made it his ambition to play there. Four years later he got his wish when the left-back signed for Tottenham from French side Lens. He spoke little English when he arrived and admits the language barrier was initially a problem but that 'English is a language that can be learned quickly.'

He was 22 years old and living alone was a new experience for him. Domestic concerns were his major issue.

'Tottenham made sure that players only needed to focus on football once they signed. I bought a vacuum cleaner but I didn't know how to use it, so I called a man who worked for the club and he came and showed me,' admits the Cameroon international. 'That shows you how much the club ensure that players only think about football and not the little hassles of everyday life.

'It was more frustrating than difficult when I first moved to London,' adds Benoît. 'When you are transferred to a new club you do not have your familiar routines and things like your favourite restaurants. Even things like not knowing what lanes to use in traffic. When you start to learn all these things, that's what makes you feel more settled and at home.'

He quickly acclimatised, though, travelling on the Tube with his Oyster card, often walking to White Hart Lane among supporters and taking to the streets in the aftermath of the

Tottenham riots in 2011 to meet those affected. He thrived at Spurs under Harry Redknapp, who subsequently signed him at Queens Park Rangers on a one-year loan.

The laidback Benoît is not your typical footballer. He has claimed that football is his job rather than passion, to the point where he often knew little about the opposition on matchday or even his own club's league position. He doesn't exactly immerse himself in the game and expressed surprise in 2013 when he discovered that Liverpool's Luis Suárez had bitten Chelsea's Branislav Ivanović, well after the incident had become a national talking point and been condemned by then UK Prime Minister David Cameron.

Typically, he's never let moves or the price on his head affect him, saying, 'The size of a transfer fee does not concern me. If there is someone who is clever enough to sell me at a certain price and someone else accepts to pay it, it concerns only these two parties and not the player. Football is a business and you have to accept to be a commodity. There are worse jobs.'

Like Frédéric Gounongbe, Raffaele De Vita was relying on school-level English when he arrived in Lancashire but he also quickly realised it wasn't much use to him in his new surroundings.

'It was a different world. First of all, there was the language,' he explains. 'I'd learned a bit of English at school but when you move to a place like Lancashire you realise that it's not the same English that you learned. I started from zero again, basically, I just couldn't understand. We had loads of Irish players at Blackburn at the time and I used to wake up every morning dreading having to talk to an Irish lad or, even, a Scottish lad! Sometimes you feel like you don't want to get out of bed, and think, "I'm just going to look stupid as they're going to ask me questions that I don't know the answer to." Even though I learned English pretty quickly I realised I wasn't very good at solving problems because I was used to always asking someone else for help.

'Now I say to my partner, who's learning English, or my brother when they come over, "It's not your problem. If you don't understand you shouldn't be embarrassed. The person you're speaking to should help you out." But, at the time, you feel like it's your fault. I didn't deal with that very well. Every time I couldn't understand something I put myself down a little bit, thinking, "I should be able to understand and I can't. And that's my own fault."'

He also encountered several culture shocks but found kindred spirits among Blackburn's cosmopolitan youth ranks at the time. 'Everything else was completely different from Italy,' he explains. 'England is a place where the days are very short. For me it was training but for other people, it's going to work and coming back from the office at 5pm and the day is pretty much over and you can't really do anything. And the shops closing at 5pm, which was something I couldn't understand as in Rome everything is open until ten o'clock at night. The food is still a big problem after 15 years! There were a lot of things I had to get used to but we had a lot of foreign lads who were in the same situation. French lads, German lads, even people from Australia, who could obviously speak the language but had the same problems as me. They didn't have any family next to them and we kind of supported each other. That was the main thing. We all lived together so, in a way, you never had time to lock yourself away in your room and feel homesick. Everything was very hectic so, in that way, I was quite fortunate.'

He missed his family, particularly in his early years, but despite the disappointment of being let go by Rovers, he has settled in the UK. In the proceeding 15 years, he played for Swindon Town, Bradford City, Cheltenham Town and Ross County, and is currently in his second spell at Livingston.

'For a 15-year-old, you feel special because all your mates are still at school and you're playing football full time. At the time you just think, "I'm the lucky one." But, obviously, after that, there are a lot of things that come into play – like being homesick and things don't always go well in football. You have setbacks. I was released by Blackburn when I was 19. There were good times but I've had to overcome tough times on my own as well,' he says.

Italy is always on his mind and I wonder if he's ever tempted to move back. Having skipped the familial path of school, university and a secure job, football is all he knows. And his homeland cannot offer him what the UK can.

'When I left Blackburn I thought I would eventually go back to Italy but I signed for Livingston for the first time in 2008. And Italy just got worse and worse in terms of the lower leagues. Obviously, if you're playing in Serie A it's different.

'There are big problems in the lower leagues back home,' he continues. 'I've got mates who play there and every time I spoke to them they say, "Stay away! You're going to end up quitting football if you come back." And I can still see it. I went back before I signed for Livingston the second time and was training with a club in the Italian Serie C, which is like League One in England. It was just a different world. The Scottish press complains about Scottish football for many reasons but compared to the lower leagues in Italy it's miles ahead. Everything is done well, even if sometimes the budgets are not great. You know you're going to get your money at the end of the month and can just concentrate on football. Back home, I was in a changing room where all that people were talking about was, "Are we getting paid this month?" It felt like people weren't enjoying football at all. The main problem was, "Am I going to provide for my family?"'

Despite being homesick, and as much as he likes the UK, it's never going to be his home. 'I realised that I'd rather be far from my family and happy with what I'm doing than go back and spend time with them and not be happy with my job. It's something that I don't really want to experience.'

It's difficult to tally the 30-year-old, fluent in English with a slight Scottish lilt, with the innocent 15-year-old described above.

But Raffaele De Vita has been through a lot in the 15 years since landing in the UK for what, he thought at the time, would be five days of fun to boast to his friends in Rome about. Even now, though, he still struggles with some aspects of British life. We spoke a couple of days after a Livingston match in the wake of the Beast from the East. 'The coldest I've ever felt in my life!' he concludes.

Most overseas players I spoke to, and indeed domestic players, expressed gratitude for the assistance provided by player welfare or liaison officers when they first arrived at a new club.

Lorna McClelland is a pioneer of the profession, becoming the Premier League's first-ever player welfare officer when the role was created by Aston Villa in 2002 following Juan Pablo Ángel's difficulties in settling in England. The Colombian striker's wife was hospitalised just days after his arrival from River Plate, while his three-week-old son Geronimo also became ill after the long flight from South America. Matters weren't helped when the family were hastily removed from their temporary hotel lodgings to accommodate guests attending a motor industry conference. Villa's manager at the time, John Gregory, was surprised that the 25-year-old 'didn't pack everything in and say he was going back home'.

Not surprisingly, Ángel's initial form on the pitch suffered. Once his off-field problems were resolved he began displaying the talent that Villa had broken their transfer record for, but Gregory's replacement, Graham Taylor, vowed not to allow such a situation to arise again.

It was a demanding role for Lorna, with the squad at the time including a melting pot of Moroccans, Finns, Swedes, Turks, Colombians, Germans, Dutch, Ecuadorians, Croatians, Norwegians and Icelanders.

One of her initial interactions was indicative of the task ahead. A new European signing arrived and Lorna met with him and his wife. Their first question was, 'Can you please help us find a company which will ship fresh fruit and vegetables from our home country to our house every week?'

'I was rather confused as to why this would be necessary, and it transpired that their friends and family had told them that supermarkets in the UK don't sell fresh produce!' she explains. 'I was incredulous, and drove them immediately to Sainsbury's, and they were delighted. It is so important to have someone around who can speak their language and also sort out any queries – otherwise, a small problem can become a huge one, and the player takes so much longer to settle.'

With such a diverse range of nationalities at the club, she called on the experiences of existing players to help their new team-mates settle in. A buddy system was created, to help the transition of a new player into a 'happy, confident and productive team member'. A former language teacher, Lorna's role was all-encompassing, even stretching to offering Spanish translations from the sidelines in training to Ecuador international Ulises de la Cruz.

'Any new signing was teamed up with a "buddy", who I felt would offer support,' she says. 'This might be linguistic if they shared a language. A fellow countryman is ideal, and he can explain any cultural differences, which can avoid embarrassment. He is someone who the new player could immediately relate to, who he could ask about the day-to-day routine, a simple point of contact. New relationships with other players were formed quickly like this.'

Lorna says that, for a newly arrived player, the first day at a new club in a new country can be pretty terrifying – particularly if he is not English-speaking. 'It can be as traumatic as the first day at school. People so often assume that new players know the routine and that they are confident – it so often is not the case. I think that it is important for a new player to feel relaxed, and that depends on whether or not he has been well informed at the start. He simply needs to slot in and start doing his job.'

It's not just the player that requires support, it's his family as well. A Rutgers University study into the marital quality of couples found the old adage, 'happy wife, happy life', to be pretty accurate. It found that a wife's happiness in a marriage is more crucial than a husband's in keeping the marriage on track. For a football club, it's just as important to help a player's wife and family settle in their new country.

'Support for the family is vital – whether it be a foreign or an English player,' explains Lorna, the founder of the National Association of Player Welfare Officers. 'Often if the wife or partner and children are happy, the player settles very quickly. Wives can often be isolated and bored so regular get-togethers with the other families provide a good self-supporting network. This means company, and these friendships can help the settling-in process a huge amount. If the girls are content, then this is a huge worry off the players' shoulders. The girls get together when there are away games, and they are not lonely. When family problems arise, the club should be ready to offer help, and the other girls can play a vital role in doing the same. Babysitting problems disappear, and the player can go out with his wife while another sits for them. They then return the favour another day. Wives sometimes want to find a job – this helps them make friends in the area, and also they enjoy doing something outside football, something for themselves.'

However, many footballers arrive in a new country at a relatively young age with no wife or partner to offer support. The parents of a player are not overlooked. 'They are often anxious that their son settles and performs well,' says Lorna. 'They also need the opportunity to speak confidentially if there are problems, and they can play a very important role in the settling-in of a player. Not infrequently, a player can struggle when moving to a new club – whether or not he is English or from abroad. Even coming from a different part of the country can mean that he leaves his parents, friends and family behind.

If he has no partner, then his whole support group has gone, and he may experience difficulties initially. With the right support, and understanding of his situation, his family and friends can be helped to organise a visit to a game to watch him play.'

Lorna also points out that managers and staff sometimes need to understand the cultural differences that a foreign player can experience. 'His reactions in certain situations may not be what they are expecting, and this can cause problems if they do not understand that in his own culture, he was expected to react or behave differently,' she says.

In the case of the African player that opened this book, he had only been to Europe previously for one match. Lorna provides a 'cultural adaptation' course for such players, tailor-made for each individual and which greatly helps the adjustment process. The first meeting with a player, as soon as he arrives, can set the tone for the rest of his time at the club.

'If he meets friendly faces, has details given to him clearly, such as the schedule or routine at the training ground and on matchdays, he will be able to settle quickly and enjoy any banter that comes his way!' she contends.

Liam Rosenior has played with numerous overseas players in the Premier League and Football League and has seen at first hand the problems they can encounter. He believes that even the best players can take time to settle in a new environment.

'I've seen players come over, who have been outstanding players in their own countries, and they look like a completely different player over here,' says the former Brighton & Hove Albion defender. 'One player from Uruguay was living out of a hotel for six months and he just didn't seem himself. He had two children back in Uruguay, over 6,000 miles away, and he's in a cold country nothing like his country of origin and faced with a completely different language. And that affects you personally and it affects your performance on the pitch. I think, sometimes, when players are signed from abroad we expect them to come here and just take off. But you look at the best foreign players – look at Thierry Henry or Dennis Bergkamp at Arsenal, for example. It wasn't the first year that they were fantastic. It was the second or third year when they had got used to the way of life. People speak about the way the game is different over here but it's the cultural things that make the difference. Where do you get your groceries from? Getting used to small details off the pitch that all add up to help your performance on it.

'The influx of overseas players makes domestic players better players and better people. Players need a lot of help. If they can come through the first six months or a year having learned the language and immersed themselves in the culture you see them grow as people. They have a lot more confidence in themselves, as do their family as well. I've moved to clubs, and that's just been around England, and it's difficult to settle in the first couple of months with a different manager and different way of playing. These players from abroad have to deal with that and, also, making sure their families move into the new country and making sure their families can speak the language. There are a lot of different things off the pitch that these players have to deal with and most of them do fantastically well,' Liam concludes.

Many of the horror stories I've heard about overseas players failing to settle, such as the Uruguayan Liam mentioned, have had a common theme – footballers holed up in a hotel with no support network in place. Lorna McClelland believes that it is vital that clubs help a player to find permanent accommodation – and quickly. 'A long stay in a hotel is not good – he needs to be able to feel settled, to have his own front door, and to be able to enjoy some solitude when he needs it,' she says. 'For players with families, finding a house means that his wife and children can join him, and normal life can begin. Homesick and worried players do not perform well. Information about things happening outside the club is vital – cinemas, shops, golf clubs, barbers or hairdressers and so on. It is good for players and their wives to meet socially and enjoy things such as golf. Clubs should organise regular events and outings for the families. This helps the settling-in of players, and they start to feel at home in their new town.'

To a generation of football fans the name Jimmy Glass is synonymous with one goal. With ten seconds of the 1998/99 season remaining, Glass's Carlisle United were staring relegation from the Football League in the face.

'The ball goes out now for a corner to Carlisle United – will they have time to take it? Referee looks at his watch. And here comes Jimmy Glass! Carlisle United goalkeeper Jimmy Glass is coming up for the kick. Everyone is coming up, there isn't one player in the Carlisle half! Well, well! And the corner comes in, and the keeper's punch ... oh, Jimmy Glass! Jimmy Glass, the goalkeeper, has scored a goal for Carlisle United! There is a pitch invasion! The referee has been swamped. They're bouncing off the crossbar!'

Glass's last-gasp goal, as described above by the late Derek Lacey of BBC Radio Cumbria, saved The Cumbrians from dropping into non-league football but it was to be his final appearance for the club. After retirement, he worked as a salesman and taxi driver before returning to football with former club Bournemouth. To a generation of footballers with The Cherries, the name Jimmy Glass is synonymous with making their lives easier. He is now a player liaison officer with the club for which he made over 100 appearances and Bournemouth's meteoric rise in recent years has meant his role is constantly evolving.

The Bournemouth squad that earned promotion from League Two in 2009/10 was mainly British, apart from Iraqi goalkeeper Shwan Jalal. Eddie Howe's side that finished 12th in the Premier League in 2017/18 included 12 different nationalities.

'Historically, we wouldn't have had many overseas players,' says Jimmy. 'It's kind of a new experience for us due to our rise in the past few years when we're bringing in bigger players to the club. The challenges with overseas players might be different but I wouldn't say they're any more difficult. You just do what you have to do, really. We'd have been dealing before with players on lesser wages, coming from all over the country. For those sort of players, on lesser wages, moving is quite a traumatic thing for them. The reality is, though, there may be a relocation allocation – a mediocre sum that they may put towards their rent or may put towards a hotel while they try to work out their next move. During my playing career, that was generally what happened. There was more of that than in modern-day football. What you end up doing sometimes is driving because you just couldn't find anywhere appropriate. So, you end up driving two hours from your home to whatever club you were playing for.'

Jimmy played with Howe at the club in the 1990s but believes his sabbatical from football has also helped him in his new role. 'I walked away from football for a long time and I've come back into it. Now I've got a set of skills from real life as well,' he explains. 'Not only do I know what they are thinking generally before they do as a footballer, because I played it for 13 years, I've also lived in the real world for 15 years and have had to live with real-world problems. Deal with families – my family, my children, my wife – and deal with businesses I've run and things like that. That's where my skills then kick in. There are people around town who I've known since my first time in Bournemouth and my wife's an estate agent so I've a network of people that I can lean on. Every player has a different need and presents a different challenge.'

He also played with Steve Fletcher, who holds the club record for appearances during almost 20 years in Dorset. Jimmy believes this longevity at one club is becoming more rare. 'It's more common that you'll do maybe a couple of seasons and move on – certainly in the modern game. The game's changed, let's be honest about it,' he says. 'Even in the lower leagues now, people are earning £1,000 or £2,000 a week. When you are earning £100,000 a year it makes a lot of things easier – and moving is one of them.

It's not so much of a panic as you can afford to pay a hotel bill. You don't want to waste your money on it but you can afford to do certain things that a player on lesser money couldn't afford to do. As you move up the leagues nowadays, you've Premier League players on 30, 40, 50, 100, 200 thousand pounds a week. And they've got people like me stepping in to make everything easy for them. It's a massive difference nowadays to what it was like five or ten years ago. It's the extremities of the wages that make it much easier for the bigger players than it is for the lesser players.'

He is usually informed a couple of days before a signing about a potential new arrival. That's when his job kicks in. 'The club will book him a hotel for a certain period of time, maybe a couple of weeks or a month,' says Jimmy. 'We're in a position now where we're a Premier League club and we have a fantastic brand-new Hilton built in the town centre. Had that not been built, I'm not sure what we'd have done. For instance, a big-name player we signed came in and we put him straight into the Hilton. He had his partner with him and we gave him a suite as opposed to a normal room. And he's in there, going to training every day, and living a luxurious lifestyle. We're not talking about a bed and breakfast in Skegness. We're talking about the Hilton, which was designed by Ted Baker.

'It's our job to get them to the hotel first and foremost, to get them settled. Give them the information they need, make sure they've the right kit they need. Then, you're trying to find them somewhere to live. And sometimes that is easy – some players are very simple in their needs and some players aren't. Some players are very specific.'

The top players may be able to avail themselves of a player liaison or welfare officer but those officers can't solve every problem. You can't learn a new language overnight. You can't learn about a new culture in a few days. Often it comes down to the individual. 'The home you can organise, the schools you can organise. How the player settles in is generally down to the player,' he says. 'Some players will gel with other players easily. Some players will know some of their new team-mates, so straight away there's a bond there – the families might know each other. Some players might never have met any of the players before and they might be a bit more introverted and not want to get involved. It's our job to keep tabs on that and understand individual players. It's usually quite easy to tell if they've not settled as their performances suffer. And then everyone will be asking questions, "Where's he living?" The manager will ask, "What's happening? What sort of life has he got? Is he settled?" So, it comes down to individual players really. We're quite lucky at Bournemouth, it's quite a happy camp. We don't have any bad eggs and people tend to settle very easily here. It's quite a young squad as well, as the manager generally tends to go for young players. And they settle in easier as they generally don't have lots of kids to move around.'

Jimmy agrees with Lorna McClelland about the importance of helping the player's family settle as well. 'We try to have a relationship not just with the player, but also with the spouse or girlfriend,' he explains. 'It's important to get the girls together, it's important that the kids are settled. At Bournemouth, we pride ourselves on being a family club – we try to be inclusive. My personal opinion is that football is very hard on families. Not just the modern game, but football in general. It has been for a long, long time. You could argue that it's very difficult on professional sportspeople in general. The whole idea of being a professional sportsperson is that you have to make sacrifices. When you're on your own, that's not a problem. But, when your family are involved, they're making the sacrifices along with you.

'The divorce rate among footballers probably tells a story by itself. If Tiger Woods, with all his hundreds of millions, can't keep his marriage together then what chance has someone got going between a few Championship or League One clubs. It is very difficult, football can be a very difficult game mentally. The players have chosen that career. But the females have come along and they don't really know what they've got themselves into. The children, certainly not. What I'm seeing more of is that players don't always move their families now. It's quite common that families will stay and players, certainly the bigger players on bigger money, will take an apartment and they'll divide their time between home and football. Take football out of the equation and put any other job into it and that would have a massive effect. But, sometimes, you have to look at the practicalities. If the kids are seven or eight years old or doing exams or settled, you have to balance it up – there are certain ages you can't just pull them out of school. As you go down the leagues there are journeymen footballers – much like I was – who are going from club to club and it'd be a very harsh and hard thing to do to take the kids with you.'

Bournemouth may now be signing bigger-name players on more money but this often leads to unusual problems. 'We had a lad come to us in the summer and he didn't have an English bank account,' Jimmy recalls. 'He didn't have a card, he didn't have any cash, he literally had nothing. Before our pre-season trip in the summer I had to take him down to the local currency exchange with a couple of grand in cash and get him some dollars. We were a day away from going away and he didn't have any money. Bear in mind he signed for big money, he's got lots of money coming to him but he'd no physical cash. I knew we were going somewhere nice where all the boys would be spending a bit of money, so I went to the club and asked for a couple of grand. Next thing you know, I'm holding his hand at the cash desk. I didn't speak much of his language and he didn't speak much English but we muscled through. Some players will have to be looked after a little bit more closely while others are quite happy and content, as they might have been at a couple of other English clubs and they're all set up and know the system. You basically do whatever you have to.'

Bournemouth goalkeeper Asmir Begović moved to England at 16 years of age and believes that the general care for young players is much better than it used to be.

'The only advice I'd give to young players moving to England is, "Don't force anything." Make sure it's the right thing to do, that your family is comfortable with it and that everybody's on the same page before you make a big move and a commitment to another country. Don't think it's going to work for sure because not everything is for everyone,' advises Asmir.

Asmir was a four-year-old when he and his family fled the Bosnian War to Germany, before settling in Canada six years later. At 16, he left his family and friends in Edmonton for a trial at Portsmouth. It was the longest he'd ever been away from home and homesickness was a problem.

'At 16, that wasn't so straightforward,' he reminisces. 'The fact I was doing it for football, which is something I'd always wanted to do, was something that gave me a comfort blanket. I went on trial for a month and signed my contract at Portsmouth, which was great. I ended up going back to Canada to finish off some schooling and also to allow time to get my visa sorted. In the first week of February, I got to England and one thing that was a saviour was the digs I was put in. The landlady was like a second mum to me. I was at the same house as when I was on trial. That was huge, as being comfortable away from home – and my family was on the other side of the world – can be tricky. That was the most important thing for me, that I was going to a nice, stable environment. It helped me out a lot.'

Team-mates who also lived in the digs returned home every weekend, while one of his parents would visit every couple of months. It left him with a lot of time by himself, which he found daunting but which helped him mature.

'It challenged my mental strength,' admits Asmir. 'Thinking back right now, it was probably for the better. Of course, at that time, I was homesick, I missed my friends, I missed my family. Football was my ultimate dream when I was very young, it was all I wanted to do, and that's kind of what helped me get through it.'

He credits the staff at Portsmouth, including academy director David Hurst, with helping him to settle in but doesn't believe they went overboard in terms of indulging him.

'I don't think they ever went above and beyond but they went and visited my parents and visited me to make sure I was alright. They did everything they could have done and they found a really good balance.'

His next move was a loan spell with Belgian side La Louvière, which he also embraced. 'I didn't know the language but had a bit of French from my time in Canada. You're living in an apartment on your own at 18, in a foreign city, a foreign country, and all these little new experiences either make you or break you. I took everything on as a challenge more than anything.'

These experiences helped make him, but he has seen them break others. 'So many kids from Canada couldn't hack it after being put in the wrong environment. Even in the UK, I've seen problems with some players from Ireland or more local countries moving digs the whole time. When things don't quite line themselves up it can be a very, very difficult environment. It really tests your mental strength and I think that's a huge challenge. And that's at an early age. When you move up the ranks it becomes more challenging when you've got family and kids,' he concludes.

When Radhi Jaïdi decided to leave Espérance Sportive de Tunis after 11 years at the club he had a decision to make: England or Germany. He'd heard about Manchester United and Liverpool before but Bolton Wanderers? Not a lot. He credits the much-maligned Sam Allardyce for helping him and his family settle in a new country that he found 'kind of strange'.

'I was probably lucky to be at Bolton Wanderers under Sam. We had two player liaison officers who tried to help the players and their families. Even with that, it was difficult as there were only two of them, and around 15 different nationalities. It was challenging,' recalls Radhi. 'But I was lucky to be in a certain environment at Bolton. Sam Allardyce was among the managers who gave importance to psychology and adjusting the environment to the foreigners. Probably because we had 15 different nationalities in that squad, but it helped. It helped a lot.'

Bolton's cosmopolitan squad at the time, which finished a best-ever sixth in Radhi's first Premier League season, included players from Brazil, France, Greece, Denmark, Nigeria, Spain, Senegal, Israel and Portugal.

While he believes his experience – he was a 28-year-old Tunisian international who had just won the Africa Cup of Nations when he made the move – helped him settle on the pitch, off the field was a different matter.

'I think it was a surprise coming to a country supposed to be in Europe, but is nothing like Europe,' says Radhi. 'In Tunisia, we are supposed to be French, or Europe-related. We have a lot of French culture. We speak languages like French, English, German and Italian. We have a lot of contacts with these countries. So, when I came to England I thought it was going to be similar to France or similar to Italy. The same mindset, the same people, the same traditions. But it was a bit of a surprise to me because it's totally different.'

It's frequently overlooked, but overseas players can often arrive from countries with totally different climates, which can have a psychological impact. This was one of the culture shocks Radhi encountered when he arrived in north-west England.

'The weather definitely has an effect on the people's state,' he continues. 'The people looked quite sad, not like in Tunisia where we wake up happy, with a smile. The sun shines there and gives people energy. We shake hands and say, "Hello" and, "Good morning". We chat about everything when we meet. When we have a coffee we speak about everything. When I came to England, I came to the dressing room and no one said, "Hello", no one said, "Good morning". People went to training sessions and probably didn't have that 100 per cent energy to enjoy it. For me, it was new and I had to adapt to it. And I had to find different ways to find that energy in myself and keep myself pushing to the next level in that environment. What I found difficult was off the pitch – settling in with my wife and kids in a new country and getting used to the daily family needs.'

As with the others earlier, Radhi was relying on English he'd learned at school but had also tried to develop his linguistic skills from listening to British music. Even then, he still found things difficult initially. 'I was probably one of the players who were most engaged with foreign languages but didn't practice English a lot as it is probably our third or fourth language,' he says. 'We speak French, we speak Arabic. But, every possibility I had to learn English, I did. So when I came to England I wasn't totally blank. I could understand the people speaking to me but I was a bit shy to speak a little bit of English back. The dialect was different, it was quick English and I had to ask people to repeat themselves two or three times to recognise what they meant.'

After 14 years in England, he now struggles to speak Arabic when he returns to Tunisia – 'I need three days to get back to normal!' he says with a laugh.

He believes his age and relative experience helped him adapt quicker than a younger player from overseas might have, and has watched other Tunisian players struggle to settle at European clubs.

'My age helped me when I arrived as I was 28. I had a lot of experience travelling abroad, seeing different people and different cultures. The football wasn't really difficult for me as it is universal,' he says. 'I know a lot of players who came to Europe and didn't succeed. And they've been in the same situation as me. They came to Europe as a star from Tunisia and found themselves unknown in these countries. They had to start again and introduce themselves, but they couldn't find a way. And that's the difference between someone who has experience and someone who doesn't. Or the difference between someone who knows how to deal with a situation and someone who doesn't. My knowledge and experience helped me to introduce myself in the right way and after that, I kicked on. Since that time, though, the demands and standards of the Premier League level means that they need the best players in this league.

'The pressure has increased compared to when I arrived,' he continues. 'When I arrived in England, it was slightly different for me compared to other players. I came as a Tunisian international, who had just won the Africa Cup of Nations. We had just qualified for the Confederations Cup. So, I came with a big name from Tunisia but when I first came to England people don't recognise, "Who is this guy from Tunisia?" So I had to introduce myself. I didn't play in the first couple of games. By the third game, Sam Allardyce introduced me to English football against Southampton at St Mary's when I won man of the match. Then I played the following game against Liverpool.'

After his spell at Bolton, Radhi moved to Birmingham City and Southampton, where he is now the under-23s head coach. He's seen young imports struggle to make an impact and believes that older, more experienced players tend to handle the transition better. This is backed up by the aforementioned study on *The Impact of Homesickness on Elite Footballers*, which found that players who were older found it less difficult to adjust to a new country or city and team environment.

'If you go through the stats – how many young foreigners have come to this country and succeeded at this level? I don't think it's a lot. The majority who have succeeded are the older ones who came and imposed themselves,' he contends.

He played against Cristiano Ronaldo during Ronaldo's early years at Manchester United and cites him as an exception to the rule. 'He was around one of the best environments when he joined Manchester United. He had Sir Alex Ferguson as manager and the quality of the players around him was crazy. Not all environments are the same as that. So, the younger guys that move to England, it's up to them and the environment they are in. It's a combination between them being professional, being disciplined, adjusting to their new country and working hard towards their objectives, and the environments of their clubs. Or they need to have enough experience to come as a confirmed player and impose themselves on the Premier League. I didn't see a lot of young academy overseas players who made it. There's not a lot.'

He supports the English FA and the Premier League's focus in recent years on helping home-grown academy players to step up a level and make it to the first team. 'The message is to give chances to English home-grown players rather than foreigners, which I believe is right. If the same happened in Tunisia, I would be saying the same thing.'

Radhi and his family are well settled in England now and he hopes to pursue his next dream in the UK too. 'At the moment I have objectives that I am trying to achieve here. Tunisia is always on my mind but I think Europe, especially England, is the highest level in terms of standards of football,' he says. 'I played in the Premier League before and want to be involved here in coaching and managing. My objective is to be a Premier League manager, if possible. I know it is not going to be easy, as a foreigner and as a minority. I have experience as a player, I've gained experience from coaching the under-23s for the past five years and have started my UEFA pro licence. Hopefully, that will help me to go to the next level.'

And, 14 years on, does he have any regrets about choosing a move to England over Germany? 'My kids were born here in England. My family are settled here and speak English daily. We discussed all our options before we moved and that's what foreign players have to do every time. I know they have a lot of support now but you have to think of what your best option is for you as a player before you listen to agents or the people around you. I think we took the right option.'

He still believes there is a wealth of opportunities for young overseas players in England but only for those with a certain mindset. 'It depends on how the player behaves during their stay in England. Some players act as if they're still in their own country, which is wrong. I think you need a certain amount of flexibility and a certain change in your behaviours because this country is totally different. As I said, I thought this was Europe. But this is England. It's not Europe. It's totally different, with different traditions and a different mindset. You need to explore and research and see a country before you act. When clubs pay a lot of money for players who are supposed to be internationals, they must have a plus, something extra. That's what the fans and the English people believe now. If you want to pay money, you need to pay it in the right place, not bringing players in just for money and image and then, that's it. There are Home Office laws where you can't be in this country without playing a certain amount of international games or have a certain amount of image as an international. This means you can't be just an average player coming to this country to play in the Premier League.

'I think the opportunities are still there. There is a lot of space to exploit in this country in terms of succeeding in your career. For the young boys to come here they need to be flexible and work hard and the benefits can be there. If they come here and think that the opportunities will come to them then they are mistaken. This country is demanding and challenging but there are lots of opportunities to exploit and benefit from. It is a good set-up for them to use to go to the next level but it has to be aligned with what they are going to bring as well to this country.'

Isaac Newell was such a pioneer of Argentine football that one of its most famous clubs – Newell's Old Boys – is named after him. In 1869 Newell left home in Kent at 16 and set sail for Argentina, where he settled in Rosario and is credited with bringing the first footballs to the country. Lionel Messi is among the club's illustrious alumni, joining *La Lepra* at six years old and going on to score over 500 goals for its youth teams before moving to Barcelona. Another alumnus followed the opposite path to Newell, landing at Championship side Barnsley, despite never having heard of the club.

Hugo Colace captained an Argentina side featuring Carlos Tevez and Javier Mascherano at the 2003 FIFA World Youth Championship. Five years later, while Tevez and Mascherano were starring for Manchester United and Liverpool respectively, a 23-year-old Colace found himself in South Yorkshire, which he unsurprisingly found 'a big change' from life in South America.

'I had been to England with Argentina Under-15s at Wembley and it was my dream to play in England afterwards,' explains Hugo. 'For me, it was very easy because I had the ambition to play in England. The weather was difficult but after one year I was fine with that. The life, the weather, discipline, everything was a lot different to back in Argentina. That is difficult for players. Sometimes you have to leave your kids, your girlfriend, to play football.'

The midfielder became a cult figure with The Tykes, winning their player of the season and player's player of the season awards at the end of his second year in England. His form declined, prompting moves to clubs in Mexico and France, among others. He returned to Oakwell for a trial in 2015 and, now without a club, would welcome a move back with open arms.

'I would love to return to Barnsley. I loved my time there,' he says. 'I speak with former team-mate Bobby Hassell all the time and I enjoyed the best form of my career at Barnsley. The supporters loved me and wanted me back.'

He last played in the Gibraltar Premier Division and, now in the twilight of his career, is eager for a new opportunity but feels his age is proving to be a barrier.

'Clubs want players under 25 or 26. Somebody called me from Italy and I'm waiting for a good offer. I've experienced not being paid in the past. Other countries don't pay on time. In England, though, it was fantastic. I don't know what country I'll be in next season. I am training in Argentina but I want to play in Europe. I am 34 years old but I feel fit and I can play like Mascherano or Tevez. They are both the same age and are still playing. The window is open for me. I want to take all the experience I've had in different countries. It's not easy for me, due to my age. I would go on trial somewhere, if necessary. I want to play now as the season is coming.'

Englishmen like Isaac Newell may have pioneered the game overseas but over 100 years on, footballers from the UK are often criticised for their lack of wanderlust. Many, like David Platt, Chris Waddle and Steve McManaman have thrived abroad. For more recent exports like Joey Barton, Ravel Morrison and Jermaine Pennant a move overseas almost felt like entering the last-chance saloon. Before the Premier League's inception in 1992, stars like Waddle, Glenn Hoddle and Gary Lineker sought clubs on the continent in the wake of English clubs' ban from European competitions following the Heysel disaster.

With the riches on offer nowadays in the Premier League, is there any motivation for British and Irish players to follow their paths?

Upon landing the England manager's job, Gareth Southgate had insisted that English players needed to, 'get off the island and learn from elsewhere'. However, not one of his 23-man England squad for the 2018 World Cup were based at clubs outside the English top flight. All but five of the 31 other countries at the tournament included players at Premier League clubs. What are the reasons behind this island mentality and hesitancy to seek foreign adventures?

The Brits and
Irish Abroad

'I'D like to play for an Italian club, like Barcelona,' said
former Aston Villa winger Mark Draper, before sort of
getting his wish – a six-month loan spell at Italian, sorry,
Spanish club Rayo Vallecano. Like several other British football
exports to Spain, Draper lasted barely longer than a package
holiday, returning to Villa after just four appearances for the
Spaniards – Vallecano having decided against making the move
permanent after his unsuccessful temporary move.

In fairness to Draper, he did try to acclimatise, learning the
Spanish translation for *pass,* to help him on the pitch. 'Permiso,
permiso,' he would shout to baffled team-mates, who wondered
why this Englishman was bellowing, 'Driving licence, driving
licence,' at them.

Perhaps longing for a spell in France, Draper ended his career
with Dunkirk. Unfortunately for the geographically challenged
winger, it was the Dunkirk in Nottingham rather than its famous
namesake in northern France.

It's become a bit of a cliché that British criminals often move
to Spain to escape the spotlight. Yet it was still a surprise when
ex-jailbird Jermaine Pennant followed a disappointing spell
with Liverpool by signing for Real Zaragoza. Despite making
25 appearances for Los Maños, Pennant's spell in Spain was

disastrous. Having turned up late for training on three occasions he was promptly sent home by coach José Aurelio Gay and never played for the club again. He did famously leave his mark in Spain, however – or, rather, his marque. Officials at Zaragoza train station became suspicious of a Porsche, displaying a P33NNT number plate, which had lain idle for over five months in their car park. It transpired that the winger had forgotten he'd even owned the vehicle. His spell in Spain is also something he'll be keen to forget.

Imagine you've waited a year for your first proper day in your new job. You're eager to impress. Your new bosses have stuck by you. If you're Jonathan Woodgate you then proceed to score an own goal on your debut before getting sent off. The English defender went on to make just eight further appearances for Real Madrid before being jettisoned back to Middlesbrough. Injuries plagued Woodgate's time in Spain and he was voted the worst signing of the 21st century by readers of Spain's leading sports daily, *MARCA*, in 2007.

Owing to cases like those above, British footballers abroad have become something of a punchline to a bad joke. Ashley Cole's awkward squad photo at Roma, where he resembled prankster Karl Power famously infiltrating a Manchester United team picture, is symbolic of many sojourns abroad.

To be fair, though, there have been success stories. The midfielder had enjoyed a successful career in England, most notably almost eight years at Spurs, but sought a new challenge. A move to Spain beckoned, where he became the linchpin of his new club's midfield, his name adorning the shirts of besotted fans who quickly penned a chant for their new hero. Vinny Samways went on to make almost 200 appearances at Las Palmas before a short-term move to Sevilla and is one of the most successful British footballing exports to Spain. Gareth Bale, who followed in Samways's footsteps to La Liga, hasn't done too badly either.

Laurie Cunningham was 24, the same age as Bale when he left Spurs, when he became the first English player to sign for Real Madrid. The left-winger scored twice on his debut and helped Madrid to a league and cup double in his first season. He also famously left the Camp Nou to a standing ovation after inspiring his side to a 2-0 win against Barcelona. However, injuries were to hamper his time at the Spanish giants. He later joined Sporting Gijón on loan and enjoyed two spells at Rayo Vallecano. However, having scored the goal that secured Vallecano's promotion to the Primera Liga, Cunningham was killed in a car crash in Madrid in July 1989. He was 33. His memory, though, lives on in Spain with former Spain boss Vicente del Bosque once claiming that Cunningham was 'as good as Cristiano Ronaldo'.

There is a perception that British footballers are reluctant to play abroad, but there are many, such as those above, who have taken the plunge. The CIES Football Observatory's 2018 *Global study on expatriate footballers* report found 165 English footballers plying their trade outside the UK and Ireland in countries as diverse as Jamaica, Luxembourg and Colombia. This figure is just slightly lower than the total number of Englishmen named in Premier League squads for the 2017/18 season. A further 21 Scots, five Welshmen and six Northern Irishmen were also furthering their careers overseas, with many more earning a living in the lower tiers of football in foreign countries. This is based on 142 leagues from 93 national associations surveyed.

What strikes you most, though, is the fact that, by and large, the majority of these far-flung footballers are not household names. What takes them out of the comfort zone of British football?

In most cases, it's simply to play football. Xander McBurnie had been released by Bradford City after his second year as a scholar when a former team-mate, Sumaili Cissa, gave him a call. Cissa had moved to Swedish club Ytterhogdals IK on a League Football Education (LFE) Erasmus+ scheme and encouraged his friend to join him. He put in a word with his manager, who seemed keen. 'Pretty much out of nothing I was getting a plane to Sweden,' laughs Xander.

He had been at Leeds United's academy for five years before his spell at Bradford and admits that young British players can sometimes be 'sort of in a bubble'. He'd spent some time on loan with an Evo-Stik League team to 'get a bit of men's football, a bit of experience' but didn't feel the standard matched his skillset so was eager to grasp an adventure overseas.

'I was playing centre-midfield and it just didn't really suit me,' admits Xander. 'I'm grateful for my time there and it helped me mature, but in terms of my future, I wasn't enjoying it. You don't really see the rest of the world as an opportunity when you're at a league club in England. When it gets real and you get released, you think that maybe you will have to broaden your horizons. What's important with a lot of players is that it's always your self-belief that gets you through. Not to sound big time, but I've never doubted my own ability. But if I didn't feel like I was good enough, I wouldn't bother doing it, I'd probably just do something else. But because I believe in my ability and think I can get somewhere, I didn't feel it was the right time to give up. Mentally, I think I did well. I was always quite strong. I've had a couple of knockbacks but all I had to do was speak to my brother or my dad to help keep me on the right track. I wasn't extremely content with going abroad but thought, "Why not give it a try?" I thought that I might as well try a new experience.'

A burgeoning expat community has helped him settle in, with 14 British players at Ytterhogdals IK alone. Also, the club's manager, Adie Costello, is English.

'It's almost like being back home but just being in a different place,' continues the 20-year-old. 'It's so good and easy to settle in. There are a few Swedish lads who are easy to get on with. It's quite a chilled country. We all live in a group of apartments together so we're always around each other. You don't really get homesick as most of the lads are British, anyway.'

Many of these have also come through the LFE scheme, which has sent over 220 players, who had been released by their English Football League (EFL) clubs, to Sweden.

'I'd 100 per cent recommend the programme,' enthuses Xander. 'Without the LFE you could always say you want to play abroad, but realistically you wouldn't have a clue how to get there, contact-wise. They make it plain, straightforward, set it all out for you and tell you exactly what you're doing, where you're going to and book it all for you. Before you know it, you're there. I can't fault it, they've helped me out a lot.'

Simon Williams, LFE's Life Skills Manager, has drawn on his own experiences as a professional footballer when assisting young players to further their careers abroad.

'I was released by Rochdale and went out to Malta,' Simon recalls. 'I had zero information on the football club and just went out there and played for Hibernians. It was absolute chaos! At least we can tell lads now exactly what it's going to be like. And it's the same with America. I also flew out to St Louis for a scholarship, with zero information on the university, what the study-level was or what the football was like. And I was willing to go and do it with no information. Knowing what I know now, I should never have even thought about going there. We're just trying to educate people and help them understand what the landscape is. If you can't manage the expectations before they go, you're going to have problems.'

LFE manages the apprenticeship programme for 16- to 18-year-olds who are attached to the majority of EFL clubs, as well as several clubs in the National League. 'The Erasmus+ scheme is an EU fund to encourage people to go and have experiences abroad,' explains Simon. 'Our core business is making sure that players in those age groups get through their apprenticeship programmes, so their education and welfare is being looked after as they train and develop as footballers. We have a remit for supporting apprentices beyond those two years as well, helping them find a positive destination. With the attrition rates the way they are, we have a duty of care to ensure that these players at 18 are supported to go to university, find a job or move to another football club. We have an exit and progression strategy for when they get to 18.'

In 2008, LFE began looking at EU funding as a way to give players an option to go abroad if they are released by their club. They now make an application to Erasmus+ annually, sending up to 30 players per year to partner clubs throughout Sweden.

'Historically, we had some contacts in Sweden, which is why we started there,' explains Simon. 'The level is good, in terms of it being a good fit with where our lads are at. Between the fourth, fifth and sixth tier in Sweden is about right for released apprentices. The lack of a language barrier is a huge thing as well. We put the application in, we get funding from the programme with the idea to get players an experience of their industry in another country – to open their eyes up to it. It means that each individual has an amount of money that can be spent against them, which covers travel, accommodation, food and other support that they need for the experience. It may go well for them and they get kept on by the club, move to another club or come back, because they've decided it's not for them or there isn't an offer for them to stay out there. We don't sell it to the lads as a last-chance saloon. It's three months for them to go and have a good experience, learn some stuff about themselves, try something new and it might go somewhere football-wise.

'We worked in Spain as well for a spell with some clubs in the fifth tier over there. For the three months that we send them out there it's structured, they're getting paid, funds are going through, accommodation is paid for – it's all done as it should be. But beyond the three months, when it becomes an agreement between the player and the club and when we're out of the picture without any control, that's when you can sometimes get issues. In Spain, things were a little bit wilder. In Sweden it's much more structured, it's a good place to be. We've had very few problems there. They have to go out there within one year of finishing their apprenticeship. So they are generally 18- or 19-year-olds who have been released by their clubs. Australia and New Zealand have become more popular and lads are starting to use football as a way to get out there. We've got links in both countries, where coaches are asking us for players. Another popular route is going to America on scholarships, which is a four-year commitment with education as well. The university package in America is massive. We had Mo Adams, who was at Derby County, who has just been drafted straight out of university by Chicago Fire. So, now he's with Bastian Schweinsteiger!' laughs Simon.

He admits it is sometimes difficult to convince young players discarded by English clubs to take a chance abroad. LFE looks after around 650 scholars every summer, with approximately 40 per cent of those winning professional contracts, and the remainder forced to look at alternatives.

'About 50 will go to universities in England, another 50 to American universities and you'd suspect a good number will go and find a job somewhere,' says Simon. 'So, before you know it, we've got to send 30 players out to Sweden and Spain from a pool of maybe 100. And you don't know whether all of them will be a good fit. And we aren't trying to force people to go. A figure of 30 per year isn't a limit but it's all about finding the people. It is always a bit of a push to fill the 30 spots. When they're released at 18, lads generally have the perception that they can go and play at another Football League club. But there's always the next age group through an academy system. When you get to 18, you've got 15 years' worth of players ahead of you in the first-team squad. The reality is that it is going to be tough. With Sweden, young players realise that they will be valued over there. They will be playing football at a senior level, which is not always the case over here. I think lads just want to be playing, want to go and do something new and be valued by a football club.

'We're trying to educate and show these hungry young men that there's more to life than just being a professional footballer over here in England. In terms of persuading lads to go to Sweden, we just give them the facts – this is how many players have gone, these are the things they've said about the experiences they've had, here's some imagery – we don't chuck it down their throats. We're just trying to give them the facts, as we want the right people to be going out there as well.'

As we spoke, Simon received an email from another Swedish club interested in working with the LFE. English players are in high demand in Sweden, regarded as hot prospects – particularly following the success of Östersund. Under the guidance of current Swansea City manager Graham Potter, the club rose from the Swedish fourth tier to the top flight, with several LFE graduates in the squad who defeated Arsenal at the Emirates Stadium in the Europa League in February 2018.

'The programme spreads like wildfire over in Sweden,' says Simon. 'The guys are doing well out there and when they get over there they are looked after. We sell it as a life opportunity with football attached rather than the other way around. That may discourage some people but it means that the ones who do go are the right ones. We've worked in Sweden for ten years now and we've fine-tuned the number of clubs we work with and the people we work with so we know the programme is fairly robust. We fly out there twice a year to check how the lads are doing and meet with the club, so we have really good knowledge on what's out there in Sweden.'

There are many success stories. Of the 220 players sent for an initial 12 weeks to Sweden, over 60 have been offered contracts.

'Players will generally ask about their chances of being kept on. It's a hard one to answer as it depends on how well they do,' admits Simon. 'But we only work with clubs who have the interest of taking lads back out there. It's hard to track as there are that many who come back to England and return to Sweden a year down the line. When you send players, their mates want to go out, too. They might not go on our programme but they head out there. I'm finding out all the time about so many lads out there who are English.

'I sent Nathan Millis, who was released by Shrewsbury a year ago,' he continues. 'Great lad, captain of Shrewsbury's youth team but just missed out on a contract. He went out there for three months and came back to England as he hadn't been offered a contract. I knew nothing about this but he went back to Sweden with his backpack, stayed with mates he'd met over there and got in touch with local clubs. He went trialling around and was offered a contract for a year. The fact that we have got individuals who are willing to go and do that – to have the courage to go and just try it – is just unreal. That's the sort of stuff that's going on that you can't measure.'

There's also a cultural aspect to the programme, with language courses and support for players arriving in Sweden. Life in the lower leagues of Swedish football certainly seems a world away from the gilded environments of English academies. Clubs are extremely community-based, with players often called upon to carry out gardening in local villages, stocktaking in supermarkets and even bingo-calling in local bingo halls.

'You name it, they do it,' laughs Simon. 'We do say that there might be all sorts going on when you're out there, but just buy into it, it's different. We do a vetting process before they go and those who are happy and willing to muck in have an amazing time and meet friends for life.

'There's other stuff like sledging in the snow and fishing trips. We make sure the club put something in place for them to keep their time fulfilled throughout the week, as some of these clubs at the lower level may just train three or four evenings a week. So there's a lot of time there where we need to make sure the lads are supported to be busy. There's all sorts going on, they'll help out in local schools, there'll be coaching with some of the younger age groups, football festivals and helping the club in the community.

'Sweden is different to England, it's unbelievably community-based out there. The football clubs are run so well in the lower levels as they're well supported by the community in terms of sponsorship, funding and volunteers. Therefore, the players are well known in the area. It's not slave labour, it's to give some support back to sponsors. They're opening their eyes up to stuff that's isn't possible back home. The humility of the players has got to show having done this sort of stuff.'

Xander has enjoyed this aspect of his experience abroad, but admits it's not an easy life for those brought up in the English academy structure.

'As the club is so small it's pretty much like a family club,' he explains. 'We make appearances at choirs and things like that. You see people every day and you're made to feel welcome. It's a really good place to be in terms of feeling comfortable and homely. You don't feel like an outsider or that you're from a different country. The team I play for is based in such a secluded area, with a population of about 900 people. There's literally nothing else to do so it has to be a certain type that will come out here and thrive. You will get bored but you have to see it as a stepping stone. I'm not here to necessarily enjoy myself, I'm here to progress as a footballer.

'From the outside, everyone thinks, "Aw, football is the perfect lifestyle." But if they saw how we live! The money's not unbelievable, as you can imagine, but that's just the sacrifices you've got to make. You just have to keep mentally strong and keep the focus on where you want to be at the end of it all. I don't mind being away from home and that, it's not really bothered me. My family haven't been over as I've not asked them. I keep in touch with them all the time but I want to concentrate on getting stuff done while I'm out here. If people start coming over I might start missing home.'

Xander made a good first impression in Sweden and was offered a contract after just five weeks, but the ambitious young man already has his sights set on his next move.

'It was great to have that security. I went back to England for about a week, which is compulsory, and then flew back out to Sweden. I saw the rest of the season out and we got promoted,' he says. 'After being in Sweden, I'm pretty much open to anything. Initially, it takes a while to get used to being on your own and not having your mum to help when you're a young lad. But I think I've matured a lot while I've been out here and would be comfortable playing pretty much anywhere now. My contract runs until the end of the season in October. Future-wise? Potentially, I'd like to get a move to a bigger club in Sweden. Preferably, I'd like to be somewhere other than Sweden, whether it's back home or elsewhere. Using my brother's contacts is always helpful.'

Xander's brother is Oli McBurnie, the Swansea City and Scotland striker. Drawing on a network of contacts across the football world for a next move was a common theme among players I spoke to and Xander agrees that furthering one's career in the game is often about who you know.

'It couldn't be more true for football,' he says. 'As it's all about opinions, you need to just put yourself out there as much as you can. I believe that I'll fit someone's criteria.'

While he may move away from Sweden, Xander believes a spell abroad can be extremely beneficial for young players often overlooked by English clubs in favour of more experienced alternatives.

'The main thing I've noticed about foreign countries is that it's a lot less harsh on young players,' contends Xander, who'd just scored a brace in a 3-2 defeat before we spoke. 'It's not an easy life by any means, but I mean in terms of your development. You're more likely to get more games as there's less money involved. In terms of growing as a player, it's extremely helpful. They're willing to play young lads, they want to play young lads, they play football the right way and, personally, it's benefiting my life on and off the field. I'd recommend it massively to young lads or even players towards the end of their careers who fancy something different.'

While Xander's future may be bright, the outlook for LFE's scheme is more uncertain. As it is funded by the EU, Brexit looms large.

'That's problem number one,' concedes Simon. 'It was discussed before the vote that it is a big part of the EU and that if we leave then that means we're out of Erasmus+. And it was discussed that there'd be something in place to replace it. But your guess is as good as mine as to whether anything will happen. We've just made a new application, which will run up until 2020. It's a good question as to what will happen then.

'Between now and then we'll be working with the Spanish FA about returning to Spain. Working with their FA means it's a bit more structured and we've got two players at Getafe at the moment – one from Barnsley and one from Millwall. At the moment, we're sending 26 players to Sweden and four to Spain per year,' he concludes.

While Xander McBurnie and the others on the LFE scheme are all graduates of the academy system, Lewis Baker took a more unconventional route to Swedish football. In 2014, he reached the final 22 out of 6,500 applicants in a Samsung competition to win a professional contract with Swindon Town or Leyton Orient.

Upon completing a sports coaching degree, he was determined to make it as a pro. He'd spent some time coaching in Stockholm and made up his mind to pursue a career in Sweden, spending weeks diligently emailing his details to hundreds of Swedish clubs.

He was offered a trial and, one week on from working part-time in Tesco, he stood in the snow in northern Sweden with a full-time contract with IFK Östersund in his hand.

'I always had that feeling that I wanted to try somewhere else,' explains Lewis. 'Football in Scotland is quite difficult to break into, especially for a young player. In my specific position, as a striker, they look for big, strong, fast players and that's not my game – I'm more of a technical player. So, I found it was tough to break in there. In Britain, it is difficult to break into a team and make a name for yourself. Nowadays, more players are realising that the best opportunities may lie abroad.'

He's regularly contacted by players back home about playing abroad and has no hesitation in recommending it. 'On LinkedIn, I get three or four players a week contacting me to gauge an understanding about a move over here, what the commitments are, what the playing style is like, what the lifestyle is like,' Lewis says. 'Every time I reply, I've got nothing bad to say about it. I guess for some people it could be more challenging but I'm the type of person that embraces that. It could be tough for some people to move to another country. Britain's hard to break into and if you want to play at a good level, I would 100 per cent recommend giving it even one year abroad. Who knows what can happen?'

He returned to Scotland for a holiday in the summer of 2018 and had an offer from a well-known Scottish Championship club. However, he sees his immediate future in Scandinavia.

'The offer did appeal to me but I'm enjoying Sweden and I'd love to move up the leagues here,' he continues. 'I have a fiancée who has been over and she loves it here too. In two or three years' time, we may still find ourselves here and I'll hopefully be playing at that higher level in Sweden, which is what I'm aiming to do. It's much easier to get a move up the leagues here than back home. Back home, teams are reluctant to recruit from the lower leagues as they almost want instant success, whereas, there is a lot more patience here. In our league last season, the top goalscorer got a move up a division. There is that opportunity to go up the leagues if you perform well enough.'

While the quote 'it was like living in another country' accredited to Ian Rush after his short-lived spell at Juventus in the 1980s is almost certainly apocryphal, the fact so many still believe it to be true hints at one reason behind the relative dearth of British football talent who have plied their trade abroad. In fairness to Rush, he's since said that his move to Turin was 'the best thing I ever did'.

According to 2014 data from the United Nations, there are over five million Britons living abroad, which equates to just under eight per cent of the UK population. The Office for National Statistics suggests that the majority of British emigrants move abroad for work-related reasons.

A 2015 Organisation for Economic Co-operation & Development report titled *Emigrants from Great Britain: what do we know about their lives?* was, according to its author John Jerrim, the first quantitative study of this issue.

It found that British emigrants tended to earn more than individuals who remained in Great Britain. Five of the top six destinations for emigrant Britons were English-speaking – Australia, the US, Canada, New Zealand and Ireland. Indeed, 70 per cent of emigrants from the UK were native speakers in their new country of residence. This tallies with the CIES Football Observatory's findings. Of the 165 English players currently playing in countries outside of the UK and Ireland, 56 – or roughly one-third – are based in Australia, the US or New Zealand. A further 21 Englishmen play with clubs in the League of Ireland.

If the majority of Britons who emigrate end up in English-speaking countries and earn more abroad, it's not a stretch of the imagination to speculate that this may influence British footballers' reluctance to move to overseas leagues. Quite simply, they can earn a lot more at home than they would by venturing to leagues in countries where English is the official or de facto language. The most lucrative of these, America's MLS, paid an average figure of $213,048 (or £159,339 at the time of writing) annually to their rostered players in 2017. Even in England's second tier, the Championship, the average annual salary is over £300,000.

Neill Collins is one player who has taken the plunge across the pond. He'd holidayed in Florida every year since he was a seven-year-old and had always fancied an opportunity to play abroad. Out of favour at Sheffield United, fate intervened in the form of a move to Tampa Bay Rowdies.

'The move over here was a coincidence, really,' admits the Scot. 'The previous year I thought there was a chance of going to New York or Orlando City but things never quite developed. Then, I knew I was coming out of contract at Sheffield United and there was quite a lot of uncertainty around the club at that time. I'd come over here on holidays for 20 to 25 years. Even when I met my wife and brought her here, she loved it. Every summer we'd come for six or seven weeks with the kids. I always fancied the opportunity to play somewhere different, especially at the end of my career. I felt the football was going in the right direction in America, it was improving, it was becoming bigger and more popular. I actually went to a Rowdies game when I was on holiday. The set-up was good. You always like to try and be as prepared as possible. I'd spoken to the manager at the Rowdies and explained my situation regarding my contract. He just said that they'd love to do something but they had to do it then. I wanted to go there and they wanted me and it just happened. It was just one of those things that came together nicely.'

When Wayne Rooney signed for DC United in June 2018 he cited family reasons for choosing Washington over a move to Los Angeles or New York. This was also Neill's priority when he decided on upping sticks from Yorkshire to the central coast of Florida.

'When you're moving your family and kids far away it's ideal to go somewhere where you can get an inkling for what it might be like,' he stresses. 'When the opportunity arose it was perfect in terms of the lifestyle and being able to bring all the kids, knowing they'd be able to settle in. They'd been over here quite often so those were the main reasons. If it hadn't been the Rowdies, it would have been somewhere else. I would have been willing to try somewhere else, even it if wasn't the US – somewhere else in Europe, perhaps. Coming to America had been my first choice though for the long term.'

Fellow Scot Steven Caldwell also finished his career in North America, having harboured an ambition to play outside of the UK from an early age.

'I'd always expected it might have been in Italy, Germany or Spain – you just assume it's going to be Europe,' he says. 'As I got older and MLS grew and got stronger and stronger, there came an opportunity to go to Toronto FC. I just thought I wanted to try something different. I probably could have played in the Championship for another few years. I was leaving Birmingham City for certain and thought I'd take the opportunity to try MLS. It was for an initial eight-week period, so I had that buffer that if the football wasn't good enough or I didn't like it I could have gone back and found another team in England. It just felt right. I just wanted to try something different and experience a different league and country.'

He went on to captain The Reds's side that included fellow Brit Jermain Defoe and would have no hesitation recommending a move abroad to any player.

'I think it really helps you as a person, obviously, but definitely as a player as well,' says Steven, who has remained in Canada following his retirement. 'I'd definitely recommend it and not just MLS. If the doors are shutting at the club you're at in the UK, I'd always recommend it.'

The transfer market, or player acquisition system, in MLS works differently to that in traditional football strongholds, with all contracts owned by the league rather than clubs. It is an extremely complex system, with a lack of transparency sometimes making it difficult to understand how a club has managed to secure the services of a particular player.

An allocation ranking order determines which club has first dibs on acquiring a player on an allocation list, which contains select US national team players and players who had been transferred out of MLS for transfer fees of at least $500,000, and takes the reverse order of the previous season's league standings.

It's an interesting system and could certainly freshen up the Premier League, but it does mean a professional football career stateside is even more precarious than it is in England.

'In the UK, you can stay at a club if you really want to,' says Steven. 'A manager might say to you, "You're out of the picture," but if you really want and you've got a contract for a couple of years, you can say, "I'm fine, I'm just going to sit here."'

'Here in North America, it's completely different. You can literally come in one morning and be traded to the other side of the country and there's nothing you can do about it,' he explains. 'You have to go. It's really weird. I've seen it a few times, where a player comes in in the morning and the general manager sends them up to the office. Next thing you know, they're flying to Chicago or Portland or wherever. There was a story about a young Argentinian lad who plays for Dallas now. We were in Portland and Toronto FC traded him and the lad couldn't get back on the plane, as he couldn't come back to Canada because of his visa. They traded him on a Saturday night after we'd played Portland Timbers and the boy had only been with us two months but couldn't come back and had to stay in Portland, and wait until his US visa was sorted out. He was waiting six or eight weeks and all his stuff was in Canada in his apartment in Toronto. So, he was playing with Portland but he wasn't able to go home and pick up his stuff until his visa was organised. That's the kind of horror story you hear and see and how transfers can really affect people. In the UK, you have that right to say, "I'm not going to move," You don't need to go.'

Former Leicester City and Watford defender Jordan Stewart joined San Jose Earthquakes in 2013 and agrees with Steven's point on the lack of player power in the US.

'In America, you can get traded at any time and you have no say,' says Jordan, who moved to Phoenix Rising after three years with the Quakes. 'You can come into training and the club can tell you that you're going to Orlando. It's different to England. When I was at Derby County, Paul Jewell got the sack and Nigel Clough came in and wanted to get the high-earners off the wage bill. He made us come in to train with the kids and things like that, which is difficult. They wanted me out of the club but I had another two years left on my contract and that's when it's good to have player power.'

Richie Ryan has had to move between four North American clubs in four years under such circumstances, but is another who is quick to extol the virtues of playing professionally outside of the UK. He spent a season in Belgium with Royal Antwerp in 2007/08, a move he credits with resurrecting his career after becoming disillusioned with the game in England. Beforehand, he had considered hanging up his boots at just 22 during a tumultuous spell at Boston United.

'I wasn't playing, didn't enjoy my time there, or enjoy playing for the manager or training,' admits the Irishman. 'I just got slated every day, I was called a five-a-side player because of the way I wanted to play the game. We were in League Two at the time and were battling relegation so there was very little technical football wanted from the manager, so I definitely wasn't his cup of tea.'

At the time the Belgian club had links with Manchester United, with over 30 young players – including John O'Shea, Jonny Evans and Darron Gibson – sent on loan from The Red Devils to The Great Old. Former United reserves manager Warren Joyce was in charge and Richie jumped at the chance to rescue his career.

'Warren was managing one of the academy teams at Leeds United when I was at Sunderland, so he knew me from playing against him. He was good friends with the old chief executive at Sunderland, who asked me whether I'd be interested in going to Belgium for a season,' he recalls. 'It was a great experience over there, the standard of football was very good, very technical. I was only there for one year, unfortunately, as the manager left. I think I'd have stayed if Warren had. Once he said he was jumping ship, I sort of knew I wouldn't be staying around either.'

Northern Irishman Henry McStay and Englishman Sean Doherty were also at the club at the time, which Richie credits with helping him to acclimatise in a country with three official languages.

'For a small country, it depends on what part of the country you're in as to what language they speak,' says Richie. 'We tried to pick up some Flemish as that was the main language in Antwerp and tried to order stuff in a supermarket. But they'd know we didn't speak it properly, so they'd say, "Do you speak English? Everybody speaks English here." So, in that respect, it was easier to settle there and I had the two lads there from the UK who'd been in similar situations to me.

'It was nice for me to get to Antwerp and enjoy football again. I had always wanted to play abroad since I was young. Even when I was playing for the Republic of Ireland under-15s and under-16s, we'd face the likes of Holland and Germany and they'd all play great technical football, so it was always in my mind to maybe go and play abroad. I think the type of player that I was, and probably still am, I was more suited at a younger age to playing abroad than playing at the higher levels in the UK. I'd recommend it 100 per cent. English is widely spoken in a lot of countries like Holland and Belgium, so for English, Irish or Scottish players it's an easy transition to go over there and it's easier to fit in. When you're there it's nice to try and blend in and learn the language because it could give you great opportunities playing in that country or even later in life. You never know – that's the beauty of football. You never know where you're going to end up.'

Now 33, Richie's thoughts are gradually turning to post-retirement and he hopes to remain in the US when his playing career ends.

'I think we'd like to stay in the States long term. I'd like to think I've made some good connections over here and have some good friendships and relationships so that, when my playing days end, I can transition into coaching somewhere,' he says. 'But, obviously, if that doesn't happen then we're going to need to work when I finish playing. I'm going to need to be involved in football somehow, whether that's in the US, Canada, Ireland or Scotland, where my wife is from. There's not really great stability in the game at all, unless you're at the top end earning big money. The level we're at, you need a job, you need to get back in quick.'

When Tom Ince left Blackpool in 2014 he had a decision to make. A host of English clubs were interested in his signature, as were the likes of Internazionale, Monaco and Olympiacos. He plumped for Hull City, claiming that, as he stood in the *Nerazzurri*'s famous San Siro Stadium, the 'English boy inside him' told him to choose the Premier League. It is an attitude that seems to be changing with Ademola Lookman spurning his Everton manager Sam Allardyce's advice in early 2018 to go on loan in the Championship in favour of a successful spell in Germany with RB Leipzig. Allardyce stated that, 'Going there and not being able to speak the language at such a young age and on your own is a massive challenge.' Lookman did his talking on the pitch, however, scoring a late winner on his Bundesliga debut and ending his temporary move with five goals and three assists in just 11 appearances. He was one of six young English players who starred in Germany's top two tiers during the 2017/18 season in what seems to indicate a sea change in attitudes among hotly tipped British talent.

Despite the influx of foreign players into the Premier League, Viv Anderson is in no doubt as to why so few British players move abroad. Viv himself was once linked with a move to Bayern Munich, which he dismisses as 'paper talk'.

'Money. The game here is awash with money,' says the former Nottingham Forest, Arsenal, Manchester United and England defender. 'I do media work all around the world and the first thing they watch is the Premier League. It comes down to the individual whether they want to experience a new culture and country. I played with Tony Woodcock for Forest, Arsenal and England and he moved to Cologne and loved it. But it only suits some players.'

He found comfort in moving to clubs where he knew players who were already there. 'At Arsenal, I knew Kenny Sansom, Paul Mariner, Graham Rix from England duty and, of course, Tony. At United, I knew Bryan Robson. It helps to settle in having people you know already at the club.'

Steven Caldwell, having played for the likes of Newcastle United, Sunderland and Birmingham City, ended his career in MLS with Toronto FC and agrees that British footballers are sometimes wary of leaving their comfort zone.

'I guess it's because we've got a pretty robust number of leagues in the UK. Why would you move unless you have the ambition to try another country or culture?' he says. 'Sometimes it's easy to stay in the environment you know and are accustomed to. To take yourself out of that comfort zone is really important as a player and a person.'

Fellow Scot Neill Collins also ended his playing career in North America and agrees with Steven that the strength of the league system in England sometimes makes it difficult to leave.

'There are a lot of reasons for players staying in England,' he suggests. 'You've got to remember that the Championship is the third or fourth most watched league in Europe, in terms of attendance. So don't underestimate what a great league it is right now. You've got two fantastic leagues with huge clubs and more big clubs in League One. You've got phenomenal clubs with so much passion from the fans, so there's so much going for the English game. I think the opportunities are not there sometimes for players that maybe should be. Clubs in England and Scotland tend to have scouting networks that are quite wide, whereas some overseas clubs don't have the resources or think it's possible for British players to make that move.'

Indeed, most British and Irish players I spoke to who had moved abroad did so as they knew someone at the overseas club. It was uncommon to find someone who had been scouted while playing in England.

'I think players are starting to consider it now because below the Championship some clubs are having to cut their costs,' Neill continues. 'So, the money's not quite what players expect so they might like to try something overseas. This thing about players in Britain being narrow-minded, I don't really buy that. I think that they're already somewhere that everyone aspires to be, so why leave? Speak to any player around the world, the majority of them – apart from in Spain and Germany – want to come and play in England. For players in Scotland, going to play in England is the holy grail, so when you get there you're not going to just give that up.

'I think British players need to be slightly more open-minded about it and European clubs could cast their scouting network a wee bit further and see if they can attract more British players. There are definitely things that British players can add to these clubs and things that they can obviously learn as well,' Neill concludes.

LFE's Simon Williams mentioned earlier the difficulties in sometimes persuading young British players to take their chances abroad. He agrees that the English league system is often seen as the be-all and end-all of the football world.

'The general perception around playing in England is that players from every other country around the world try and get to England to play football,' he says. 'That it's the best place to be to play football. And I think the lads here realise that this is a good country to be if everyone else is trying to get here to play. Financially-driven maybe, but also because we've got so many professional levels which I think a lot of European countries are envious of. We're already at a stumbling block there.'

Intermediary Gary Mellor, whose agency Beswicks Sports represents over 170 players, believes that, while the Premier League may well be the place to be now, that might not always be the case. 'The latest TV rights money is still somewhat unknown and then there's Brexit, where sterling has taken a hammering. So the English market is not quite as attractive as it was before,' argues Gary. 'That might have a positive in terms of younger English players getting a chance. Every country has a duty to develop their youth and not enough money goes into grassroots football. The vast sums going out of the Premier League to the likes of Italy, Spain and Belgium does worry me. We're making these countries stronger, which encourages them to develop their players to sell to the Premier League.'

Xander McBurnie, an LFE graduate, is in agreement that some players don't necessarily want to take themselves out of their comfort zones. 'They're happy at home with their friends and families,' says the youngster. 'They're not really open to sacrificing all that just for football. They don't think it will be worth it and are not willing to take the risk in case they don't enjoy it. I think that is the case with a lot of people back home.'

Birmingham-born Jordan Stewart had spells in Greece and the US before retiring in 2017. Now settled in Arizona and the holder of an American Green Card, he is often contacted by fellow players for advice on potential moves stateside.

'It's difficult for a lot of people to move abroad and settle,' says Jordan. 'Family is a big factor. It gets more complicated when you've got a family. I didn't want to commit to anything when I was playing for those reasons. It's kind of selfish but I wanted to focus on my career before settling down. Some people just like being close to home. Others think it's too big a change. Some may not think that the league is good enough for them. I have out-of-contract players ringing me saying, "Jordan, what's it like over there?" They hear about the lifestyle and want to come but I always say to them, "You're used to going to Los Angeles, Las Vegas and Miami but if you sign for Columbus Crew, for example, it's a different world."'

Having played in the UK for 15 years, Italian midfielder Raffaele De Vita lends an outsider's perspective. 'I've played with so many British players and it's difficult the way they think, especially Scottish players. They've got a different mentality to other European countries. And, of course, everything works well here,' he argues.

That's not to say that many British and Irish players who have spent their careers close to home have not considered a spell abroad. Sometimes red tape, family reasons or just lack of opportunities scupper any ambitions.

'I was always looking to play abroad,' says Liam Rosenior, who has made over 400 appearances during his career in England. 'There were a couple of occasions when I could have gone to certain countries but my wife is from America, so her visa wouldn't have allowed me to go and play there. Going abroad would have been a fantastic experience for not just me, but me and my family – being together in a different environment.'

He has often looked at foreign team-mates and their success at making a life for themselves and their families in England and pondered what the lifestyle would be like for him and his own family in another country.

'For example, Spanish defender Bruno has been at Brighton for seven years,' says Liam. 'He absolutely loves it, his wife loves it in England and his children speak perfect English and Spanish. Moving abroad could be an amazing experience. A completely different way of life and a different way of football. To be honest, though, the money is here in England. So, if you are an English player and you can live with your family and can earn great money and don't have to move, then it would take a brave person to go just for the sake of moving.

'I think that's part of the problem. That's a huge element of it. If the money wasn't here, players would go where the money is. It's a short career and you have to maximise it and one of the things that comes into it is finance. And, at the moment, the Premier League is the richest league in the world. If you're fortunate enough to be English and play in it, earn good money and be with your family then there isn't really a better way of life. I understand that. For me, though, I always wanted to go abroad just to experience the football and have a different way of seeing the game. We're a bit behind tactically in England but because of the financial rewards on offer, we don't go and learn. We don't go and take different experiences from the continent or from South America or places like that. Different isn't better but it gives you a broader skillset, a broader encyclopaedia of football to look back on and make decisions moving forward.'

Northern Ireland goalkeeper Michael McGovern, who has spent his career in Scotland and England, has also had the opportunity to move abroad but, for him, family came first.

'It was a really good contract that I was offered,' says the Norwich City keeper. 'I spoke to my wife and we both decided that we weren't going to bring the kids away to that particular country. I talked about doing it myself but it was just going to be too hard to be away from them. It's different if you move about in England. You can commute or you can stay overnight for one or two games a week. But if you're talking about going to another country that's not as accessible and you're away from your family then you're not really part of the family. You're really out of the loop.

'If you look at England, it's about money. The Premier League is the richest league in the world. The Championship, I believe, is in the top five or six wealthiest leagues in the world as well. I think that's the number one reason. Footballers are funny. I think if more players started to do it then other players would follow. You find that with footballers, a few people will try something and others will go, "Oh look, he's gone to MLS." I've seen a few going to MLS recently. Johnny Russell went to Kansas in January, and Danny Wilson went over there from Rangers. So, you never know what might happen in the future.'

Mark Roberts, who has played for a dozen clubs across England, regrets never having the opportunity to play outside of his home country.

'If I'd my time again it's something that I would probably consider,' he says. 'I do love to travel – my wife and I share that passion and try and instil it in our young family and try and take them to as many places as we possibly can. To be able to combine the two things that you love – travel and football – I'm sure is a wonderful thing. You realise when you move away from home – although you may be in the same country – that you can go months or possibly longer without seeing people you know and care about. I know players who have had wonderful experiences in going abroad and plying their trade in different countries and cultures. It depends on the individual. It's probably something that's never been an option for myself but you can never say never.'

While China has earned a reputation in recent years for luring foreign players with exorbitant contracts, it is other Asian countries that British players have tended to journey to. At the time of writing, there were Brits ensconced in the likes of India, South Korea, Saudi Arabia, Japan, Indonesia, Singapore, Malaysia, Hong Kong and Thailand. The latter appealed to Leroy Lita after he turned down a move to China.

'I actually went to China and didn't like it; I couldn't see myself moving there,' admits the former Premier League striker. 'When I was in China, I got a call informing me that a club in Thailand were interested in me so I decided to go and check it out.'

Leroy acknowledges that there were a lot culture shocks when he initially moved to south-east Asia, in addition to the language barrier. He most recently played for Thai League 1 side Sisaket, before returning to the UK after a season in north-eastern Thailand. His have-boots-will-travel attitude meant a move to south-east Asia was an easy decision for the former England Under-21 international, who was born in Kinshasa but moved to England as a five-year-old and is 'as British as they come'.

'I didn't want to end up playing League One and dropping down the divisions,' explains Leroy, who previously spent a season at Greek side AO Chania, 'You lose motivation if that happens, if you're just playing for money – especially if you've played in the Premier League. No disrespect to them but you're not going to fancy going to Accrington Stanley, for example, when you've played at the top. You don't have anything to prove to anyone in League One or League Two. I believe you're better off going abroad as it gives you a boost and that drive and hunger again. You need drive and ambition if you want to have a good career, so why not do it in another country? You can help others learn about the way we are and the way we play. I'm not speaking for everyone but that's how I see it.

'British players don't move abroad for many reasons,' he continues. 'Some players don't want to leave home; everyone's different. A football career is very short, so I believe that if you have an opportunity to live and play somewhere else, take it. But not everyone's the same.

'There are not many British players abroad, full stop,' Leroy continues. 'It's one nation that doesn't really leave their domestic leagues, apart from one or two. If you look at our leagues back home, you've got many Spaniards, many Italians, many Brazilians – they all come to us, but we don't go anywhere else. It's going to get harder for British youngsters to come through now, so, instead of them playing that silly under-23s league, why not go to a foreign team and play some first-team football, get some experience and get some confidence? Then go back home and play first-team football and you'll be ready. You'll feel like a professional. It's not their fault, though, it's the way the system is. I think some British players are just comfortable. People often say to me, "You've played at a lot of clubs," but when I've been at a club and I've not been playing I've always gone on loan because I've wanted to play football. You should be playing as your career is as a footballer. I can't just sit on a bench, because football is my passion.'

It's a passion shared by Charlie Sheringham, who took himself outside the comfort zone of English football for a spell in Bangladesh. Again, it was a contact from back home that prompted the move for a player who had enjoyed a loan spell in the US while a youngster on Crystal Palace's books.

'I knew Saif Sporting Club's coach Ryan Northmore from England,' explains Charlie. 'I'd played against his teams back home. I'd been sort of toying with the idea of playing abroad for six months, really. At the end of last season I was talking to a few people and a couple of opportunities came around. I almost signed for a team in Thailand, which didn't work out in the end. Ryan got in contact and it seemed to be a good deal for me at the right time.

'I was over for the second half of their season. I joined in October and their season finished in the middle of January. We qualified for the AFC Cup, the Asian equivalent of the Europa League, and had a couple of games in that and were then knocked out, so I'm back home,' he adds.

Despite his earlier spell in the US, he wasn't prepared for the culture shock of life in Dhaka, a city of over 18 million inhabitants.

'This was a bit different because, obviously, it's a completely different culture and language,' says Charlie. 'Then there's the food, the people, the traffic, the weather – it's just completely on its head compared to living and playing football in London.

'It was a bit more difficult than the US, put it that way! I enjoyed it but was out there for three and a half months and think that was enough, to be honest. I'm glad I did it and have no regrets about doing it. I scored a few goals and played well so I'll see what happens.

'They kind of had to help me settle in or else I really would have been in trouble!' the Londoner continues. 'All the players lived in an apartment block, with a chef there as well, so I was with the team a lot of the time. The club picked us up at the bottom of the apartment block for training every day and when we had a match they took us from the apartment block to the coach. They look after you, in that respect, so you're not on your own a lot of the time. It was only really in the evenings or after training that you had to fill your time with whatever you wanted to do – exploring the city or testing out the culture. Everything was set up for you.'

Football-wise, it was also poles apart from life as a professional footballer in England. Charlie played in the Bangladesh Premier League, where the majority of games are played at one ground in the capital with many clubs not having their own training facilities.

'That was obviously a big difference,' he says. 'It was very different to how you'd expect it to be in England in a top professional league. In a lot of the Asian leagues you have the majority of players from the national country and then you're allowed a certain number of foreign players. In my team, we were allowed three foreign players and the rest of the squad had to be Bangladeshi nationals.'

He is quick to recommend a spell abroad but can understand why some British players are hesitant about such moves.

'From my point of view, the level I was playing at as a lower English Football League and National League player, it was kind of a no-brainer, really,' says the former Bournemouth striker. 'I was playing in the National League, I got an opportunity to play at the top level in Bangladesh, be paid well and then potentially play in their equivalent of the Europa League, which I wouldn't get to do in England or most parts of Europe. So, wow, why not take the opportunity and enjoy it while I'm still young enough and still able to play? At the end of this season or next season, I'll still be able to find a club at the National League level. I know enough people at that level – managers, agents, and so on – to get me a team, so when this opportunity came up it was kind of like, "Let's do it, let's have a crack and if it doesn't go well I'm going to be back in a few months anyway."

'It's a big change, though. Going out there, usually not knowing anyone. I was lucky that I knew the coach a little bit so I could talk to him, he could tell me all about it, what it was like and give me an insight into it. For English players moving abroad to a foreign country where they don't speak English, sometimes on the back of an agent or a contact they don't really know, it can be difficult. Or just being chucked into Thailand, Bangladesh, India, Malaysia, wherever you want to go – especially that part of the world – is a big thing. It's not an easy one to say, "Yes, I'm going to do it" and think nothing more of it.'

Even for players without children, a move away can be difficult. Charlie's long-term girlfriend didn't join him in Bangladesh, an environment he felt wasn't ideal for her to live in.

'She did come and visit a couple of times and I think that was enough for her; she definitely didn't want to come and move out there with me,' he says. 'It's difficult to set down plans as a footballer. Even now that I'm back in England, I'm sort of trying to figure out where I go to next, what I do next. There's no real easy option. You can't make too many long-term plans, that's for sure.'

When we spoke, he was still under contract with Saif Sporting Club but was in the process of negotiating an early termination. As for his future, as with most footballers, it is uncertain.

'I have an agent and I know a lot of contacts that I played for, especially around London, and there's been a few people in touch already,' says Charlie. 'It's a funny one. The season in Bangladesh is quite short. It doesn't start again until September, so there's a big gap. So I'm probably going to look elsewhere. If they offered me another contract, I'd think about it but, if I'm honest, I'd a good time over there and enjoyed the experience but I don't really want to go back there. I'd like to go somewhere else, if possible, a different country but preferably not Bangladesh.'

As Richie Ryan mentioned earlier, 'You never know where you're going to end up. That's the beauty of football.' True, but you can often end up on the ugly side, too. While the majority of players in this chapter enjoyed their spells abroad, for others a move to foreign climes can cause their careers to spiral downhill.

The Global Game

'I'VE played at the very top. And I've played at the absolute bottom. I've seen corruption and match-fixing, not been paid and was forced out of a country Mafia-style.'

To say Rohan Ricketts is a well-travelled footballer is a bit of an understatement. He has taken in 20 clubs in 18 years – in 11 countries and four continents. If you chart his career from its beginnings at Arsenal to his latest club in Canada it totals 81,160km – or just under a quarter of the distance from the Earth to the Moon. It's fair to say that there's been some turbulence along the way.

Ricketts fell in love with football as a kid, growing up in a block of flats between Stockwell and Brixton in south London. He fell out of love with the game in the more unlikely surroundings of a hotel room in central Moldova. Quite a lot happened in between.

Ricketts is one of just a handful of players to leave The Gunners to join north London rivals Tottenham and had notions of playing abroad from an early age. He didn't, however, expect to end up travelling to training on a rickshaw, having to avoid elephants sprawled out in the middle of the street as they basked in the Bangladeshi sun.

'I was always a player who had an appetite for playing in a country like Spain, because of the technical level required. When I was 14 years old I was wanted by Ajax, so I always had an appreciation for clubs like that,' he explains. 'I didn't see it as something I would do so soon, it's just something I thought, "Maybe one day I'll play in Spain" but it wasn't in the front of my mind.' He will readily admit, though, that as a teenager, he never dreamed of playing in the likes of Hungary, India, Hong Kong, Thailand or Ecuador.

After leaving Tottenham, he had spells at Wolverhampton Wanderers, Queens Parks Rangers and Barnsley before the opportunity of the first leg of an unplanned world tour arose.

'I was going to sign a deal with MK Dons under Paul Ince, who was my captain at Wolves,' recalls Rohan. 'We had become good friends. They were in League Two, though, but I rated him as a coach. I loved him but I didn't really want to go to League Two as I knew if it didn't really work out it would be difficult to come back. Football is very harsh like that. It's ruthless. I was in and out of the team at Barnsley, and also had the opportunity to go to clubs in the likes of Spain such as Deportivo de La Coruña, in Switzerland and in MLS. And I said, "Yes to America". I was on my way; I loved it.'

MLS was growing at the time, with a certain fellow Englishman named David Beckham in his second season at LA Galaxy. Rohan enjoyed two seasons at Toronto FC, winning a Canadian Championship along the way, but felt like a forgotten man upon his return to England.

'I came back from MLS a better player, a better person, more mature, yet I couldn't get a trial in the Championship,' he reveals. 'A trial! I'm not saying you have to give me a trial but I played in the Premier League and did well there. I did well in the Championship. But then you can't get a trial? You can't even get looked at in your own country? My problem was I went away. If I'd spent the 18 months or two years I was at Toronto FC in the Premier League, even with a small club, and didn't do that well I'd be able to get a trial in the Championship. And it's all down to perception.'

He cites the example of John Bostock as someone who's had to leave England to successfully rebuild his career. Courted by the likes of Barcelona and Manchester United as a teenager, Bostock is both Crystal Palace and Tottenham's youngest-ever player. However, he was released from the latter after a series of loan spells and moved to Royal Antwerp under Jimmy Floyd Hasselbaink. His form with The Great Old earned him moves to fellow Belgian side Oud-Heverlee Leuven and French club Racing Club de Lens, where he won Ligue 2 Player of the Year in 2016/17. The upward trajectory continued when he signed a two-and-a-half year contract with Turkish Süper Lig side Bursaspor in early 2018.

'Outside of England, things aren't as professional in certain countries,' states Rohan. 'At the same time, I would tell players to consider it if you have run out of options. That's when English players need to look abroad. What did John Bostock do? He went abroad where he was brand new. Nobody knew him. They looked at his CV and went, "Hmm, Tottenham" and took him on. He went to Belgium and did really well. Then he gets bought by a team in France and does exceptionally well there. No one's even talking about this boy in the English press! Then he moves to a big team in Turkey and, still, no one in England is talking about him!'

A month after we spoke, Bostock signed a three-year deal with Ligue 1 club Toulouse. In keeping with Rohan's sentiments, the transfer hardly registered a mention in the English football press.

'If you see your career going downwards and you go, "Hold on a minute, I'm a Premier League level player", you better jump abroad quickly. Go when your stock is higher. When I had Arsenal and Tottenham on my résumé, clubs were all over me. Then you start going down and they see Toronto FC and say, "Oh, he's in MLS. Mickey Mouse league." Whereas now they're signing players from MLS.'

Rohan's next move was to the unlikely outpost of Diósgyőri VTK in the Hungarian League. He played just one game in Hungary, where he claims to have witnessed match-fixing for the first time. The next stop was his ill-fated move to Moldova. He played in a friendly for FC Dacia Chişinău and, after scoring a hat-trick, the club were only too eager to sign him – under the false impression that he was a striker.

'They were like, "Oh, we've got the next Pelé!" laughs Rohan. 'But the real games came and they saw that I wasn't a striker, I was a midfield player. Then they didn't want to pay me. We drew a game and they said, "Well, we're not paying the whole team." After about a month they said they wanted to renegotiate my contract. I replied, "Renegotiate? You haven't even paid me a penny."'

He remained in Chişinău for three and a half months, unpaid, and was unable to sign for a new side as the Moldovan club held his registration. A stand-off ensued before 'some serious guys' called to Rohan's hotel room and gave him a deadline to leave the country.

Eventually, Rohan, with the assistance of the PFA, was awarded US$100,000 in damages by the Court of Arbitration for Sport (CAS). A Macedonian team-mate received US$250,000 after going through a similar experience. But Dacia weren't finished yet. It is commonplace in some countries to sign up players to two contracts for tax reasons and the club argued that a second document had not been signed by them.

'I won the case but they appealed it and said they didn't sign the real contract. They said they only knew about a US$200 a month one and didn't know about the real one. But how did I get it? CAS awarded them the victory and said they didn't have to pay me. If CAS were using their brain they would have seen they dealt with the same club the week before. It's like a guy arrested for robbing a house turning up at a police station and the police say, "Oh, he's back again!" My friend got paid for a similar thing. When I saw the result come through I didn't want anything more to do with this sport. I didn't want to play. I was tired and angry.'

In 2015, FIFPro expressed 'serious concerns' about CAS, questioning its lack of independence, equal representation and accessibility.

'They owed me a lot of money and I'm still hurting about that,' Rohan continues. 'I still want to find out if I can reopen the case but someone told me it would cost about £25,000 to do that. The initial case cost £40,000 to £50,000 in legal fees. A team hasn't paid me and said I had two contracts. They said I agreed to work for US$200 a month. That I flew in and said, "You know what? I'm gonna play for you guys for 200 bucks a month for three years." And they gave me five grand up front, saying that was part of the salary, so basically, they said they were gonna pay me around US$7,000 over a three-year period, US$5,000 of it up front. So I was supposed to sit in the country for three years waiting for US$2,000 to be spread out monthly! How does that case even get attention?'

While the move proved disastrous for Rohan, others certainly did well out of it, with two agents sharing US$30,000 for moving him to Moldova. 'They got more than me to move me, put it that way,' he says. 'But agents are useful as they are gatekeepers to certain clubs. You need to know them as they're the ones that are spending their time flying around and meeting clubs. I love the game, it's the business that I'm not in love with. I like the art form and love teaching kids but the business and the politics and the lies? I'm not into that. I just want to play football. You're dealing with crooked agents and now it's getting worse. Agents are realising that kids really want to make it and are selling them a dream. They're asking for US$500 for a trial! Trials are meant to be free and the agent only gets paid if it works out. It's happening a lot in North America. These guys are doing this with ten kids and getting five grand. It's a business.'

Meanwhile, an offer from FC Ingolstadt 04 in Germany was withdrawn as the Zweite Bundesliga club were unwilling to wait a month for Rohan to get his International Clearance Certificate (ICT). Under FIFA guidelines clubs can be 90 days late paying players without consequences. After 117 days a player can cancel their contract.

'But they're also asking, "Why did he go to Moldova?" Then, I go to another team at a lower level in Germany as they were willing to wait the 28 days for FIFA to release my ICT. And this is a smaller team,' explains Rohan. 'The next club are asking, "What league in Germany was that?" They're not looking at who I am or what I can do. They're looking at what league I was in.

'They don't want to sign me so I go to a club that's going to respect my Arsenal and Tottenham background and then they don't pay me. And I'm like, "Oh my gosh! Where do I go now?" It's a mess. I'd gone to Germany, but almost immediately I'm on the hunt again for a new club. I'm down all that money and now I've got Hungary and Moldova on my CV. And I'm on the hunt yet again.'

His next port of call was the League of Ireland, with Shamrock Rovers and a reunion with the club where he made his name. In 2011, The Hoops became the first Irish team to reach the Europa League group stage, where their opponents included Tottenham.

'The only reason I signed for Shamrock Rovers – and I needed to sign somewhere – was that it was a straight contract and we were in the Europa League,' admits Rohan. 'Plus, I was going to play against my old club, Spurs. I got to reconnect with Harry Redknapp and asked if I could go back and train with the club to stay in shape after my spell in Ireland.

'I was training well and standing out and the Premier League players I was training with weren't even aware that I couldn't get a trial in the Championship. When I was first at Spurs I won a young player of the year award at the club. I took the option to go to Wolves and dropped down a level as Glenn Hoddle loved me. But once I'd done that, Hoddle got sacked and a new manager came in who didn't play me. All these little things that no one thinks about add up. I couldn't get a trial because of my track record. My track record of, "Where have you been lately?" Before you know it you're flying to India and selling your soul to get money.'

Before we spoke, I assumed Rohan's global adventure was all down to his love of the game. I put this to him and he replied that it was one of the reasons but not the major factor. He then queries my employment background. I go through my career since university, which was going quite well until the global economic crash in 2008, which hit Ireland particularly hard. Three months after moving to a larger house to accommodate our growing family and to be closer to work, I was made redundant. I was desperate for employment and took a role I wouldn't previously have considered.

'Why did you take the job?' Rohan asks.

'Money, I suppose,' I reply sheepishly, understanding what he was getting at.

'Exactly,' he says. 'And that's what people forget about footballers. It's a job! People look at it and go, "Why did he go there?" It's literally how we get paid. So I can say, "This is going to look bad on my CV so I'm not going to go." But how am I going to pay my bills? I'm not a multi-millionaire and neither are most players. I moved to these places because I needed to get paid. This is how messed up it is. If you don't take up an offer and are looking for a club for five months, the next club will ask, "Well, where have you been for five months?" You're damned if you do and you're damned if you don't. They want a guy that's been playing. And, then, if you are playing, they ask, "Why did you sign for that team?" They're not even looking any more at your actual talent. They're looking more at what's on paper.'

I can empathise with him on this. A low-profile person, like me, can omit the embarrassing jobs from our CV or LinkedIn profile. A five-month gap between jobs? Career break. A professional footballer? Their résumé is on Wikipedia, press reports and the tips of potential suitors' tongues.

'People need to understand that football is a business. It's ruthless,' he explains. 'When you get in there, yes, you love it but you need to understand it's a job and you've got a short window of opportunity. These things aren't really discussed and players need to be educated. Outside of the Premier League and the Championship, it's crazy. I went to India purely for money. They offered me tax-free money.'

Based on his own experiences, Rohan can understand why British players are sometimes reticent about moving abroad. 'When you speak about England, the Premier League and the Championship is where it's at,' he continues. 'But that's probably about 20 per cent of the leagues that exist there. It's not a fair description of what's out there. There are players at a lower level who could play in the Championship or even the Premier League but they don't get the opportunity. They get criticised for not moving abroad but moving abroad comes at the risk of going through the things I went through – not getting paid on time or not getting paid at all, having to accept signing for clubs that are not really at your level. They're not going to look good on your CV and that's going to affect your next move. Language barriers are a problem but I was fine with that as I learned Spanish and have always loved languages.

'The English players have everything in England. I can understand why they don't travel abroad. I went through a situation where CAS didn't protect me. FIFA protected me but CAS overruled FIFA and ruled in the club's favour. I never got paid. I never broke any rules. So how can a club that is known as an offender get away with not paying me and then win the appeal? It's ridiculous. My friend, who was in a similar situation to me, won his case against the same club.'

It's not just in non-traditional footballing countries where these problems exist. In 2011, Spanish footballers went on strike over demands for guarantees on unpaid wages. The players' union, led by Luis Rubiales – who went on to become Royal

208

Spanish Football Federation president and sack Julen Lopetegui on the eve of the 2018 World Cup – demanded central funds to cover unpaid wages to its players. The league offered €10m per year, a lot less than the €50m-plus that had gone unpaid the previous season. The union stated that 200 players had not been paid in full, or at all, in the preceding two seasons. Three years later Racing Santander's players staged an on-pitch protest, claiming not to have been paid for a number of months. The squad had threatened not to contest a Copa del Rey tie against Real Sociedad and stuck to their word, standing arm-in-arm in solidarity in the centre circle while their opponents kicked the ball between themselves.

In 2017 Argentine players also declared strike action as some had not been paid for four months. A year later Panathinaikos's players failed to turn up to training, claiming they had not been paid by the club for several months. The Greek Super League also docked the club three points over failing to settle an unpaid wages dispute with their former defender Jens Wemmer. The Athens-based club were subsequently handed a three-year ban from European competitions for failing to pay their debts.

Closer to home, Bolton Wanderers players boycotted a pre-season friendly against St Mirren in July 2018 in support of members of the squad who had not received wages or bonuses the previous month. A statement issued by the squad noted that players had not been paid on time on numerous occasions over the course of the previous two years with 'no notification or an explanation as to why'.

It's clear that Rohan's case, which took several years to be heard, still rankles greatly with him. He believes that stricter penalties need to be put in place to ensure that what happened to him doesn't happen to other players in the future. 'It's simple, and the same thing that I'd say about knife crime in the UK. They need to have severe measures. Cases need to be dealt with much quicker and have ramifications,' he argues.

'They're giving clubs years to prove their case and that can't be fair. It doesn't make sense to me. The consequences need to be stronger and more immediate. Clubs should be scared to pull this kind of bullshit, to violate the rules. That's what needs to happen. I don't know how much FIFA really care about that, though, as that part of the market doesn't run in order anyway. They pull a lot of money from the Premier League, La Liga and the Bundesliga but are you going to talk to them about Vietnam, Thailand, India and Moldova? They ain't got time for that. Didier Drogba didn't get paid in China. He left but his case was after my case, but I guarantee his case was dealt with before my case. My case was left in limbo for a while and I couldn't sign for anyone else.

'The Moldovan club were forcing me out of the country. They came into my room and gave me a document but took it back from me. They forced me out of the hotel but I had nowhere to go. I thought they were going to do something to me because these guys were serious guys.'

It's not all been lows though. Now that his career is drawing to a close he can look back on his globetrotting with a smile, thankful that he got to see the world doing something he once loved.

'What does having a good career mean? Does it mean playing in the Premier League or does it mean you made good money?' he asks. 'We forget when the money comes in that we're doing something we love for a living, irrespective of what you earn. We've seen players in the Premier League get stressed and depressed. The true beauty of it is we're doing something we love for a living. If you're earning £1,000 a week but you're smart with it you can still create a nice lifestyle.

'Playing football professionally across the globe is very hostile, very unstable but very exciting. I had an adventure. I saw the world. I went to training on my moped in Thailand and explored some private islands in the afternoon. We'd start training at seven o'clock in the morning and by nine o'clock we were finished. I had the whole day then to spend around a private island on a speedboat. I experienced Songkran, a national holiday over there, with my friends. I lived in Goa in India and got to see different parts of the country with monkeys and snakes.'

It comes as a surprise when someone as well-travelled as Rohan mentions he doesn't like flying, with one particular awayday in India taking its toll.

'I went to an away game where we had to fly from Goa to Mumbai to Kolkata to Sikkim. That was three flights and then a five-and-a-half-hour jeep ride up one of the steepest mountains in the world. All this for one game! There was no barrier and the driver was on his mobile phone, driving close to the side where you could fall off the highest point I've ever been in my life! I was shitting myself!'

So, what does the future hold for Rohan Ricketts? He's returned to Toronto, to be in his four-year-old son's life and seems happy now with his lot.

'I'm not officially retired but I'm not going to play again. I've been coaching and I love that. I got a good education from Arsenal and Spurs, which I'm now passing on to young boys over here,' he enthuses. 'I'm more settled now. I've got peace now. I know where I'm going to be next week. I've done it. I've played at the top under Wenger and Hoddle, played against Cristiano Ronaldo. I've done it at the top and then I've seen the bullshit. I have a bit more control now over what I'm doing. I'm happy and content here.'

David Low is another footballer whose nomadic football career has taken him to 11 countries. The Singapore-born midfielder grew up in South Africa and has chased his dream across five continents. His travels have included spells in Mongolia, Cameroon and Australia. He's also seen at first hand the realities of life as a professional footballer away from the gilded European leagues.

211

'The road was not an easy road. I am compassionate toward other people, especially people from poorer backgrounds or people who are struggling. I know what struggle is. Professional football is cruel,' he concedes.

His peripatetic career began back in Singapore, where he'd returned for 28 months of compulsory National Service. His perseverance ensured this did not halt his ambitions, as it had done to others before him.

'The National Service affects a lot of footballers in Singapore. After it, a lot of them quit the game or they try to make a comeback but they are not good enough. And most lose heart for the game and retire,' he explains. 'For me, I was very persistent and always had a goal to make it as a professional footballer.'

After his mandatory military service, he trialled with a few teams and played with two clubs in Singapore, where racism and political issues were widespread. Rather than be disheartened, it strengthened his ambition to challenge himself internationally.

'If you look at the national team and look at the number of races throughout the population of Singapore, it's a sensitive issue,' he explains. 'I experienced racism and a lot of unprofessionalism. It was a bit corrupt and I didn't want to waste my time trying very hard to break into the game in Singapore where people at the management level don't even care about you as a footballer. All that they care about is to try to use you for their own selfish gains. They are not bothered about developing and helping players there so I decided to take myself abroad. Even if I'd made it in with a Singapore side or the national team I still wouldn't have been satisfied due to the low FIFA rankings and low level of the domestic league. As a footballer, you have to be tested to the best of your ability. I wanted to be challenged in high-level leagues, which made me very persistent and took me abroad to play.'

He knew that his background could count against him overseas but was determined to prove people wrong and make it as a professional footballer.

'There is a stigma about Asian footballers,' he contends. 'Wherever you go, they are looked down on and I've nothing against that. It makes me want to challenge myself even more, to prove people wrong. I'm not the fastest, I'm not the most skilful player, I'm not the most physical player but I take a part of each attribute and form it into my own weapon. I'm an ordinary player but what set me apart was the willingness to develop myself and to challenge myself. I came to football pretty late because of National Service and because of my parents. Asian parents don't really support their kids to be a professional footballer. They are more into, "Study well, get a job, settle down with a family." I knew it was going to be very difficult because some consider other countries' sportspeople to be mentally and physically stronger compared to Asians. Growing up in South Africa made me stronger, too. I tried to make as many contacts as I could, especially from foreign players and coaches.'

It was through one of these acquaintances that his journey began, taking him first to Western Australia before he started a youth coaching role in the US. 'I met some players there, who brought me to their clubs to train. That was how my network grew and how I travelled around the world to play football. One thing led to another, I didn't plan for it,' he admits.

His set of contacts continued to grow, as did the number of stamps on his passport. A Singaporean agent landed him a club in Mongolia, where a Japanese team-mate put him in touch with former Cameroon international Emmanuel Maboang, who played in two World Cups and, notably, against England for the Indomitable Lions in a World Cup quarter-final at Italia 90.

'He brought me to play with his Cameroon team. He was very surprised that I could adapt and play with Africans very well,' says David. 'The most important thing was adaptation, being mentally prepared. Going to a very strong footballing country like Cameroon is not a walk in the park. I knew I was going there to accomplish my goal, which was to sign for an Elite One team, Canon Yaoundé.

I was very pleased but, as a footballer, I wanted more. I moved to another Elite One club in Cameroon called Cosmos de Bafia the following year. I left mid-season to go to Portugal but things didn't go well due to the incompetence of the club president, who was a Portuguese FIFA agent based in Singapore.'

Money was not the main driving force for David, but he recognised at Yaoundé that financial issues among the players were rife and decided to speak up for his team-mates when FIFPro arrived to survey footballers on their working conditions.

'During my football career, the salary that I earned was not a lot of money but was decent enough for a single man like me. It kept me going from one club to another and gave me some savings to contribute to my family and some savings for when I was injured,' explains David.

'That's how I survived but, of course, you get some clubs that are very unscrupulous. They don't want to pay the players on time. They halve the salary when you are injured or when you are not playing well. When I was in Cameroon I spoke up for the local players when the local players' union visited our training session. When I was there they paid me because I was a foreign player and were afraid that I would go and speak to FIFA and all this sort of thing. I was not too bothered about the salary, once it kept me going. The most important aspect was the level of play. Money comes and goes but to prove you can play at that level is something that money cannot buy. That, to me, was more important than a big salary.

'They didn't give me exactly what they promised,' he continues. 'They'd give me half of it or three-quarters of it. I didn't complain, I just took whatever they gave me. When FIFPro came to Cameroon to do a survey with the players they were very surprised to see an Asian player there so they wanted to interview me.'

David was just one of 14,000 professional footballers in 54 countries across the world surveyed by independent assessors from the University of Manchester in what is believed to be the world's largest survey of professional athletes in any sport using direct participant data.

'I tried to help my fellow team-mates because they are there every season and they are suffering because they are not getting paid on time and some don't get paid for a few months or even for almost the whole season,' he says. 'They have a lot of internal problems there so I spoke up for them to FIFPro. I wanted to be a voice for them so maybe something could be done.'

He heard recently from one of his former team-mates there that things are improving as FIFPro are now involved with a local football players' union in Cameroon responsible for players' welfare. 'I hope things can get better for them. It was an eye-opener for me, seeing how tough the football was and the hardships most locals face daily. That's why the hunger and desire to succeed is there,' he stresses.

David witnessed the problems first hand in Cameroon and is adamant that these sorts of issues are a worldwide problem affecting professional footballers outside of the elite.

'It is not only in Africa. It's happening in Asia, Eastern Europe and South America. It even happened recently in Western Europe, in Denmark at Lyngby BK. The players don't complain because they want to keep their job and use it as a platform to go to another club. They know they are being mistreated, though. I went to Portugal and a lot of players were not getting paid. It's only those at top clubs like Porto, Braga and Sporting Lisbon who are getting paid.

'One of my football friends signed a contract in the Portuguese top tier and never got paid a single euro. He played a whole season there for free just to try and catapult himself into another league. It didn't happen for him and he went back to Indonesia, where there are problems, too.'

As an example, the players at Portuguese second division side SAD Olhanense threatened strike action and issued a collective notice of termination of contract in early 2015, having gone without their salaries for more than three months.

'In south-east Asia, the mentality of management is often very backward,' David continues. 'They are very fickle-minded when it comes to foreign players. When they get a foreign player they expect instant success or else they sack the player immediately and want a replacement. They don't realise that it takes time to adapt to a new culture, that it takes time to adapt to the playing style.'

He cites a case of a South American footballer who died in Indonesia after going unpaid for more than four months. Diego Mendieta was a Paraguayan forward with Persis Solo, a club based in Central Java who reportedly owed him US$12,000 in back pay. He was subsequently unable to afford his hospital care or a much-longed-for return to South America. The 32-year-old died on 3 December 2012 reportedly after contracting typhoid and suffering a cytomegalovirus infection, over 15,000km away from his wife and three children. Prior to his death, he had struggled to pay for food and accommodation, relying on the goodwill of friends and fans. A few days after his passing his salary arrears were paid to his widow. The club went unpunished.

David reiterates that it is a global problem, not limited to Indonesia, Cameroon or Eastern Europe.

'In south-east Asia, a huge number of local and foreign players are not getting paid properly. In Eastern Europe players are not getting paid properly. It's all over the world,' he maintains. 'I highlighted Cameroon as I played there and saw it with my own eyes. I have travelled around the world and spoken to many players in many countries and they told me the same thing – that they are suffering. Modern football is like this. It's only the top clubs where the players get paid. There's an injustice in the wage system. The rich get richer and the poor get poorer. Very soon there will be a huge imbalance and you will see clubs spiralling out of control. It is a very unstable career.'

He has also seen former team-mates forced out of their clubs against their will, although he points out that being involved with any club is not completely straightforward. He has made the best of each opportunity, with a move to New Zealand his only regret. However, for David, the good experiences outweigh the bad.

'I made a mistake signing for a club in New Zealand. I should have been more patient. The style of football, especially in the southern part of New Zealand, is very direct. They don't really play football, it's football in the air,' he laughs. 'Chivas USA folded while I was there briefly. Then I went and played with a Mexican club in the US fourth tier with the hope of going to a club in Mexico. It was a little bit difficult and Mexico is not a very safe country and I was warned not to go there on my own. I was in Italy, too, with a free-agents team, Equipe Lombardia, under the management of the late Emiliano Mondonico, who played pre-season games against Serie A, B, C, D and E teams with the view to getting a contract with a club. Italy was very difficult because of the rules relating to my non-EU background. It was nonetheless a great experience.

'Mongolia was also another good experience. The players there are developing very quickly to become a good footballing country. There's been an influx of foreign players and coaches in their league. They have a very strong futsal background as it is a cold country. I think they spend more time playing futsal than football, which is how they develop their technique and close control. I spent some time with a lower-league team in Germany, a Swiss tier-two reserve team and in the USL, which helped me to develop as a player.

'Now that I am semi-retired I can look back and have no regrets. The best moments were when I signed in Cameroon, won the Mongolian Cup, when I had a chance to train with Chivas USA in MLS and my time in Italy. I also had the privilege of training under former Celtic player and Hibernian manager John Hughes. I am very proud of my journey, that I am a real professional footballer who went around the world and tested myself at a high level.'

His playing career may be coming to a close but I wouldn't bet against David Low coaching in a dozen countries in the next decade or so. 'I had some injuries and have since semi-retired. I just got my AFC C coaching licence and Holland might be my next stop. Things are winding down now as I'm 35 in November. I still love to play and want to make it as a coach. I just hope that all my experiences of playing abroad will help me transition into a very good coach. I have the passion to coach abroad and recently had an interview with Chinese soccer academies. Hopefully, things can move forward,' he says.

He's not ruling out one final adventure as a professional footballer, though. 'I still keep myself fit as I believe in football anything can happen. You never know,' he concludes.

After speaking to David, I couldn't help but be reminded of a quote from Pelé – "Success is no accident. It is hard work, perseverance, learning, studying, sacrifice and most of all, love of what you are doing or learning to do."

The aforementioned 2016 report by FIFPro, in which David took part, studied the working conditions in the professional game, including the role of the transfer market.

This Global Employment Report split the global football market into three tiers, with the top tier made up of a global elite of players with superior talent and skill.

The second tier included a large number of professional footballers playing for clubs offering more moderate but decent employment conditions in well-regulated and relatively sustainably financed markets. Finally, the third tier represented the majority of players, who are under constant pressure to extend their careers in the game and face precarious employment conditions, including a large degree of personal and contractual abuse.

The aim of the survey was 'to raise awareness of the realities faced by footballers – especially those who are not among the elite of the sport – with a view to understanding and improving conditions in the industry.' The findings were certainly a world away from transfers announced in tandem with grime artists and the glitz of Sky Sports's deadline-day coverage. Some of the revelations are certainly eye-opening.

The report revealed that 29 per cent of players who moved for a transfer fee said they were pressured to go to another club or did not go to the team they wanted to, despite having an ongoing contract. Over 20 per cent were aware of players being forced to train alone, a tactic used by some clubs to try and force a player to move elsewhere. Around 45 per cent of participants earned less than US$1,000 per month, while a similar figure reported experiencing delayed salary payments over the previous two seasons. The global average length of a player's contract was just over 22 months, with those earning least having the shortest contracts. The report followed on from a study in 2012, which looked at the working standards of professional footballers in 12 countries.

Jonas Baer-Hoffmann, FIFPro Europe's Secretary General, says, 'At that point, the focus was on employment relationships, the non-payment of salaries, violence and discrimination. It was quite a successful report but was quite a specific region. We expanded it as we had been going through the same kind of discussions for years with our counterparts in clubs, UEFA and FIFA about some of those problems. We wanted to take it from a question about, "Does this really happen?" to "Okay, it happens but how do we resolve it?" It was a tool to give us insight into what type of mechanisms to put in place to help players better and to get a feel for different markets so that we can help our unions if their players were offered a contract there.'

The aim was to use first-hand feedback from players worldwide to provide a balanced and realistic overview of the conditions and experiences of footballers throughout the industry, and will be repeated every few years. Almost one-quarter of FIFPro's 65,000 affiliated players were surveyed. The Premier League and some other elite leagues were not included, but Jonas doesn't believe this will have skewed the results.

'We were missing some of the major markets but we spoke to the researchers about what that would do to the data,' he explains. 'But they said, "It might change it slightly. For every England that is not included, we also have five other smaller markets that are not included", so it would not make such a significant difference.'

The study divided the global football market into three broadly defined tiers, with the top tier comprising players predominantly based in the big five European leagues – the Premier League, Bundesliga, La Liga, Serie A and Ligue 1.

'The 98 per cent are in the middle and bottom tiers,' says Jonas. 'The reality is that we have a very small piece of the industry who, because they are the best in the world and because we live in a capitalist society, are able to demand incredibly high wages for what they do. However, if you look at our pyramid of membership you really see the three tiers. The top tier can command a lot for what they do. Then we have a middle section, which is made up of less-wealthy players but who are in very stable economies, such as the Scandinavian countries, the US or Australia. And then you have all the rest, which accounts for about 45,000 of the 60,000 footballers that we represent. Their careers are very precarious, they go from contract to contract on fairly low wages with very high frequencies of contract breaches. It's a very, very tricky environment for them to know where they'll be next year and where their career will be going.'

At this end of the football pyramid, FIFPro observes a lot of abuse. 'For example, in Serbia, more than 80 per cent of the players said their agent decided where they were going. The players don't actually have much choice as to where they continue their careers,' says Jonas.

Accounts of both physical and psychological abuse of players are common. One in ten players surveyed reported experiencing physical violence while almost one-sixth had been victims of bullying or harassment. Overseas players were more than twice as likely to suffer discrimination and also more likely to experience physical violence. Jonas is under no illusions as to the reason for this.

'Around issues like discrimination and abuse, we know that our numbers are just the tip of the iceberg,' he maintains. 'The background to this for me seems to be quite obvious – that there is still a pretty large degree of racism out there in the football community.'

Over 20 per cent of players reported being forced to train alone, a method often used by clubs to pressure players into ending, changing or signing a contract or even to force them out. Another 15 per cent had seen this happen to team-mates. This was more prevalent among players in the higher – but not the highest – salary scales.

'Clubs will bring in high-earning talent at the beginning of the year, speculating on certain sporting success but the moment that doesn't materialise their budgets don't hold to pay those players their wages. They will then resort more frequently to those techniques and say, "Look, either you accept to play for half the money that we promised or you just better get out of here." That's why those higher earners are maybe more likely to have those kinds of experiences,' explains Jonas.

As we saw earlier in Rohan Ricketts's case, secondary contracts are commonplace in some countries and usually cover payment for the use of image rights. However, these are often misused by clubs, particularly in developing footballing countries.

'What we've been looking at is that, to the disadvantage of the player, a large part of their remuneration is taken out of the employment contract and put in the image rights contract to avoid tax contributions,' says Jonas. 'The problem with that is the player doesn't have the benefit of social security contributions when he retires but, more importantly, it is very, very difficult to enforce the payment of the image rights contract if the player gets into difficulty with his club. You usually end up just getting the employment contract as the courts do not always recognise the image rights contract as part of your employment conditions.

'These guys are sometimes on a national minimum wage in their employment contract and maybe a couple of thousand extra in the image rights contract. But, thinking about who these guys are, it is also quite preposterous to think their image rights are that valuable because there is not a lot of marketing activities going on there.'

In late 2017, FIFPro dropped a legal bid against FIFA to abolish the current transfer system but is still in intense negotiations with the world governing body, along with the European Club Association and World Leagues Forum. Progress has been made but Jonas admits that there's still a lot of work to be done on protecting players worldwide from some of the issues we've seen.

'The problem is that we've created a market in which two clubs are bidding and negotiating about the value of a player's services. It's a trading market. When you go back to 2001, and the history of when this system was established, it should be a negotiation between an employer and an employee about when, and under which circumstances, someone can terminate a contract,' says Jonas. 'We do need some rules to ensure that this shouldn't happen right in the middle of a season, that you can't just walk away from your club three games before the end of the season and join a competitor, and you need to have a commitment to a large part of the contract. But, if you have a five-year contract, FIFPro has long held the view that there needs to be a period within that contract where if the player accepts to pay a reasonable amount of compensation to terminate the contract then that door must be open.

'That door is effectively closed now for the player, while contract breaches by clubs are commonplace. And the consequence is that the only way you move between two clubs is a transfer. And that has created this market between the clubs where these extreme amounts are being negotiated, where we have no real fair distribution of the talent and, often times, many players who are not in the elite do not even have a choice where they are going.

'We think that if we don't change the triggers within the market and why people act the way they do – what motivates them, what their commercial and sporting interests are – we will not be able to regulate the transfer system effectively. If the club decides to breach the contract – which, as you see from the report, happens all the time in the form of non-payment – then the consequences for the club also need to be severe. That's what we've been negotiating, especially at the end of 2017, and we've been able to make some improvements.'

A six-year cooperation agreement has been signed with FIFA, which FIFPro stated 'has helped set in motion the biggest changes to football transfer rules since 2001'.

'At the end of 2017 we had very intense negotiations with FIFA, the European Club Association and the World Leagues Forum around what is really the abuse of contracts for players – non-payment, being pushed to terminate their contracts or accept lower pay because they've been made exempt from the team and made to run through the snow for six hours a day, for example,' Jonas continues.

'We've been able to find an agreement on these sorts of things and tighten them up, improve the arbitration system and a few other parameters around it. Hopefully, this will lead to more players having better tools to protect themselves and, hopefully, the clubs understanding that there are higher consequences for their actions and, therefore, may think twice about rejecting a player and not paying him any longer.'

Things were going well for Rhema Obed at Arsenal. He was part of the club's famed academy, which won two consecutive Premier Academy League titles, and had represented England at under-16 level. Just a few years later he found himself relying on his Romanian team-mate's mother for food.

He'd never even considered playing abroad but when he ran out of options in England he began to broaden his horizons. It was a decision that took him to Singapore, Israel, Greece, Slovenia and a nadiral move to Romania.

'The idea of playing abroad was a bit far-fetched as a youngster as you always have the ambition of making it in England,' Rhema admits. 'Having grown up in London, Arsenal was all I knew when it came to football. And even if it didn't happen there, something else in England would have made a bit more sense to me.'

His eventual release from The Gunners coincided with his parents' separation, but he still had a fierce ambition to make it as a professional footballer.

'I didn't consider retiring as I always have confidence in myself,' he says. 'It was a bit hard, it was a big setback. I was going through a lot of personal issues at the time. My parents' separation played quite a part in the way I was viewing things, the way I was viewing life. Even though it was pretty late compared to separations in other families, at 17 years old it still had an effect on me. I had to mix that with the fact that I was no longer at Arsenal. I was still very determined to make it somehow. If not here, anywhere was better than nowhere. So when the opportunity came to play abroad I grabbed it and didn't look back.'

The offers weren't forthcoming at home so he began to look at the alternatives, vowing that if it wasn't going to work out for him in England, he'd make it work elsewhere. After 12 months without a contract, he packed his bags for a club in the Singapore Premier League. Just a year, and two clubs, later he found himself in the Romanian capital, being asked to leave his hotel room.

Rapid Bucharest had scouted Rhema when he was playing for a Greek side and were desperate to add him to their squad for a promotion push, having been demoted to the second tier due to their financial situation.

'I didn't know it at the time but they were going through a semi-crisis,' Rhema laments. 'I wasn't aware of that when I signed. All I knew was that Rapid Bucharest were a club that I used to see all the time in Europe. They had been in Europe the year before I arrived and I remembered that. So when the name came up I just remembered them as a European regular. I did a bit of Googling on the stadium and the fans and things like that. But the nature of their situation, I was not aware of at all.'

It was an inauspicious start to life in Romania. On his first day, hotel staff approached him and told him his room had not been paid for and that he'd have to leave. The issue was finally resolved and, shrugging it off, Rhema made his way to training with his new club. When he arrived he discovered that the players were planning a strike and were not going to play until they got paid. He hadn't even made an appearance for the side at this stage.

'I had to pay for the room and the food that I was eating, as I'd been under the impression that since they bought me and had put me in a hotel until I signed a contract that they were paying for it,' he recalls. 'They then put me in a *cantonament*, which are places they stay when they have games. And then I heard about the strike. The game got cancelled but, eventually, they did get paid.

'When I was made aware of this, I told my agent that, "I don't think this is right, there's something fishy about this." They were lying to him and lying to me. Telling me that we're going to get paid, the money's coming in. So they kind of sweet-talked me into signing the deal, not knowing what was ahead. I did get money to start off with. I got money for a deposit for my house. I think I got one month's salary at the beginning, in August or September. I got one salary so I was under the impression that it would continue. I didn't see anything then until just before Christmas. My then girlfriend, and now wife, came along with me and she was working as an English teacher in a private school. So that was helping to fund the rent. And, luckily, I had a landlord who was very kind to me at the time as he knew the situation. As you can imagine, that situation wasn't one that anyone would want to be in. When I spoke to friends and family, they couldn't believe it.'

Financial concerns intensified when they learned just before Christmas that Rhema's partner had fallen pregnant. After an extended winter break, due to adverse weather conditions, he returned to Romania to utter turmoil. He was frozen out of the team and the club began isolating him from training. He had signed a contract worth up to €100,000, including bonuses, over three years, so stood his ground.

'They were telling me to, "Sign this, sign that." So I knew what the score was from then. They were really trying to force me out,' he reveals. 'There was no way I was going to let that happen. So, once I realised, I tried to compromise. I was still training, and training well. But the manager who originally signed me was demoted and a club legend was brought in.'

Viorel Moldovan, who had a brief spell at Coventry City in the late 1990s, took over and Rhema was not part of his first-team plans.

'The financial situation wasn't working, I wasn't playing and I was being forced out. They were trying to get me to sign things I knew I wasn't supposed to be signing in order to get me out. It was just getting worse and worse,' he explains. 'I had very few friends there but had one friend in particular, who I still speak with, out of gratitude for what he did for me.'

Goalkeeper Dragoș Plopeanu, who is now an assistant coach with the Mongolian national team, took Rhema under his wing and brought him home every other day for his mother's traditional Romanian cooking.

'I used to go to his house after being forced to train with the youngsters,' Rhema recalls. 'He wasn't part of that situation but he would always sympathise with me. Out of grace and love, he offered to give me food. I never tasted it before but I'll never forget it as it kept me going. He's the only man I still talk to from that time.

'At the time he was helping me out, I realised that they were not going to pay me anything so I told my wife to pack her bags and go back home where she'd be more comfortable. We had found out that we were expecting twins so it got more intense! It got to February and we were surviving on her money, which was around €1,000 a month, but I thought it was best for her to go home to be closer to family. And, also, the situation I was going through wasn't ideal for us.'

Rhema could have left at any time but, of course, that was what Rapid wanted. He didn't leave until he had made the decision to sue the club.

'I went straight to FIFA and that is how the case got publicised. The club wanted me to go through their country's courts, but their court system means the clubs can keep the players even though their contracts are not being respected,' he explains. 'They're allowed to keep the players as they're seen as assets because the club was under administration, so they can profit from them even when they're not being paid. They were smart as they weren't paying us our full salary but they would give us something. They gave me nothing, but the squad members that were playing, they were doing what they could to keep them happy. It wasn't a full salary but at least they were going home with something. In doing this, of course, it created a lot of division between players who were not being paid anything. And I was one of those players. When my wife left, I did most of the dealings with FIFA on my own. When they responded to me, that's when I decided to leave.'

After a two-year wait, Rhema won the case and was awarded almost half of his contract. The club were also warned by FIFA that if they didn't pay him they would be deducted six points, a potentially devastating penalty for a club in pole position for promotion to the top tier.

'The year I was there, they'd got promoted but had since been relegated again so were back in the second division. They were on top of the league and the decision was given about a month before the season was due to end. They only had three or four games left so the threat of them losing six points meant they panicked,' says Rhema. 'They were calling me and trying to negotiate with me, offering me more money if they got promoted, for example. My agent told me not to sign anything and eventually they paid me. They were about to go bust.'

One month later, Rapid Bucharest were declared bankrupt by a Romanian court. It'll be a while before they'll be European competition perennials again, with the club's current incarnation currently languishing in the third level of Romanian football.

It was the worst experience of his career but it didn't put Rhema off his travels. At his most recent club, though, in the Slovenian Prva Liga, he also encountered problems.

'I did have issues there but it wasn't as bad as it was in Romania,' says the Londoner. 'They would always pay but they paid whenever they wanted. They would never respect the date that they put in contracts. And I find this lack of respect for contracts is common in a lot of Eastern European countries.'

Now a player intermediary, he would still recommend a spell abroad for young, British players but admits he'd have reservations about particular countries.

'I'd be very sceptical on the destination,' he admits. 'Based on my experience, I would never advise any of my players to go to a place like Romania, and even half of the Greek top division can be a bit dodgy. If it was any of these nations that I know have financial issues, it would have to be to one of the top two clubs in that country. When I was in Greece, half of the top-flight teams weren't paying properly. They were late with payments and it was creating problems for a lot of players. My agent at the time, who is now my business partner, is Greek and a lot of dealings they do now are outside of Greece because of this issue. You see a lot of British players these days going to Germany, which is the complete opposite. If it was somewhere like that, I would definitely push them towards that. I'd just be very wary of countries where you know there's a chance you're not going to get your money.

'It's not worth the hassle when all you want to do, as a player, is play football. You don't want the stress of not knowing when you're going to be able to pay your bills or send money home. I know certain players who were in the exact same situation as me but their families relied solely upon them. The pressure got on top of them as they weren't able to provide.'

Former Leicester City defender Jordan Stewart can attest to that. He was holidaying in Los Angeles in 2010 when an agent, claiming to represent Greek club Skoda Xanthi, phoned him out of the blue to inform him that Sheffield United had accepted a bid for him.

'It didn't really make sense to me as no one from Sheffield United had contacted me about it,' Jordan recalls.

He'd always harboured an ambition to play abroad and, realising his first-team opportunities would be limited with The Blades, agreed a deal with the Greek Superleague side. The players were paid by cheque, which they had to cash in a bank themselves, and alarms bells rang a few months into his stay.

'I took my January cheque to the bank and the teller was pointing at the date,' he recalls. 'I wondered what was wrong but looked at the date and it was 15 February. I went back to the club and asked, "What's going on? We're supposed to get paid." They blamed problems in the wider economy but assured me that I'd get my money. I just let it fly that time as I'd heard a few things before.

'February's payment was also late, though, which I told the club was unacceptable. I'd always been paid on time elsewhere and expected the same process in Greece. I'd signed a contract and expected the club to abide by it. After the third time it happened, I left. I'd signed a two-year deal there but I couldn't go through the uncertainty over being paid any more.'

He enjoyed his time in Greece and admits he would have stayed longer were it not for the salary issues. 'Where I played in Greece was beautiful,' he enthuses. 'It was ten minutes away from the sea. The food was nice and the people were friendly. You're used to getting paid on time and then, all of a sudden, it's almost like you're working for free. I think if you look at the economy of Greece as a whole – how much debt they've gotten into and the way the country is run – it all trickles down. Football is a sport but it's still a business. It's a disorganised country, which is a shame because it's a beautiful place.'

To paraphrase Jordan, football is the world's most popular sport, but it's still a badly run business in many countries. It may be too late for Rohan Ricketts, too late for David Low's Cameroonian team-mates, too late for Rhema Obed and too late for Diego Mendieta, but FIFPro's efforts should provide some relief to its 45,000 members struggling on the lower rungs of the global game.

The Past and
the Future

D ESPITE his remarkable success at Manchester United, Sir
Alex Ferguson had a mixed record in the transfer market.
For every Cristiano Ronaldo, there was a Bebé. For every
Peter Schmeichel, a Massimo Taibi.

His final signing at Old Trafford, before handing over
the reins to David Moyes, was the £15m capture of Crystal
Palace's exciting young winger Wilfried Zaha. However, Zaha
struggled to break into the first team under Moyes, making just
four appearances for United before returning to Palace for an
undisclosed fee.

Ferguson's first signing at the club was a lot more successful.
When the Scot moved to Old Trafford from Aberdeen he
immediately identified the need to strengthen the right-back
position. So he got his captain to put out the feelers.

'I got a call from Bryan Robson,' recalls Viv Anderson. 'We'd
roomed together for England and had become good friends. He
knew my contract at Arsenal was up and had suggested me to his
new manager, who asked him to give me a call.'

Anderson was 31 at the time and initially believed Robson
was pulling his leg about a return to his boyhood club, which
he'd been released from as a youngster. 'I wasn't really that

disappointed at being let go by United in my teens. They had Best, Charlton and Law at the club when I was first there. But it was great to get an opportunity to go back.'

The circumstances surrounding Ferguson's first signing at United, however, proved farcical. 'I met them in a hotel room in Nottingham. The chairman at the time, Martin Edwards, came in and asked had I seen the manager. He left and Alex came in another door and asked had I seen the chairman. This went on for 15 minutes!' laughs Viv.

When it came to the decision to move, Anderson – like most footballers when considering their careers – had to think about number one. 'We'd just bought a house in London and I went home to my wife and said, "Come on, we're moving." You have to be selfish and put football first and family second.'

Anderson had no agent when he signed for United, relying on an accountant who did all his paperwork. By the time he'd moved into management with Robson at Middlesbrough, he noticed a sea change in the game.

'Agents had become more prominent. By the time I'd left Manchester United to go to Sheffield Wednesday, gone to Barnsley and gone to Boro with Bryan Robson, the agent culture was everywhere. It was practically a given by that stage. Invariably, you had to go through an agent to get the player you wanted,' he recalls.

He was also at the forefront of the changing face of English football, whose riches were now attracting big-name players from overseas. He's in no doubt that the vast sums of money coming into the game were a huge factor in the changing demographic of Premier League players. Sir Alex Ferguson famously signed Eric Cantona from Leeds United after a phone conversation about another player and, similarly, Boro's astonishing capture of Fabrizio Ravanelli also came about by chance.

'We went to visit Juventus really to see Gianluca Vialli. And then, in a conversation at dinner later on, Fabrizio Ravanelli's name came up. He'd just scored the winning goal in a European Cup final for Juventus and they said, "Make us an offer." We couldn't believe it and went back to Steve Gibson, the Boro chairman, who made an offer and got the player,' recalls Viv. 'Now, to convince the player to go to Middlesbrough when he'd just scored the European Cup winner and thought he'd be at Juventus for the rest of his career was quite tricky! But he came and he really embraced it. He brought a different culture to Middlesbrough with his fitness regime and the things he used to do, which helped the players around him. It was interesting, to say the least. Juninho was another one, who left Brazil to come to the cold north-east. He's another one who embraced the idea and the fans took to him with their hearts, so it was a good thing for his career. He subsequently came back time and time again.'

Ravanelli, known as The White Feather and who Robson hailed as 'one of the best strikers in the world' cost Boro £7m in 1996 – the third-highest transfer fee in English history at the time. It actually looked a bargain when he bagged a hat-trick on his league debut against Liverpool.

What, though, would a talent like Ravanelli cost nowadays? Using the Bank of England's inflation calculator, his fee would equate to just under £12.5m in today's money, or £2.5m less than the club paid for Nottingham Forest's Britt Assombalonga in July 2017. In other words, a snip. Using the standard rate of inflation is unsatisfactory, though, as it's clear that the level of football inflation outperforms that of the wider economy.

Paul Tomkins first tried to work out a comparison for transfer fees across eras when analysing five decades of Liverpool transfer activity for his book *Dynasty: Fifty Years of Shankly's Liverpool.*

'For each manager, I wanted to look at what they spent, but how could you compare £60,000 being a huge fee in the mid-1960s to 2009 when it was often less than a week's wage?' recalls Paul.

He came up with what he called the Relative Transfer System, which compared every deal to the English record fee of the day. So if a transfer fee was 90 per cent of the 1962 record of £115,000, it would equate to 90 per cent of £15m in 1997.

'Then, after reading the book, accountant and analyst, Graeme Riley, got in touch to suggest a better system, which would be to recreate the Retail Price Index but with footballers instead of a basket of produce,' Paul continues. 'And so we created the Transfer Price Index. From a starting point of the 1992/93 season, as going back any further was problematic, we took all the transfer prices for anyone who changed clubs that season, and found the average price. So in the first season of the Premier League era this was around £500,000.

'This could then be compared to subsequent seasons. If the average price of a player rose by a certain amount, this would be reflected in the index. Then you could retrospectively work out what it would cost in today's money, or what we called the Current Transfer Purchase Price. The average almost always rises, but following the collapse of ITV Digital and during the global financial crisis, the average did dip as well.'

In January 2017, the index valued what Boro paid for Ravanelli at £36.2m.

'In my opinion that is far, far too cheap. You've now got centre-backs going for £50m so, with that in mind, I would pay at least £50m,' argued Viv Anderson at the time.

Paul agreed. 'Ravanelli looks an absolute bargain at £36.2m in today's money, given his 31 goals in his single season at Middlesbrough. I think I saw him saunter about at Anfield in a 5-1 defeat, so his work rate and attitude may not always have been desirable, although his opening-day hat-trick against The Reds lives painfully long in the memory. Boro were one of the first clubs to import younger, top-class foreign talent, rather than bring in ageing big names. I imagine some of those earlier imports had to do more adjusting than they do now, with more cosmopolitan teams and managers. Ravanelli cost less than half what Alan Shearer did at the same time, so he had to have seemed cheap at the time, too. Viv is also taking the anchoring point of John Stones, it seems, and the belief that centre-backs should be cheap. Rio Ferdinand twice broke the English transfer record – young centre-backs aren't always cheap. Ferdinand to United works out at around £95m in today's money. He cost an absolute fortune back in the day.'

Fast-forward 19 months to August 2018 and Ferdinand's deal seems even more extravagant, with a Current Transfer Purchase Price of almost £198m. Ravanelli's adjusted value, meanwhile, looks a lot more realistic at just over £75m.

'Much of it depends on what any particular season was like overall, in terms of what a player would now cost,' explains Paul. 'So in 2004, when Chelsea were spending around £25m on individual players, that was in a depressed market; most other clubs were topping out at £15m max. So with less money sluicing around in general at the time, Chelsea's spending, which came from external funding, now seems even greater. So we can say that a £25m player in 2004 was very expensive at that time, based on how low the average that year was. So in today's money that will always remain a higher figure than, say, in other seasons when £25m was less of a big deal.

'Whether or not people think the fee makes sense in today's money, they're all calculated in the same scientific way. As of 2016, the average price of a Premier League player was 13 times what it was in 1992/93, whereas standard UK inflation is not even twice what it was 24 years ago. So football inflation runs more than seven times faster than normal inflation.'

Looking through the Current Transfer Purchase Price for the top 100 Premier League buys is certainly eyebrow-raising, but many current values seem pretty fair. It's not unrealistic to imagine Ed Woodward shelling out the guts of £225m for a Dwight Yorke and Andy Cole strike force.

However, several figures immediately jump out. Shaun Wright-Phillips cost Chelsea £21m in 2005, which equates to an eye-watering figure just north of £150m in today's money.

'Wright-Phillips was an interesting one, given that, as a Liverpool fan, I remember loads of Reds thinking we should sign him around 2004,' recalls Paul. 'But it just never happened at Chelsea and now we might forget how promising he looked. I even coined a theory inspired by Wright-Phillips, which was about how a young player, or cheap buy, can be gently introduced to a team with little pressure and imperceptibly improve and adapt, only to then struggle once sold for a big fee. Initially, he has time to get to know the club where he is slowly emerging, knows his team-mates, knows the ideas and the tactics. He presumably has a settled life. He may be nervous at first but no one really knows his name, and over time he gets a taste of what's expected and adjusts. Within a year or two he's showing his true qualities and is improving with experience.

'Then he gets yanked from that stable bubble and moved to a new club, which starts with upheaval in his personal life. The fee means that there is no settling-in period. He has to get to know the new tactics, new team-mates and is burdened by new expectations and this sudden need to prove he's worth a small fortune. If he's bought to be a squad player he no longer has the rhythm of playing that he had before and people will expect him to break into the team and do great things – but when he emerged at his first club the process was so low-key. Do his new team-mates expect more from him, as he cost a lot and is therefore also presumably on high wages? It's almost a sink-or-swim situation.'

Despite currently holding the British transfer record, Paul Pogba's move back to Manchester United ranks in 16th place on Paul's top 100. While some deals like Wayne Rooney and Rio Ferdinand to United, and Didier Drogba and Michael Essien to Chelsea proved value for money, the amount of flops in the top 15 is remarkable.

Andriy Shevchenko's £50m move to Chelsea tops the list, now valued at four times that amount, while Fernando Torres's deadline-day transfer to Stamford Bridge also features. The names of two Argentinians, Juan Sebastián Verón and Ángel Di María, who both failed to make an impact at Old Trafford, also stand out.

Paul has analysed over 3,000 moves and has come to the conclusion that only 50 to 60 per cent of the most expensive transfers succeed, for various reasons.

'Every expensive player bought during the Premier League era had to have done some pretty special things in the past for people to pay a high fee, but almost half go on to fail,' he says. 'Any time there's a major change, a player's fortunes can change; so if a player is at his original club and a new manager arrives, his fortunes can change for the better or for the worse. If another player is sold, perhaps the one who set up his goals, his fortunes can change for the worse. But a move of club for a big fee means that every single area of his game – his relationship with other players, his home life, his training regime, his role within the team and so on – all automatically change. There are so many elements that can go wrong.

'I know Stan Collymore felt he wasn't helped much by Liverpool when he joined,' Paul continues. 'He had his own issues as well, but the club didn't go out of its way to make him feel settled, and tactically he seemed to be told to "Go and do what we bought you for", which was the old Liverpool way.'

Collymore's move to Liverpool from Nottingham Forest is now valued at just over £90m, slightly less than his subsequent sale to Villa two years later.

'I think his fee holds up really well for the ability he had, which seemed limitless, and he's also an interesting case because, once adjusted for inflation, the £8.5m Liverpool paid for him in 1995 will always work out less in current day money than the £7m they sold him to Aston Villa for in 1997, given that average

237

prices had fallen by the time he was sold. So, in a deflated market, £7m was relatively more than £8.5m had been when fees were generally higher.'

I remember thinking the world had gone mad when Manchester United shelled out around £7m for Andy Cole in 1995. Of course, nowadays it wouldn't get you half a Daley Blind. During every transfer window fans vent their spleen at the rise of transfer fees, but Paul believes this is simply down to a form of cognitive bias known as the anchoring effect.

'The anchoring heuristic came from the work of Amos Tversky and Daniel Kahneman,' Paul explains. 'They realised that if they asked someone to quickly give an estimate for the sum 1x2x3x4x5x6x7x8 they would get a much lower guess than if they asked them to estimate 8x7x6x5x4x3x2x1, which is, of course the exact same question, just in reverse order. Starting with the number one anchored the reply to a lower figure. Similarly, they asked their students to guess how many countries there were in Africa, but only after they'd picked a random number in a seemingly unrelated act. However, if the random number was higher, they guessed higher for the number of countries in Africa, and if it was lower they guessed lower. Whatever their random number was it anchored their guess to that kind of ballpark figure.

'So we can be anchored with football fees – in terms of what someone is "worth" – by transfers from a year or two ago. We get fixated on that being the going rate. But whenever there's a new TV deal – say one that doubles the amount of money pumped into football – then the average price of a footballer will also double within a couple of years.'

It's not a recent phenomenon. When Falkirk smashed the world transfer record in 1922 for West Ham's Syd Puddefoot, one newspaper editorial raged, 'We are amazed that any club should pay such an astounding price for his transfer. When will this folly on the part of football clubs come to an end? What is to be the limit? Is there to be a limit?' It is thought that The Hammers asked for the then-exorbitant figure of £5,000 – or double the previous record fee – in the knowledge that Falkirk would not be able to match it, akin to what Barcelona believed was a prohibitive release clause in Neymar's contract 95 years later. However, Falkirk fans helped raise the fee for the Englishman who subsequently failed to settle in Scotland, with one journalist writing, 'He has learned the old, old lesson that money is not everything, and he spends his days (and some of his nights) sighing prodigiously for London.' Syd's brother Len followed him to The Bairns but made only one or two appearances, a bit like that time Crystal Palace signed Jonathan Benteke.

The 57-year-old Diego Maradona lives quietly in Harrogate after a relatively successful career with Sheffield United. He enjoys the odd glass of ale in his local, The Fat Badger, and regularly cheers on the pub's darts team. Unlikely? Not overly so. In 1978, the then United manager Harry Haslam was impressed with a 17-year-old Maradona on a scouting trip to Argentina. A £200,000 bid was put in place but the deal collapsed due to further financial demands. Haslam signed fellow Argentinian Alex Sabella instead, who was sold two years later to Leeds United as The Blades dropped to the fourth tier of English football.

Super-agent Jon Smith, who represented the Argentinian for three years, believes a young Maradona would now fetch a world-record fee. 'In the current market, with the hype that would surround him, Diego, at that age, would be worth over £190m plus add-ons,' says Jon.

When Paul Gascoigne joined Tottenham for a British record transfer fee of £2.2m in 1988, a pile of fan mail awaited him. He excitedly opened the first letter, which turned out to be from Sir Alex Ferguson, slamming him for reneging on a gentleman's agreement to join Manchester United. Gazza's record fee equates to just under £6m today, using the UK inflation calculator. A little on the low side for the player Ferguson was most disappointed about not signing while manager at Old Trafford.

Tony Cottee's move from West Ham to Everton broke the record again just a month later, in a deal brokered by Jon Smith. He believes a player like Gascoigne would also be worth a world record-breaking figure in 2018.

'He'd be worth a huge amount now,' he contends. 'What would Spurs sell Harry Kane for now? £200m? You'd be looking at something similar. Fred got transferred to Manchester United for £50m and it didn't even make a headline, just a little paragraph in the *Daily Express*. I've just had a new knee and I'm probably valued at £10m!'

Gary Mellor agrees. 'It'd be huge, wouldn't it? Gazza at his peak was phenomenal. You can't imagine what eye-watering numbers he'd have made in today's game. My fear for the English market is that most of the money is going out of the country. The English game has had a bit of a boost with some of the results its underage sides have produced. I'm hoping that success is because they're around the likes of Paul Pogba and Mo Salah. The marketplace is saturated with players from overseas, which is blocking the path for players like Paul Gascoigne to come through. Would he have played for Newcastle United as early as he did in today's market? I hope he would.'

I asked a few stars from Gazza's era, who featured in Team Tactix, what they might be worth in 2018 but they were too modest to estimate. 'Bryan Robson? £100m. Me? £1m,' laughs Viv Anderson, for example.

Faustina Asprilla, however, could never be accused of reticence. The former Colombia international cost Newcastle United £6.7m in February 1996 and was sold back to Parma two years later at a slight loss. The flamboyant forward claimed in early 2018 that, nowadays, he'd be worth, 'as much as Neymar, €200m for sure'. The Transfer Price Index puts the current money purchase price of his move to St James' Park at a slightly more moderate sum of £79.5m – the same as Dennis Bergkamp's transfer to Arsenal and Liverpool's January 2011 deadline-day capture of Luis Suárez.

With ever-increasing TV deals, which have led to 14 of the 2017/18 season's Premier League clubs being listed among the richest 30 clubs in the world, where might transfer fees end up?

Paul Tomkins admits it's difficult to predict how things will go. 'The massive explosion of money in football, and the increased television deals, seems to reach a point when people think it has peaked, and then it rises again,' he says. 'But, like anything, there will come a point where it slows down or regresses. All I can say is that there will probably be dips in the market again, but on past evidence it will come strong again. Obviously, changes to laws or regulations could mean that transfer fees are eventually deemed unlawful and then it will all become about the wages.'

Dr Raffaele Poli heads the CIES Football Observatory, which analyses the transfer market and the performance of players. The group has been regularly contracted by organisations and clubs such as FIFA, UEFA, City Football Group, Chelsea and Benfica and has become well respected for its scientific estimation of transfer values.

The week we spoke, Pierre-Emerick Aubameyang moved from Borussia Dortmund to Arsenal for a fee of €63.75m. The CIES Football Observatory had valued him at €64.7m. They boast an 80 per cent correlation between estimated fees and those actually paid by clubs since 2013, with Philippe Coutinho's move from Liverpool to Barcelona an example of one player they undervalued.

'Depending on the financial situation of the club or the need to have a very specific player, they can overspend or they may not match the "fair value",' explains Raffaele. 'We had a valuation of €122m, which is below the actual cost, as that included add-ons. You could say they paid perhaps 20 per cent too much. Perhaps it's inflation or the real need to send a message after the Neymar sale. Then, of course, it's also in anticipation. They know that there is inflation, the player is still quite young, he could help them to win the Champions League, that he might be more expensive after the World Cup. After the transfer, for example, Coutinho was valued at over €130m because we re-evaluate considering the book value of the player which has dramatically increased.

'The Spanish league is not as rich as the English one but Barcelona is more successful than Liverpool,' Raffaele continues. 'This is a positive factor. He also has a longer contract, even though he already had a long contract at Liverpool. That's why there is a value before and after every transfer as we have new conditions – contract, book value, league and club. Also, the prices are dependent on the buying club. €122m is the coefficient of the most likely buying club. This also gives a margin of error. If we introduced Barcelona, which is a very specific club, then it may well be that the right price would be €150m. When a club contacts us to ask how much the value of the player is, if we know the potential buying club then we can say the fair value for this club.'

Indeed, they're often commissioned by clubs to determine a fair value for players in contract negotiations.

'Clubs read what we publish,' he says. 'We publish to be credible and we have no strong competition in the market so far. Clubs mandate us in cases of disputes, negotiations, sell-on fees and so on, they ask for our consultancy.'

As of August 2018, Harry Kane was the CIES Football Observatory's most highly valued footballer on the planet at €203.5m. So, where does Raffaele see the market going? Could we see the first €300m footballer in the coming seasons? He doesn't rule it out.

'There is definitely a premium added if the buying club is English or if the player is English, but it depends on the player. It's always relative to the other values.

'We can say that there was an annual inflation rate of 15 per cent on average over the past six years. This means that the same player would cost about twice as much today as they did five years ago. So, of course, within a year that value could be €240m; within three years it could reach €300m. It is an eventuality of course,' he concedes.

Manchester United are often criticised for a perceived overspend on Paul Pogba and Romelu Lukaku but Raffaele believes they got value for money, with the pair now valued at over €300m between them. Indeed, according to Raffaele, it was another José Mourinho signing that they seemingly paid over the odds for.

'Neither were overspending on United's behalf, but there was clearly an overspend on Eric Bailly – almost double the estimated value when he moved,' he contends.

The CIES Football Observatory is not the only organisation used by football clubs when conducting their transfer business. Social media has become an important part of a club's overall marketing strategy, with Manchester United boasting 73 million fans on Facebook, over 18 million followers on Twitter and a further 23 million on Instagram. While Manchester United's pursuit of Viv Anderson back in 1987 consisted of Bryan Robson casually asking him if he'd fancy a move, clubs have become a lot more sophisticated when sounding out potential signings.

London-based Cicero Group advise clients on their media relations, digital aspects and their public affairs and several football clubs are among their clients.

'We launched the sport offering in February 2017,' explains Ben Wright, account manager with the firm. 'Broadly, we found that clubs are recruiting on a four-pillar model. So when they look at a player they're considering technical ability, tactical ability, social and psychological aspects. We supplement those latter two sides of the recruitment process. What that involves is doing a deep dive into an individual's entire online history. We'll go way back through their social feeds on Facebook, Twitter, Instagram and so on. We also mine through all the fan forums and we'll weigh up anything that's ever been published online, which allows us to give a profile of that player. Ultimately, we'll come up with a report that enables that club to decide if the player's for them. That could be in terms of what they're like as a person.'

We spoke in January 2018 and he cites Arsenal's Alex Iwobi as an example. 'He was out the other night in Soho, which is usually fine but when you lose to Forest in the FA Cup the day after it suddenly becomes more of a problem,' says Ben. 'In a reporting sense, we can see when they're posting, where they're posting from, when they're active and offline. You get an idea of whether they're out a lot at night.'

One client was very interested in signing Watford's Troy Deeney and a report was produced which hinted at a lively nightlife.

'It showed that back in 2010 through to early 2013 he was incredibly active very late at night and in the small hours of the morning and was posting from various cities that weren't cities he was based in,' explains Ben. 'So he was going out on the razz all over, but by early 2013 he had grown up and stopped, and that had very much changed.

'The other side is real-time monitoring, which allows clubs to track players' activities in real time. We weren't working with Arsenal but, for instance, when Alex Oxlade-Chamberlain had retweeted an ArsenalFanTV video calling for #WengerOut last year, we would have alerted them immediately to that and they could have got it down hopefully before the *Daily Mirror* found it.'

When we spoke, Swansea City's Alfie Mawson had been heavily linked with a move away from The Swans. He subsequently joined Fulham in August 2018 but previous suitors had commissioned a report, which wasn't exactly glowing.

'He's tipped for great things. But earlier on in his career, there were a number of sexually explicit tweets and a number of tweets where he was calling fans the 'c' word and everything else. It is finding those and getting those removed where it becomes more useful. Yes, someone may have a screenshot but, if you can get rid of the original, that will greatly reduce the risk,' says Ben.

It is often an agent who will commission the services of Cicero Group, hoping to exploit their client's social profile to justify a pay increase or transfer fee.

'We've found that the agency world is getting more and more competitive,' explains Ben. 'It used to be that the player had the same agent for their entire career but, increasingly as we're now seeing with the Dele Alli stuff, agents are working on a far more transactional basis. So they're approaching players and saying, "Let us represent you for X, Y & Z transactions" – either a move or a salary negotiation or a sponsorship negotiation rather than a long-term model. As a result of this, agencies are looking for points of differentiation and points that illustrate that they can get the best deal for the player. So they'll come to us and perhaps want us to support them in proving the marketability of a player.'

Conversely, clubs are often reluctant to invest in a player with negligible promotional appeal. As an example, he mentions Torino centre-forward Andrea Belotti, who a number of clubs were interested in signing during the 2017 summer transfer window.

'Clubs were reluctant to spend the money that they needed to spend on him, you're probably talking €60m, because, of his 30,000-plus social media following, the majority of them were Turin-based,' Ben declares. 'Furthermore, there was no spike in activity on social media, fans' forums and so on when he, for instance, made his Italy debut or scored his first goal for Italy. There was very little chatter around the key hotspots. He was linked with Manchester United and the Manchester area had something like a couple of hundred posts a day – there wasn't much excitement about a possible new arrival, and the same was true of Chelsea fans. But, actually, you're probably not going to bring many of those 30,000 followers and convert them into shirt sales or merchandise sales at a new club because they're following Belotti because they're Torino fans and not because they're Belotti fans.

'Whereas you've got other players like Paul Pogba, who Manchester United were quite right to spend £89m on because his marketing value is absolutely huge. He really did have a global following beyond just your traditional United fan, and they've been rewarded financially for signing him and been vindicated in their decision.'

He admits that the marketability of a player is obviously not the number one priority, but it can be a deciding factor when two targets are on broadly the same level in every other aspect that is being considered.

'Say, for instance, you're Chelsea and you're looking at Álvaro Morata and Andrea Belotti. You've concluded that they're a similar age, have a similar profile, have a similar shot conversion rate, similar style of play – everything else is largely on par. You then look at the marketability of them and see indicators that you're going to get a better return from Morata. So it makes sense to spend the money on him.'

When Joey Barton signed for Burnley in 2015 a tweet he wrote the year before stating, 'We may be really overrated but at least we don't have to live in Burnley!' was dragged up. It was the perfect example of the kind of thing that Cicero Group include in any reports on players requested by an interested club.

'There's the psychological/social profile – what are they like as a guy – and then we cross-reference them with 15 or so members of the squad currently in place,' Ben explains. 'Are they similar? Will they get on or are they likely to clash? The likeliness of any issues flagged – that could be issues in terms of their lifestyle, or it can be issues in terms of, "Yeah, they're great now while the going's good but will they snap when they're under pressure?" And then there's what we call the red flags,

246

such as comments online that they'll have to remove before you sign them.

'For example, Barcelona signed Sergi Guardiola in 2015, but he had tweeted anti-Catalonia content a few years beforehand, and he was sacked just hours after signing. We'll also look for generally unacceptable stuff like racism, sexism and abuse to fans.'

It's not uncommon for content posted by footballers before they became famous to come back and haunt them. Former Burnley striker Andre Gray was banned for four matches in 2016 for homophobic comments made on Twitter four years previously, when he was playing non-league football. They were subsequently deleted but it was too little, too late.

'In the bulk of instances, footballers' social media accounts are pretty tame,' Ben acknowledges. 'And that's when it's important to delve a little bit deeper back. They weren't being so tame when they were 15 or 16 years old. This is especially true nowadays for the youngsters. So you look at guys like Bobby Duncan, who was at Manchester City before recently joining Liverpool. He was captain of the under-16s, is a cousin of Steven Gerrard and is a hot England prospect for the future. To an extent, they're so heavily media-trained now that it's just anodyne, like a picture of a rainy training field with a caption, "Tough weather today but we keep going." We also offer a supplementary service to train them – it's not the, "Don't do this, don't do that," because they switch off – it's to inject their personality à la Peter Crouch or Benjamin Mendy, who's particularly funny, while also being safe.

'It varies from club to club. You look at a club like Southampton, who've got an internal team of 10 to 15 people constantly watching and monitoring the players – nudging them and prodding them and making sure they're on-brand and on-message. Even the big, big clubs still aren't properly watching the kids. You get a sense that City give young players certain posts to push out – very staged photos of the Etihad training village and all that sort of stuff. But what they're missing is that these youngsters are posting pictures of themselves in the showers after games and stuff like that. It's fine when they're 15 or 16 and nobody knows who they are, but if they ever do rise to stardom, it'll come back to haunt them. It's quite scary because this is the first generation that are growing up in the public eye,' Ben concludes.

Tottenham manager Mauricio Pochettino was ridiculed on social media when he cited Brexit as one of the reasons for his club's lack of transfer activity in August 2018, claiming it had led to a 30 per cent increase in the cost of procuring overseas players. Spurs had become the first-ever Premier League club to fail to sign a player in a summer window since its inception in 2003. The Argentinian had a point though, as specialist sports lawyer Dan Lowen explains.

'Transfers of players moving from Europe to English clubs have become more expensive for English clubs,' says Dan. 'We are a net importer of talent so the outcome of the 2016 referendum had an appreciable knock-on effect for clubs. The most obvious immediate impact for clubs was the drop in the value of the pound – put simply, it costs more to acquire and contract with international talent.'

The long-term impact on football of the vote for the UK to withdraw from the EU remains to be seen.

'Currently, European players are subject to the same free movement rights of other European workers and, therefore, are not subject to additional work-permit rules,' Dan explains. 'Clubs can sign European talent as if the players were from the UK. Those from outside the EU need to obtain a work permit and the FA's governing body endorsement, which can be tricky in this country. We have one of the most restrictive work-permit systems for footballers in the world.

'What happens once Brexit becomes a reality depends to a large extent on what form Brexit takes. The various stakeholders in the game will however be in discussion with the FA and the

Government with regard to whatever new work-permit system will apply in respect of footballers. There are of course significant competing interests, with the Premier League desperate to protect its status as one of the world's top leagues, attracting the best talent from around the world, but with the FA trying to safeguard the development of football in this country and therefore wanting to protect against an influx of foreign players. It is possible that it will become easier for players outside of the EU to move to and play for clubs in England, while becoming more difficult for European players to move to English clubs – a significant percentage of European players currently playing in England would not have met the work-permit criteria that would have applied had they come from outside of the EU. We'll know a lot more in 2019.'

Another potential impact of Brexit is that certain FIFA regulations, which only apply to national associations within the EU, would no longer apply.

'One of the big issues concerns the international transfers of minors,' Dan continues. 'FIFA prohibits the international transfer of minors unless the transfer meets one of the few exceptions to that prohibition. One of these is that a player who is 16 or 17 is permitted to move cross-border within the EU/European Economic Area (EEA) provided that the new club has sufficient educational, football training and mentoring facilities. That is the system through which English clubs have traditionally signed many European players. If we are no longer part of the EU/EEA then those rules would arguably no longer apply. It may be that the regulations are adapted in some way, but at this point in time, there's a lot of uncertainty.'

Agent Rob Shield believes that Brexit may have a positive impact on the opportunities for young British players.

'Long term, it depends if the Premier League adopts what the Government's process will be. It's all up in the air really. Day to day we don't know how it will pan out, never mind regarding football,' Rob concedes. 'Currently, around 75 per cent of international players in England are non-EU players. There are going to be fewer lower-quality foreign players, which will be better for the UK players, long term. I'm not saying it's going to improve the national team but it's definitely going to improve the playing times of UK players.'

Simon Chadwick, Professor of Sports Enterprise at the University of Salford, sits on several sport groups that are part of Government ministries where these kinds of issues are being discussed.

'I kind of know that the British Government have started to think about this already,' reveals Simon. 'The British Government set up, in the summer of 2017, something called the Sports Business Council, which is basically to ensure that the British sport industry remains globally competitive. And the person co-chairing this is Richard Scudamore, the outgoing Executive Chairman of the Premier League. So these things are being talked about already. And clearly, in this particular case, Scudamore has manoeuvred himself into a position where he is co-chairing a very influential post-Brexit Government panel on the future of the British sport industry.

'Regarding the bodies that I am associated with, there seems to be no directive at all from central Government. It's more a case of these groups of people knowing that something is going to happen and, essentially, being left to their own devices to make sense of it all. Rather than the Government saying, "Right, this is what we want you to do," what seems to be happening is these groups are saying to Government, "Right, this is what we think needs to happen." In many ways, they are leading the conversation and telling the Government what to do. There seems to be an absence of leadership at that top level.'

He agrees that the impact of Brexit remains to be seen but is sure that the Government will have to protect, if not enhance, the status of the Premier League.

'Clearly, this will have to be worked through,' he says. 'My view on this is that, for Great Britain, the Premier League is an important economic industry and cultural asset. I believe that rumours of lots of players being deported because they don't meet visa regulation requirements are naive and wildly misplaced. Prior to even the Brexit vote, we've seen that the Premier League and the British Government are prepared to negotiate arrangements for player visas that are outside the normal visa regulations. It really wouldn't surprise me if the Premier League actually comes on quite strong with the British Government. And we may actually see a relaxing of visa regulations, potentially to enhance the power and strength globally of the Premier League and to make sure that it's still as easy as it is now for EU players to come here, but potentially also to make it easier for the next big star from Brazil or Argentina to move here than it is to, for example, go to Spain. La Liga is being really, really aggressive right now in the way that it competes with the Premier League.

'I think that the post-Brexit visa regime for the Premier League will potentially be even more relaxed than it is at the moment. I would be more concerned about what happens further down the league pyramid, where I wouldn't really see this being the case. I wonder whether we'll get a two-tier system with certain visa regulations for the Premier League and different visa regulations for everyone else,' he concludes.

The future of the transfer market may be uncertain, but what of the players it impacts? Since I started writing this book, thousands of footballers worldwide have moved house, moved clubs, moved cities and moved their families – often through no choice of their own. The fast-moving pace of the transfer market has meant that the situations of many I spoke to have changed in the intervening months.

Following their promotion to the Premier League, Cardiff City released Frédéric Gounongbe. Still unsure as to whether injuries incurred during his time in Wales would lead to a premature retirement, he enjoyed a first family holiday in ten years in August and has enrolled on an asset management degree course in Brussels with the aim of helping professional sportspeople deal with their finances.

Mark Roberts has also turned to academia after his contract with Forest Green Rovers ended in the summer of 2018. After deciding to return to the north-west, he enrolled on a CEO of a Sports Organisation MBA at the University of Salford while continuing to play part-time with Warrington Town.

David Low hasn't hung up his boots just yet, with Holland becoming country number 12 on his global journey.

Neill Collins's time in Florida has been extended, although his playing career has come to a halt. In May 2018 he moved from player to manager at Tampa Bay Rowdies.

Liam Rosenior has also hung up his boots 'privileged to have earned a living doing something I love'. He's looking forward to a new chapter as a coach at Brighton & Hove Albion and analyst with Sky Sports.

Raffaele De Vita enjoyed promotion to the Scottish Premiership with Livingston but is currently watching from the sidelines. He suffered a cruciate injury in a play-off match against Dundee United and is working on his rehabilitation, having undergone an operation in June.

Charlie Sheringham's Bangladeshi adventure is over for now as he's moved back to the National League South with Dartford, a level he was confident he could return to after his Asian sojourn.

Xander McBurnie remains in Sweden, where his club lies third in the league following seven straight wins. He's helped more British arrivals settle in Scandinavia, ensuring they realise the opportunity they have been given and grab it with both hands, as he has done.

Whatever their current club, role or transfer status, I have become more mindful that each of them – like tens of thousands of other footballers across the globe affected by the transfer market – is not just a name, not just a transfer target, not just a commodity. They're each, 'living a life as vivid and complex as your own – populated with their own ambitions, friends, routines, worries and inherited craziness – an epic story that continues invisibly around you like an anthill sprawling deep underground, with elaborate passageways to thousands of other lives that you never knew existed, in which you might appear only once, as an extra sipping coffee in the background, as a blur of traffic passing on the highway, as a lighted window at dusk.'

Acknowledgements

Firstly, a huge thank you to all the current and former footballers who shared their experiences of the transfer market. Each participant was a key signing for the book and I couldn't have wished for a better squad. They include, in order of their playing positions, Asmir Begović, Michael McGovern, Jimmy Glass, Viv Anderson, Benoît Assou-Ekotto, Timm Klose, Radhi Jaïdi, Steven Caldwell, Neill Collins, Mark Roberts, Liam Rosenior, Jimmy Dunne, Jordan Stewart, Richie Ryan, Raffaele De Vita, Rhema Obed, Rohan Ricketts, David Low, Xander McBurnie, Leroy Lita, Rudy Gestede, Frédéric Gounongbe, Niall Quinn, Charlie Sheringham, Hugo Colace and Lewis Baker. I'd also like to thank those who discussed their experiences, but wished to remain anonymous.

I'd like to express a huge sense of gratitude to everyone else who contributed including, in no particular order, Dan Lowen of LEVEL, Gary Mellor of Beswicks Sports, Rob Shield of Evolve Sports Management, @WeahsCousin, the guys at FootballTransferLeague.co.uk, Tom Hopkinson of the *Sunday Mirror* and the *Sunday People*, Paul Tomkins, John Jerrim, Declan Varley, Sean Cummins, Ben Wright of Cicero Group, Jim White of Sky Sports & talkSPORT (for his contribution and kindly penning the foreword), Jonas Baer-Hoffmann of FIFPro, Dr Martin Roderick, Kevin Harris-James of Harrison Clark Rickerbys, Raffaele Poli of CIES, Jon Smith, Thomas Lintz of TransferMarkt.

co.uk, LFE's Simon Williams, Professor Simon Chadwick of the University of Salford, the guys at Playonpro, Lorna McClelland and Clifford Bloxham. I sincerely apologise if I've missed anyone.

I also wish to acknowledge Emmett Murtagh, David Sheehan, Colin Howard, Duncan Olner, Derek Hammond, Cath Harris, Ivan Butler, Jim Burke, Rory Callan, George Kinane, Aidan Homer, Chris Clarke, Martin McGahon, Eamonn Murphy, David Moran, David Faul and Paddy Faul for their time and help with the project. Will Reilly was, again, of enormous assistance in helping to get the book into shape in its closing stages. A special mention too for my aunt Carmel – and Patrick Kavanagh – for some much-needed inspiration just when I needed it most.

One person I thought about a lot while writing this was Ken Meegan. You are sorely missed, Ken.

Paul and Jane Camillin at Pitch Publishing were a joy to work with again and I sincerely appreciate their continued support.

My parents, Tom and Eileen, have been a huge support – not just while writing this book, but throughout my life. I am extremely grateful for everything they do for me. And thanks to my brothers David and Thomas, who I probably forced to play Team Tactix with me for months on end.

The book took a few transfer windows to research and write, during which time my wife, Tracey, was a shining light as always. It's difficult to convey how much I appreciate her patience, support, sacrifices and love. I couldn't have done it without her. And, finally, thanks to my amazing children Daisy, Noah (a budding goalkeeper who would like to thank Asmir Begović for his words of encouragement!), Joel and our new arrival Alice for their inspiration and, more importantly, just for being themselves. I'm a very lucky man.